PEARSON   ALWAYS LEARNING

Mike Johnston, CPhT

The Pharmacy Technician
Foundations and Practices
Lab Manual and Workbook

Third Custom Edition for Condensed Curriculum International

Taken from:

*Lab Manual and Workbook for The Pharmacy Technician:
Foundations and Practices*, Second Edition
by Mike Johnston, CPhT

Taken from:

Lab Manual and Workbook for The Pharmacy Technician: Foundations and Practices, Second Edition
by Mike Johnston, CPhT
Copyright © 2014 by Pearson Education, Inc.
New York, New York 10013

This special edition published in cooperation with Pearson Education, Inc.

Pearson Education, Inc., 330 Hudson Street, New York, New York 10013
A Pearson Education Company
www.pearsoned.com

Printed in the United States of America

2   17

000200010272075311

EEB

ISBN 10: 1-323-58080-8
ISBN 13: 978-1-323-58080-6

Contents

Preface

The Pharmacy Technician: Foundations and Practices, 2nd edition addresses today's comprehensive educational needs for one of the fastest growing jobs in the United States—that of the pharmacy technician. The pharmacy technician career is ranked number 19 among the 100 fastest-growing jobs in the United States. According to the U.S. Bureau of Labor Statistics, the pharmacy technician career is growing at approximately 32%, a much higher rate than other jobs in the health professions. This equates to an anticipated net increase in employment opportunities of 108,300 between 2010 and 2020.

In addition to the tremendous workforce demand for pharmacy technicians, professional regulations and requirements are being established for pharmacy technicians across the United States. With many state boards of pharmacy either considering, or having already enacted, requirements for mandatory registration, certification, and/or formal education, the need for a comprehensive and up-to-date pharmacy technician textbook such as *The Pharmacy Technician: Foundations and Practices, 2nd edition* has never been greater.

This *Workbook/Lab Manual to Accompany The Pharmacy Technician: Fundamentals of Practice, 2nd edition* is designed to give you additional practice in mastering the varied skills that will be required of you as a pharmacy technician. It is organized to correspond with the 38 chapters in the textbook. Each workbook/lab manual chapter includes:

• Learning objectives from the textbook, with references to related activities within the workbook/lab manual.

• An introduction that summarizes the main themes from the textbook chapter.

• Review Questions that evaluate your comprehension of the textbook chapter content. Question types include multiple choice, fill-in-the-blank, matching, and true/false.

• Pharmacy Calculation Problems that will give you additional practice and help increase your comfort level in using the math skills you will need on a daily basis as a practicing pharmacy technician.

• PTCB Exam Practice Questions related to the chapter's specific content will help you prepare for the Pharmacy Technician Certification Exam.

• Activities in each chapter challenge you to explore facets of the chapter material more thoroughly and offer a variety of exercises, including anatomy worksheets, case studies with critical thinking questions, Web research problems, and role-playing scenarios.

• Hands-on Lab activities in certain chapters give you the chance to practice procedures, work with equipment, or perform additional research.

MyHealthProfessionsLab for The Pharmacy Technician

The ultimate personalized learning tool is available at www.myhealthprofessionslab.com. This online course correlates with the textbook and is available for purchase separately or for a discount when packaged with the book. MyHealthProfessionsLab for the Pharmacy Technician is an immersive study experience that includes pretests and posttests to asses the skills the student learns in each chapter. Videos focused on math and other special topics, games, and anatomy & physiology activities round out the experience.

Learners track their own progess through the course and use a personalized study plan to achieve success. Visit www.myhealthprofessionslab.com to log into the course or purchase access. Instructors seeking more information about discount bundle options or for a demonstration should contact their Pearson sales representative.

About NPTA

The NPTA is the world's largest professional organization specifically for pharmacy technicians. The association is dedicated to advancing the value of pharmacy technicians and the vital roles they play in pharmaceutical care. In a society of countless associations, we believe that it takes much more than just a mission statement to meet the professional needs of and provide the necessary leadership for the pharmacy technician profession—it takes action and results.

The organization is composed of pharmacy technicians practicing in a variety of practice settings, such as retail, independent, hospital, mail-order, home care, long-term care, nuclear, military, correctional facilities, formal education, training, management, sales, and many more. NPTA is a reflection of this diverse profession and provides unparalleled support and resources to members.

NPTA is the foundation of the pharmacy technician profession; we have an unprecedented past, a strong present, and a promising future. We are dedicated to improving our profession while remaining focused on our members.

Pharmacy technician students are welcome to join more than 60,000 practicing pharmacy technicians as members of NPTA.

For more information:
call 888-247-8706
visit www.pharmacytechnician.org

CHAPTER 1
History of Pharmacy Practice

After completing Chapter 1 from the textbook, you should be able to:	Related Activity in the Workbook/Lab Manual
1. Describe the origins of pharmacy practice from the Age of Antiquity.	Review Questions, PTCB Exam Practice Questions
2. Discuss changes in pharmacy practice during the Middle Ages.	Review Questions, PTCB Exam Practice Questions
3. Describe changes in pharmacy practice during the Renaissance.	Review Questions, PTCB Exam Practice Questions
4. List significant milestones for pharmacy practice from the 18th, 19th, 20th, and 21st centuries.	Review Questions, PTCB Exam Practice Questions
5. Discuss the role biotechnology and genetic engineering could have on the future of pharmacy practice.	Review Questions

INTRODUCTION

The practice of pharmacy has ancient roots. The word *pharmacy* comes from the Greek word *pharmakon*, meaning "drug," and the origin of pharmacy practice goes back to ancient times, more than 7,000 years ago. The role of a pharmacy technician can be traced back to 2900 BCE, in ancient Egypt, where echelons were gatherers and preparers of drugs, similar to the modern-day pharmacy technician; chiefs of fabrication were the head pharmacists.

The history of pharmacy practice may seem to be unnecessary to you as you prepare to become a pharmacy technician. However, if you are to understand many of the concepts, theories, and practices covered in this workbook/laboratory manual and the textbook, you need to understand the evolution of the pharmacy profession. Many of the principles used in pharmacy thousands of years ago are still practiced today. Understanding the historic roots will also help you appreciate the areas in which the profession has evolved and how professional guidelines and regulations have developed. As you will discover, the responsibilities of and opportunities for pharmacy technicians continue to evolve, along with the profession of pharmacy itself.

REVIEW QUESTIONS

Match the following.

1. __e__ pharmacogenomics
2. __f__ pharmacy
3. __d__ prescription
4. __a__ apothecary
5. __c__ biotechnology
6. __g__ pharmacopoeia
7. __b__ compounding

a. Latin term for pharmacist
b. Producing, mixing, or preparing a drug by combining ingredients
c. Use of living things to make or modify a product
d. An order to prepare/dispense
e. Study of genetic differences in responses to drug therapy
f. Art/science of preparing and dispensing medication
g. Book of products, formulae, and directions for preparation

Choose the best answer.

8. The word *pharmacy* comes from which ancient Greek word for drug?
   a. pharmakos
   b. pharmakopeia
   c. pharmakon
   d. pharmakot

9. The Latin word *recipere* or recipe means _____.
   a. Heal, Thou
   b. To Heal
   c. To Make
   d. Take, Thou

10. The Age of Antiquity refers to which time period?
    a. 8000 BCE up through 699 CE
    b. 5000 BCE up through 499 CE
    c. 3000 BCE up through 899 CE
    d. 4000 BCE up through 599 CE

11. The "father of botany" is considered to be:
    a. Shen Nung.
    b. Echelon.
    c. Theophrastus.
    d. Charaka Samhita.

Match the following scientists with their accomplishments.

12. __e__ Fleming
13. __b__ Mithridates
14. __a__ Hippocrates
15. __c__ Pedanios Dioscorides
16. __d__ Galen

a. developed the theory of humors
b. poisons and poison preventatives
c. rules for drug collection, storage, and use
d. established principles of compounding
e. discovered penicillin

Choose the best answer.

17. The first apothecaries, or privately owned drugstores, were established in the late 8th century by the:
    a. Arabs.
    b. Greeks.
    c. Romans.
    d. Italians.

18. The first pharmacy technicians in ancient Egypt were known as:
    a. slaves.
    b. ebers.
    c. echelons.
    d. chiefs of fabrication.

19. The _____ is an ancient Indian manuscript, originating in approximately 1000 BCE, which records over 2,000 drugs.
    a. *De Materia Medica*
    b. *Charaka Samhita*
    c. *Pen T-Sao*
    d. *Corpus Hippocraticum*

20. The first school of pharmacy was:
    a. the Philadelphia College of Pharmacy.
    b. the University of Pennsylvania Pharmacy College.
    c. Boston University.
    d. the Massachusetts School of Pharmacology.

21. John Winthrop established the first apothecary in the American colonies in:
    a. 1617.
    b. 1729.
    c. 1640.
    d. 1751.

22. The *United States Pharmacopoeia* (USP) was first published in:
    a. 1820.
    b. 1877.
    c. 1822.
    d. 1869.

23. Gregor Mendel is known as the Father of Modern Genetics. He was an Austrian:
    a. pharmacist and scientist.
    b. priest and pharmacist.
    c. scientist and priest.
    d. priest and author.

24. The practice of pharmacy began to be regulated by the federal government:
    a. in the early 1900s.
    b. in the late 1800s.
    c. in the late 1900s.
    d. pharmacy has always been heavily regulated by the federal government.

25. Pharmacogenomics is the use of:
    a. genomic or genetic information to predict a drug's efficacy.
    b. personal DNA information to track patients.
    c. gene splicing to produce effective medications.
    d. a study of future drugs and their possible uses.

26. Colonial America's first hospital was established in:
    a. Boston.
    b. Jamestown.
    c. New York City.
    d. Philadelphia.

Match the following.

27. __C__ Clinical Era
28. __d__ Pharmaceutical Care Era
29. __a__ Traditional Era
30. __b__ Scientific Era

a. formulating and dispensing drugs
b. developing and testing drugs
c. dispensing information, warnings, and advice
d. positive outcomes of therapies

PHARMACY CALCULATION PROBLEMS

Calculate the following.

1. 12.7 + 58.3 + 91.2 + 0.4 = 162.6

2. 120 mL + 60 mL + 80 mL + 40 mL = 300 mL

3. 750 mg − 150 mg − 75 mg = 525 mg

4. 14.25 oz. + 11.5 oz. − 3.25 oz. = 22.5 oz

5. 9.8 mL − 5.4 mL + 12.9 mL = 17.3 mL

PTCB EXAM PRACTICE QUESTIONS

1. Which ancient civilization provides the earliest record of apothecary practice?
   a. Babylonian
   b. Chinese
   c. Indian
   d. Aztec

2. Who is credited with developing the polio vaccine?
   a. Wilson
   b. Marshall
   c. Fleming
   d. Salk

3. In what city was the first American school of pharmacy founded?
   a. Boston
   b. Baltimore
   c. Providence
   d. Philadelphia

4. Which organization is responsible for setting standards for pharmacy education and continuing pharmacy education?
   a. APHA
   b. NABP
   c. ASHP
   d. ACPE

5. Hippocrates, often referred to as the "Father of Medicine," was part of which ancient culture?
   a. Egyptian
   b. Greek
   c. Roman
   d. Chinese

CHAPTER 2
The Professional Pharmacy Technician

After completing Chapter 2 from the textbook, you should be able to:	Related Activity in the Workbook/Lab Manual
1. Summarize the educational requirements and competencies of both pharmacists and pharmacy technicians.	Review Questions, PTCB Exam Practice Questions
2. Describe the two primary pharmacy practice settings and define the basic roles of pharmacists and pharmacy technicians working in each setting.	Review Questions
3. Explain six specific characteristics of a good pharmacy technician.	Review Questions
4. Demonstrate the behavior of a professional pharmacy technician.	Review Questions
5. Explain the registration/licensure and certification process for becoming a pharmacy technician.	Review Questions, PTCB Exam Practice Questions

INTRODUCTION

Pharmacy is an industry consisting of professionals: pharmacists and .pharmacy technicians. Many claim—with good reason—that pharmacy is the most trusted profession in America. As with any profession, employment in this field requires you to be educated, trained, diligent, and ethical. You must maintain specific competencies, undergo specialized education and training, and exhibit key personal characteristics. The process of preparing for your future includes formal education and training, registration/licensure, national certification, and involvement with a professional organization. The benefits of your hard work and dedication are the tremendous career opportunities awaiting you as a future pharmacy technician.

REVIEW QUESTIONS

Match the following.

1. ___h___ certification
2. ___b___ licensing
3. ___a___ registration
4. ___j___ attitude

a. process of listing/being named to a list
b. government permission to do something
c. located on site where patients reside
d. common name for health system pharmacy

✱ 5. ___f___ compassion   e. feelings of concern and understanding

✱ 6. ___e___ empathy   f. deep awareness and sympathy

7. ___i___ ambulatory pharmacy   g. retail pharmacy

8. ___g___ community pharmacy   h. nongovernmental verification of competency

✱ 9. ___c___ health system pharmacy   i. chain, drug/grocery store, mail-order, home health care pharmacies

✱10. ___d___ institutional pharmacy   j. way of acting, thinking, or believing

True or False?

11. Historically, there were only two recognized professions: law and medicine.

     T   (F)

12. Pharmacy technicians must be licensed in all states.

     T   (F)

13. Today, pharmacy practice is based upon delivering direct patient care.

     (T)   F

14. Most institutional pharmacies are open 24 hours.

     (T)   F

15. Your body language can hide your true feelings and attitudes.

     T   (F)

Choose the best answer.

16. Which of the following tasks is most likely to be performed by a pharmacist?
     a. insurance billing   (c.) patient counseling
     b. patient private information maintenance   d. inventory ordering

17. Which of the following is considered an ambulatory pharmacy?
     a. hospitals   (c.) home health care
     b. extended-living facility   d. retirement home

18. The set of qualities and characteristics that represent perceptions of your competence and character, as judged by your constituents, is called your:
     a. attitude.   c. professionalism.
     (b.) professional image.   d. demeanor.

19. Which of the following attire would be unacceptable for a pharmacy technician?
     a. tie   (c.) shorts
     b. lab coat   d. scrubs

20. Since 2001, pharmacists are required to complete _____ years of college.
     a. 4   c. 7
     (b.) 6   d. 8

21. Which is an example of adapting to change?
     a. changing priorities, strategies, or methods   c. handling stress properly
     b. maintaining effectiveness   (d.) all of the above

*22. _____ accredits pharmacy technician training programs.
   a. AAPT
   b. ACPE
   c. APhA
   d. ASHP

23. Which of the following is not a common eligibility requirement for technicians?
   a. no felony conviction(s)
   b. high school graduate or GED equivalent
   c. a two-year college degree
   d. certification

24. Pharmacy technicians are in the business of:
   a. selling drugs.
   b. patient care.
   c. patient consultations.
   d. making money.

25. Which of the following is considered an institutional pharmacy?
   a. retail drugstore
   b. home health care
   c. mail-order facility
   d. long-term care facility

List the four basic steps to problem solving.

26. _____

Name four sources of continuing education (CE) for pharmacy technicians.

27. _____
28. _____
29. _____
30. _____

PHARMACY CALCULATION PROBLEMS

Calculate the following.

10) 1hr
11) 1hr
12) 1hr
1) 1hr
1) 1hr
2) 1hr

1. Bobby has completed 16 hours of CE. How many more hours does he need to complete to meet the PTCB requirements?   4

2. If Judy worked 36.5 hours one week and 39 hours the next week, how much would her gross pay be for those two weeks if she were paid $13.05 per hour? $(13.05)(36.5) + (13.05)(39)$
   905.28

3. A customer has three prescriptions and owes a co-payment of $15.00 on each one. How much will the customer be charged for all three prescriptions? $15 \times 3 = 45

4. A technician works the third shift at a hospital for seven days in a row, followed by seven days off. She is scheduled to work Sunday through Saturday from 10:00 P.M. till 8:00 A.M., every other week. If the pay period starts on Sunday, how many hours will she work in two consecutive weeks?
   70 hrs

5. A medication order calls for a special mouthwash that the pharmacy must make. It contains 50% diphenhydramine syrup and 50% viscous lidocaine. The physician ordered 12 ounces. How much of each ingredient will you need to make this?
   6 oz

1   2   3   4   5   6   7
Sun Mon Tues Wed Thu Fri Sat

1. When a pharmacy student graduates from an accredited college of pharmacy in the United States, what degree does she or he receive?
   a. Bachelor of Science (BS)
   b. Bachelor of Arts (BA)
   c. Doctor of Pharmacy (PharmD)
   d. Master of Science (MS)

2. In the United States, pharmacy technicians are often required to be registered or licensed before they may perform the duties of a pharmacy technician. This requirement is mandated by which government agency?
   a. Food and Drug Administration (FDA)
   b. State Board of Pharmacy (SBOP)
   c. Drug Enforcement Agency (DEA)
   d. United States Pharmacopoeia (USP)

3. When a pharmacy technician successfully completes a certification examination to become a CPhT, this signifies to others that he or she is:
   a. smart.
   b. polite.
   c. empathetic.
   d. competent.

4. An extended living facility is an example of a(n) _____ pharmacy.
   a. ambulatory
   b. institutional
   c. retail
   d. community

CHAPTER 3
Communication and Customer Care

After completing Chapter 3 from the textbook, you should be able to:	Related Activity in the Workbook/Lab Manual
1. Describe and illustrate the communication process.	Review Questions, PTCB Exam Practice Questions
2. List and explain the three types of communication.	Review Questions, PTCB Exam Practice Questions
3. Summarize the various barriers to effective communication.	Review Questions, PTCB Exam Practice Questions
4. List and describe the primary defense mechanisms.	Review Questions
5. Describe specific strategies for eliminating barriers to communication.	Review Questions, PTCB Exam Practice Questions
6. Summarize the elements of and considerations in caring for patients.	Review Questions, PTCB Exam Practice Questions
7. List the Five Rights of medication administration.	Review Questions

INTRODUCTION

Communication is simply the process of transferring information, although it is not a simple process. You communicate to get your message across to others clearly and unambiguously. Communicating takes effort from everyone involved, including the sender (the person who initiates the communication) and the receiver (the person or group the sender is addressing). The communication process often breaks down, and errors may result in misunderstandings and confusion.

As a pharmacy technician, you will need to communicate effectively with a variety of people, including your immediate coworkers, customers or patients, health care personnel, suppliers, drug representatives, health insurance representatives, and many others. Pharmacy technicians work as frontline employees in the pharmacy, which means that both your management and your patients will rely on you to be an effective communicator and to identify and eliminate communication barriers as they arise. Remember that becoming an effective communicator is a lifelong process that gets easier with experience and time.

REVIEW QUESTIONS

Match the following.

1. __c__ context
2. __d__ projection
3. __a__ inflection
4. __b__ denial
5. __j__ feedback
6. __g__ channel
7. __c__ kinesics
8. __i__ defense mechanisms
9. __f__ proxemics
10. __h__ pitch

a. a change in the tone of voice

b. defense mechanism of refusing to acknowledge painful realities

c. body language

d. defense mechanism in which one's own attitudes are attributed to others

e. the situation or environment in which the message is delivered

f. the study of measurable distance between individuals as they interact

g. gesture, action, sound, written or spoken word used in transmitting information

h. how high or low the voice is in sound wave frequency

i. unconscious mental process used to protect the ego

j. the return of information back to the sender

Choose the best answer.

11. Directly related to the effectiveness of communication are:
    a. customer service and pharmaceutical care.
    b. speed of medication delivery and customer care.
    c. patient satisfaction and sales.
    d. pharmacy profitability and customer service.

12. The situation or environment in which a message is delivered is called:
    a. channel.
    b. feedback.
    c. context.
    d. verbal.

13. In communicating with patients, it is best to use a:
    a. monotone, impersonal tone.
    b. condescending patient tone.
    c. sympathetic caring tone.
    d. tone that mimics the patient's.

14. Effective communication will involve all of the following except:
    a. pleasantness.
    b. active listening.
    c. professional tones.
    d. aggressiveness

15. When leaving a voicemail for a patient, it is important not to:
    a. provide personal patient information.
    b. provide your name.
    c. provide your pharmacy's phone number.
    d. repeat information you have already given.

16. Facial expressions, eye contact, posture, and silence, are forms of:
    a. communication barriers.
    b. nonverbal communication.
    c. intimidation.
    d. not as effective as the spoken word.

17. Which of the following is not a barrier to communication?
    a. inaccurate information
    b. language
    c. overly lengthy message
    d. translators

18. If a patient does not speak good English, a technician should:
    a. see if a translator is available.
    b. speak the patient's native language if possible.
    c. provide instructions in the patient's native language.
    d. all of the above.

19. Defense mechanisms share two common properties:
    a. repression and sublimation.
    b. denial and displacement.
    c. unconscious trigger and distortion of reality.
    d. projection and rationalization.

20. When an individual transfers his or her own negative emotions to someone who is unrelated to those feelings, it is called:
    a. rationalization.
    b. displacement.
    c. denial.
    d. projection.

21. A patient who is prejudiced against minorities, and complains that an Asian-American technician showed him disrespect, may be using:
    a. regression.
    b. sublimation.
    c. projection.
    d. displacement.

22. The best strategy a technician can use for pharmacy conflict resolution is to:
    a. hold one's ground.
    b. demand respect.
    c. identify who has a problem.
    d. involve the supervisor.

23. In the Five Rights, the "right time" refers to the:
    a. pick-up time.
    b. drop-off time.
    c. time to fill the prescription.
    d. administration time(s).

24. The Patient's Bill of Rights includes being treated with courtesy and respect. It was passed by Congress in:
    a. 1905.
    b. 2005.
    c. 1995.
    d. 1955.

List and describe five common defense mechanisms:

25. Reaction Formation: A defense mechanism characterized by actions at the opposite extreme of one's true feelings or overcompensation for unacceptable impulses.

26. Intellectualization: A defense mechanism used to protect oneself from the emotional stress or anxiety associated w/ confronting painful fears or problems.

27. Sublimation: A defense mechanism in which unacceptable instinctual drives & wishes are modified to take more personally & socially accepted forms.

28. Rationalization: a defense mechanism whereby one's true motivation is concealed by explaining one's actions & feelings in a way that is not threatening

29. Displacement: a defense mechanism characterized by an unconscious shift of emotions, affect, or desires from the original object to a more acceptable or immediate substitute.

PHARMACY CALCULATION PROBLEMS

Calculate the following.

$$\begin{array}{r} 246.80 \\ + 38.85 \\ \hline 285.65 \end{array} \qquad \begin{array}{r} 10 \\ \times\ 2 \\ \hline 20 \end{array} \qquad \begin{array}{r} 285.65 \\ 20.00 \\ \hline 265.65 \end{array}$$

1. At retail price, two prescriptions would cost $38.85 and $246.80, respectively. The customer has insurance and only pays $10 per prescription. How much money did the customer save with her insurance?

    $ 265.65

2. It costs the pharmacy $46.16 for 32 ounces of guaifenesin syrup. How much does it cost per ounce?

    $\dfrac{46.16}{32}$ $1.44

3. If a customer pays 30% of the retail price for a medication, how much would the customer pay for a prescription with a retail price of $200?

    $(200)(.3) = 60

$\begin{array}{r} 12 \\ \times 1.5 \\ \hline 18 \end{array}$

4. A technician gets paid $12 per hour for the first 40 hours worked in a week. He gets traditional overtime pay that is 1.5 times more than his regular pay for the hours he works over 40 hours. How much will he get paid if he works 48 hours in one week?

    $12 \times 40 = 480$
    $18 \times 8 = 144$ $480 + 144 = 624

5. Jane works the second shift at a hospital. Her base pay is $13.25 per hour. The hospital gives a shift differential of $1.00 per hour for every hour worked on the second shift. How much will her weekly paycheck be if she works 32 hours?

    $456

    $32 \times 13.25 = 424$
    $32 \times 1 = 32$ $\begin{array}{r} 424 \\ + 32 \\ \hline 456 \end{array}$

PTCB EXAM PRACTICE QUESTIONS

1. Which of the following best describes the protection of a patient's privacy (identity and health information)?
    a. Compatibility
    b. Conformity
    c. Compliance
    d. Confidentiality

2. Some patients may feel uncomfortable if the pharmacist or technician stands too close or touches them. Other patients may initiate a handshake or pat on the back. These kinds of differences might be considered:
    a. genetic differences.
    b. cultural differences.
    c. physical differences.
    d. physiological differences.

3. You have a patient who is less than 12 years old. This patient would be categorized as what kind of patient?
    a. geriatric
    b. neonate
    c. pediatric
    d. ambulatory

4. An important communication concept, which refers to the situation, environment, or circumstance in which a message is communicated, is:
   a. projection.
   b. context.
   c. intellectualization.
   d. rationalization.

5. Which of the following is NOT one of the *Five Patient Rights*?
   a. Right Medication
   b. Right Price
   c. Right Strength
   d. Right Time

CHAPTER 4
Pharmacy Law and Ethics

After completing Chapter 4 from the textbook, you should be able to:	Related Activity in the Workbook/Lab Manual
1. Classify the various categories of U.S. law.	Review Questions, Lab 4-1
2. List the regulatory agencies that oversee the practice of pharmacy and describe their function(s).	Review Questions, PTCB Exam Practice Questions, Lab 4-1
3. Summarize the significant laws and amendments that affect the practice of pharmacy.	Review Questions, PTCB Exam Practice Questions, Activity 4-1, Lab 4-1
4. Recognize and use a drug monograph.	Review Questions
5. Define ethics and moral philosophy.	Review Questions, Activity 4-1, Activity 4-2
6. List and explain the nine ethical theories.	Review Questions, Activity 4-3
7. Summarize the Pharmacy Technician Code of Ethics.	Review Questions, Activity 4-3

INTRODUCTION

Federal and state laws, as well as professional ethics, regulate the practice of pharmacy. The regulations on pharmacy practice in the United States have evolved over the past hundred or so years, and their number has increased as legislators responded to demands from citizens to serve and protect the public interest. The government began to take the initiative in regulating pharmacy practice toward the end of the 18th century. Over time, the profession of pharmacy has become increasingly more regulated. In the United States, a professional degree is a requirement for any individual who wishes to practice pharmacy. This requirement was established to protect the public and set minimum standards, so that citizens could rely on pharmacists having at least a standard level of education and competence.

Many of the regulations pertaining to practice as a pharmacy technician are established and enforced by your specific state's board of pharmacy. In general, federal laws govern the manufacturing of pharmaceutical products, and state laws govern the actual dispensing of those products. It is imperative that you familiarize yourself with both the federal laws and your state's laws pertaining to pharmacy practice. In addition, you should fully understand the basic ethical theories and *Code of Ethics for Pharmacy Technicians,* in preparation for ethical dilemmas and questions that will arise in the pharmacy setting.

REVIEW QUESTIONS

Choose the best answer.

1. The quality of keeping a promise is:
   a. beneficence.
   b. ethics.
   c. fidelity.
   d. veracity.

2. A drug that has been misleadingly or fraudulently labeled is referred to as:
   a. adulterated.
   b. a felony.
   c. a monograph.
   d. misbranded.

3. A system of principles often associated with a profession is:
   a. civil law.
   b. consequentialism.
   c. ethics.
   d. criminal law.

4. Most laws pertaining to pharmacy were enacted to:
   a. limit the scope and practice of pharmacy.
   b. protect the public interest.
   c. lower the number of drug addicts.
   d. protect drug manufacturers.

5. Which is not a type of law in the United States?
   a. legislative intent
   b. constitutional
   c. government policy
   d. statutes

6. Which set of laws would take priority?
   a. federal
   b. state
   c. municipality
   d. local codes

7. Statutes are laws that are passed by:
   a. the federal government.
   b. state governments.
   c. local governments.
   d. all of the above.

8. Legislative intent is often referred to as:
   a. common law.
   b. case law.
   c. civil law.
   d. all of the above.

9. Regulations:
   a. have the force of law.
   b. are guidelines.
   c. refine laws.
   d. are not connected to laws.

10. Crimes are classified as either _____ or _____.
    a. infractions, misdemeanors
    b. infractions, violations
    c. infractions, felonies
    d. felonies, misdemeanors

11. Professional liability insurance is:
    a. currently available only to pharmacists.
    b. available to both pharmacists and pharmacy technicians.
    c. required by most states.
    d. required by the federal government.

12. Which agency/administration is not involved in the practice of pharmacy?
    a. CMS
    b. HIPAA
    c. HCFA
    d. FEMA

13. Which agency/administration is responsible for protecting the privacy of patients?
    a. CLIA
    b. SCHIP
    c. HIPAA
    d. DEA

Match the following.

14. __d__ Drug Enforcement Agency
15. __c__ Food and Drug Administration
16. __e__ Federal Bureau of Investigation
17. __a__ State Board of Pharmacy
18. __b__ Joint Commission
19. __f__ Occupational Safety and Health Administration

a. regulates and registers pharmacy technicians, pharmacists, and pharmacies
b. establishes and enforces standards for health care organizations
c. assures the safety, efficacy, and security of drugs
d. regulates the legal trade in controlled drugs
e. the administrator of the DEA reports to this chief
f. assures the safety and health of American workers

Choose the best answer.

20. The Food and Drug Administration was created by the:
    a. Food, Drug, and Cosmetic Act of 1938.
    b. Pure Food and Drug Act of 1905.
    c. Controlled Substances Act of 1970.
    d. FBI's need to expand to combat prevalent drug abuse.

21. "A display of written, printed, or graphic matter upon the immediate container of an article" refers to the:
    a. label.
    b. labeling.
    c. package insert.
    d. patient information sheet.

22. Which of the following information is not a labeling requirement for a dispensed prescription?
    a. NDC
    b. serial number (Rx number)
    c. date of fill
    d. prescriber's name

23. Which of the following information is not required to be on the manufacturer's label of a prescription-only drug?
    a. route of administration
    b. name and quantity of active ingredients
    c. date of fill
    d. federal legend

24. Which of the following information is not required to be on the package insert?
    a. dosage
    b. indications and usage
    c. adverse reactions
    d. unique lot or control number

Fill in the blank.

25. The amendment signed in 1951 that required the "federal legend" to be printed on all prescription drugs was _Durham-Humphrey Admendment_

26. The Kefauver–Harris Amendment, signed in 1962, is also referred to as the _Drug Efficacy Admendment_.

Match the following.

27. _C_ OBRA '90

28. _d_ Pure Food and Drug Act of 1906

29. _d_ Food, Drug, and Cosmetic Act

30. _b_ Durham–Humphrey Amendment

31. _g_ Schedule I

32. _h_ Schedule II

33. _i_ Schedule III

34. _e_ Schedule IV

35. _f_ Schedule V

36. _m_ DEA Form 224

37. _n_ DEA Form 225

38. _j_ DEA Form 363

39. _l_ DEA Form 222

40. _k_ DEA Form 41

a. limits interstate commerce in drugs to those that are safe and effective

b. established "federal legend"

c. focused on funding Medicare and Medicaid

d. neglected to ban unsafe drugs

e. low abuse, limited dependence

f. lowest abuse potential, lowest dependency

g. no accepted medical use, high abuse potential and high dependency risk

h. high potential for abuse and dependency

i. mostly combination drugs, moderate dependency

j. needed to compound narcotics or conduct narcotic treatment

k. used to report lost or stolen C-II drugs

l. needed to order C-II drugs from distributor

m. needed to dispense

n. needed to manufacture or distribute

True or False?

41. A P.O. Box address is not permitted on a C-II prescription.

   T   (F)

42. C-II prescriptions must be kept separate from all other prescriptions.

   (T)   F

43. All prescription drugs must be distributed in childproof containers.

   T   (F)

Choose the best answer.

44. The NDC number identifies which of the following?
   a. drug
   b. manufacturer
   c. package size
   (d.) all of the above

45. Anabolic steroids (except estrogens, progestins, and corticosteroids) are classified in which schedule?
   a. C-I
   b. C-II
   (c.) C-III
   d. C-IV

46. A moral philosophy is a(n) _____ set of values or value system.
    (a.) individual
    b. professional
    c. community
    d. none of the above

47. Which agency/administration maintains a closed system for the distribution of controlled substances?
    a. CMS
    b. FDA
    (c.) DEA
    d. HHS

Match the following.

48. __C__ indication
49. __b__ warnings
50. __a__ contraindications
51. __d__ precautions

a. lists types of patient who should not use the drug
b. lists remaining possible side effects
c. specific conditions that the FDA has approved the drug to treat
d. serious side effects and what to do

Match the following.

52. __e__ fidelity
53. __C__ beneficence
54. __d__ veracity
55. __a__ justice
56. __b__ autonomy
57. __i__ ethics of care
58. __h__ rights-based ethics
59. __g__ principle-based ethics
60. __f__ virtues-based ethics

a. acting with fairness or equity
b. acting with self-reliance
c. bringing about good
d. telling the truth
e. keeping a promise
f. the idealization of morals
g. more personal approach
h. democratic view of individuals
i. focus on kindness, tact, etc.

PHARMACY CALCULATION PROBLEMS

(1)(2)(14) = 28

Calculate the following.

1. A prescription states that the patient is to take one tablet by mouth twice daily for 14 days. How many tablets will you need to dispense for a 14-day supply?

   28 tablets

2. An antibiotic suspension is dispensed in a 150 mL bottle. If the patient takes 5 mL by mouth three times a day, how many days will the antibiotic last?

   (5)(3) = 15 $\frac{150}{15}$

   10 days

3. A customer gives herself one enoxaparin injection every day. If enoxaparin comes in a 10-count box (a box of 10 single-dose syringes), how many boxes will the customer need for 30 days?

   3 boxes

4. A patient with a chronic pain condition applies one fentanyl patch every 72 hours for pain relief. How often does the patient need to apply a new patch?

   Every 3 days

5. If the patient in question #4 needs enough patches to last 30 days, how many patches should the pharmacy dispense?

   10 patches

PTCB EXAM PRACTICE QUESTIONS

1. Vicodin is an example of a Schedule _____ drug.
   - a. II
   - b. IV
   - c. III
   - d. V

2. HIPAA regulations were established to safeguard and maintain patient privacy. In the law, PHI stands for which of the following?
   - a. personal health information
   - b. protected health information
   - c. private health information
   - d. programmed health information

3. In response to incidents of fatal poisoning from liquid sulfanilamide, which of the following laws required proof that new drugs were safe before they could be marketed?
   - a. Food and Drug Act of 1906
   - b. 1938 Food, Drug, and Cosmetic Act
   - c. 1951 Durham–Humphrey Amendment
   - d. The Kefauver–Harris Amendment of 1962

4. The Combat Methamphetamine Epidemic Act requires that OTC cold and allergy medications that contain which of the following drugs be kept behind the counter?
   - a. antihistamine
   - b. methamphetamine
   - c. ephedrine and pseudoephedrine
   - d. dextromethorphan

5. Which law required childproof packaging for most prescription drugs?
   - a. Food, Drug, and Cosmetic Act
   - b. Poison Prevention Packaging Act
   - c. Durham–Humphrey Amendment
   - d. Kefauver–Harris Amendment

ACTIVITY 4-1: Case Study—Legal Matters and Patient Confidentiality

Instructions: Read the following scenarios and then answer the critical thinking questions.

You and your spouse are having dinner out one evening. As usual, you both discuss events from the day at work. Frustrated, you begin sharing with your spouse, "I had this one patient today, Sharon Eckels, who nearly put me over the edge. She came into the pharmacy and handed us her empty bottle for her antipsychotics, and demanded that we refill it right away. Why can't people call ahead before they run completely out?!"

"That's ridiculous," your spouse responds.

It just so happens that Mr. Eckels, a prominent attorney in the community, is having dinner with a client at a nearby table, and they both overhear your comments. Initially embarrassed, Mr. Eckels is now outraged by the breach of patient confidentiality.

1. What, if any, law or regulation was violated by your dinner conversation?

   _____

   _____

   _____

2. Does Mr. Eckels have a legitimate lawsuit pertaining to patient confidentiality? Why?

   _____

   _____

   _____

3. Could you be liable for your actions? Could the pharmacy be liable for your actions? Explain.

_____

_____

_____

_____

4. What would have been an appropriate way to express your frustration at dinner?

_____

_____

_____

_____

ACTIVITY 4-2: Case Study—Medication Errors and Liability

Instructions: Read the following scenario and then answer the critical thinking questions.

Note: Based on an actual event.

A pharmacy technician who worked at the inpatient pharmacy of a children's hospital made an error when preparing an IV bag. Instead of using a prepackaged saline solution containing 0.9% NaCl (salt), the technician prepared an IV bag with a solution that was 23.4% NaCl.

The IV was reviewed and verified by the staff pharmacist. Although the technician did raise several questions about the product, it was approved and dispensed for administration. The patient to whom it was given, who was two years old, died three days later.

1. Who is responsible for the medication error: the technician, the pharmacist, or both?

_____

_____

_____

_____

2. Who could be held liable for the medication error: the technician, the pharmacist, or both?

_____

_____

_____

_____

3. What do you think would be an appropriate judgment in this scenario: for the parents of the child, for the technician, for the pharmacist, and for the hospital?

_____

_____

_____

_____

4. Research online for a story containing a pharmacy-related medication error. Attach a copy of the article and answer questions 1–3, listed above, concerning this error.

_____

_____

_____

_____

_____

_____

_____

_____

_____

_____

ACTIVITY 4-3: Case Study—Ethical Considerations

Instructions: Read the following scenarios and then answer the critical thinking questions.

Scenario 1

A young man comes into the pharmacy and asks to purchase a box of syringes. When you inquire if he has a prescription for insulin or syringes on file at the pharmacy, he quickly says that he usually fills his prescription at another pharmacy. You also notice that he has not requested a specific size or gauge of syringe. Your intuition tells you that this young man wants to purchase syringes for recreational drug use. If you sell him the syringes, it could be argued that you are enabling his drug use. However, it could also be argued that if you do not sell him the syringes, he will likely still continue to abuse drugs, possibly with dirty or used syringes.

Scenario 2

During the peak of cold and flu season, the manufacturer of one of the best over-the-counter remedies is back-ordered on its products, with an expected delay of six weeks for shipments. You are aware that all the other pharmacies in town are already completely out of stock on this product, but your pharmacy has one package left. An elderly woman comes into the pharmacy, clearly suffering from a nasty cold, to ask if you have any of the medicine available. You promised your next-door-neighbor that you would hold the last package for his family; although they have not yet gotten sick, they want to have the medicine on hand.

1. In Scenario 1, would you sell the young man syringes as he is requesting? Why?

_____

_____

_____

_____

2. In Scenario 2, would you sell the last package of the cold remedy to the elderly woman, or would you reserve it for your neighbor as promised? Why?

_____

_____

_____

_____

3. What ethical theory or moral principle discussed in Chapter 4 of the text are you using as the basis of your decision in both questions? Explain.

_____

_____

_____

_____

4. Describe another ethical consideration, not discussed in the book, that you could imagine occurring in pharmacy practice. How would you handle the situation?

_____

_____

_____

_____

LAB 4-1: Creating a Pharmacy Law Timeline

Objective:

Review and remember the major laws that pertain to the practice of pharmacy in the United States.

Pre-Lab Information:

Review Chapter 4, "Pharmacy Law and Ethics," in your text.

Explanation:

It is important for pharmacy technicians to have an understanding of pharmacy law. Many of our current laws were enacted because of an injury to persons using medications. The progression of laws related to the practice of pharmacy through American history can give you a better perspective on current laws and regulations.

Activity:

Using the following chart, complete the timeline by filling in the correct year in which each law was passed.

Law	Timeline
The Pure Food and Drug Act	
The Prescription Drug Marketing Act	
The Occupational Safety and Health Act	
The Orphan Drug Act	
The Medical Device Amendment	
The Affordable Care Act	
The Poison Prevention Packaging Act	
The Omnibus Budget Reconciliation Act	
The Kefauver–Harris Amendment	
The Health Insurance Portability and Accountability Act	
The Controlled Substances Act	
The Combat Methamphetamine Epidemic Act	
The Medicare Modernization Act	
The Durham–Humphrey Amendment	
The Drug Listing Act	
The Anabolic Steroids Act	
The Food, Drug, and Cosmetic Act	
The Dietary Supplement Health and Education Act	
The Drug Price Competition and Patent Term Restoration Act	

1. Name four broad categories of law in the United States and provide a brief definition of each.

_____

_____

_____

_____

2. What is the difference between criminal and civil law?

_____

_____

_____

_____

3. Name six of the regulatory agencies that oversee the practice of pharmacy in the United States and describe their function(s).

_____

_____

_____

_____

_____

_____

CHAPTER 5
Terminology and Abbreviations

After completing Chapter 5 from the textbook, you should be able to:	Related Activity in the Workbook/Lab Manual
1. Identify selected root words used in pharmacy practice.	Review Questions, Activity 5-3, Lab 5-1, Lab 5-2, Lab 5-3
2. Identify and correctly use selected prefixes and suffixes in conjunction with root words.	Review Questions, Activity 5-3, Lab 5-1, Lab 5-2, Lab 5-3
3. Recognize and interpret common abbreviations used in pharmacy and medicine.	Review Questions, Pharmacy Calculation Problems, PTCB Exam Practice Questions, Activity 5-1, Activity 5-2, Lab 5-1, Lab 5-2, Lab 5-3
4. List abbreviations that are considered dangerous and explain why.	Review Questions, PTCB Exam Practice Questions
5. Recognize and list common drug names and their generic equivalents.	Review Questions, PTCB Exam Practice Questions, Lab 5-1, Lab 5-2, Lab 5-3
6. Recall and define common pharmacy and medical terminology.	Review Questions, Activity 5-3, Lab 5-1, Lab 5-2, Lab 5-3

INTRODUCTION

To understand the pharmacy industry and profession, you must learn its language, which consists of medical terminology, abbreviations, and drug names. Most medical terms derive from Greek and Latin and consist of a root word, prefix, and/or suffix. It is unlikely that you will remember all the information contained in Chapter 5 of the textbook, but by learning selected roots, prefixes, and suffixes, you will be able to understand words you may have never seen or heard before. Over time, with experience and practice, you will develop a strong working knowledge of medical terminology.

REVIEW QUESTIONS

Match the following.

1. __f__ pneum
2. __n__ arthr
3. __e__ hemo
4. __g__ my
5. __d__ oste
6. __m__ ectomy
7. __c__ rhin
8. __l__ ante
9. __b__ dys
10. __h__ hyper
11. __a__ tachy
12. __j__ itis
13. __i__ cyte
14. __k__ dipsia
15. __o__ intra

a. fast
b. abnormal
c. nose
d. bone
e. blood
f. lung
g. muscle
h. too much
i. cell
j. inflammation
k. thirst
l. before
m. surgical removal
n. joint
o. within

Choose the best answer.

16. The part of a word that helps identify its major meaning is the:
    a. prefix.
    b. suffix.
    c. root.
    d. origin.

17. A part of a word that is attached at the beginning of the term is a:
    a. prefix.
    b. suffix.
    c. root.
    d. origin.

18. Which of the following are on the Joint Commission's "do not use" list?
    a. qhs
    b. SC
    c. QOD
    d. all of the above

19. ADR is the accepted abbreviation for:
    a. average drug response.
    b. adverse drug reaction.
    c. antibiotic-related dietary restriction.
    d. acute drug release.

Match the following.

20. __f__ dispense as written
21. __h__ after meals
22. __i__ as needed
23. __k__ before meals
24. __b__ as directed
25. __l__ left ear

a. AU
b. u.d.
c. apap
d. NPO
e. gtt
f. DAW

26. ___j___ twice daily   **g.** NKA
27. ___a___ both ears   **h.** pc
28. ___g___ no known allergies   **i.** prn
29. ___e___ drop   **j.** bid
30. ___q___ milliliter   **k.** ac
31. ___n___ aspirin   **l.** AS
32. ___o___ potassium   **m.** Na
33. ___p___ penicillin   **n.** ASA
34. ___d___ nothing by mouth   **o.** K
35. ___c___ acetaminophen   **p.** PCN
36. ___m___ sodium   **q.** mL

Match the following brand drugs with their generics.

37. ___m___ Accutane   **a.** zolpidem tartrate
38. ___r___ Zoloft   **b.** piroxicam
39. ___x___ Flexeril   **c.** meperidine
40. ___v___ Toprol XL   **d.** warfarin
41. ___g___ Allegra   **e.** etodolac
42. ___h___ Zithromax   **f.** propranolol HCl
43. ___f___ Inderal   **g.** fexofenadine HCl
44. ___b___ Feldene   **h.** azithromycin
45. ___k___ Aldactone   **i.** clonidine HCl
46. ___d___ Coumadin   **j.** donepezil HCl
47. ___e___ Lodine   **k.** spironolactone
48. ___c___ Demerol   **l.** meclizine
49. ___a___ Ambien   **m.** isotretinoin
50. ___n___ Fastin   **n.** phentermine
51. ___l___ Antivert   **o.** clarithromycin
52. ___p___ Halcion   **p.** triazolam
53. ___w___ Lamisil   **q.** valsartan
54. ___j___ Aricept   **r.** sertraline
55. ___i___ Catapres   **s.** clopidogrel
56. ___u___ Phenergan   **t.** amoxicillin and clavulanate potassium
57. ___q___ Diovan   **u.** promethazine HCl
58. ___t___ Augmentin   **v.** metroprolol tartrate
59. ___s___ Plavix   **w.** terbinafine
60. ___o___ Biaxin   **x.** cyclobenzaprine

PHARMACY CALCULATION PROBLEMS

Calculate the following.

1. A prescription reads: "Cephalexin 500 mg: 1 cap qid × 10d." How many capsules should you dispense?

   4 times daily   10 days

   (4)(10) = 40 capsules

2. If a patient takes 5 mL of albuterol syrup BID, how many mL should you dispense for a 10-day supply?

   2 times daily

   5 × 2 = 10 mL for 1 day

   (10)(10) = 100mL

3. How many drops of timolol ophthalmic solution is a patient using per day if the instructions read: "2 gtts ou tid"?

   drops both eyes   three times a day

   2 × 1 = 2 × 2 = 4 × 3 = 12 drops

4. A prescription reads: "Azithromycin 250 mg: Take two tablets by mouth once daily for the first day, then one tablet on days 2–5." How many tablets will you dispense?

   2 3 4 5 = 4   *6 tablets*

5. A bottle of fluticasone nasal spray contains 120 metered doses. If the directions state: "Use 2 sprays in each nostril BID," how many days will the spray last?

   2 times daily

   2 × 2 = 4 × 2 = 8

   15 days   *8⟌120*

PTCB EXAM PRACTICE QUESTIONS

1. Tobrex ophthalmic ung refers to: *ointment*
   - (a.) an ointment used for the eye.
   - b. a solution used for the eye.
   - c. a topical ointment for external use only.
   - d. an ointment used for the ear.

2. If a medication is to be taken a.c., it should be taken:
   - a. in the morning.
   - b. around the clock.
   - c. after meals.
   - (d.) before meals.

3. Which of the following abbreviations is considered acceptable for use when writing medication orders?
   - a. Q.D.
   - b. Q.O.D.
   - (c.) Q.I.D.
   - d. U

4. What is the generic name for the drug Cataflam?
   - a. cimetidine
   - b. diltiazem HCl
   - (c.) diclofenac sodium
   - d. cytarabine

5. What health care accreditation organization has created a list of "do not use" abbreviations?
   - a. APHA
   - b. APA
   - c. NABP
   - (d.) Joint Commission

ACTIVITY 5-1: Case Study—Lost in Translation

Instructions: Read the following scenarios and then answer the critical thinking questions provided.

Scenario 1

A patient brings in a new prescription for Glucophage XR 500 mg. When you are processing the prescription into the pharmacy computer, you quickly select Glucophage 500 mg from the drop-down list of medications as you scroll down. The prescription is filled and dispensed, as neither you nor the pharmacist notice that the prescription was written for Glucophage XR (extended release) as opposed to Glucophage.

Scenario 2

When writing up a compounding formula sheet, you put down that .5 mg of active ingredient is to be used per dose. The following month, however, another technician is reviewing the formula to prepare the patient's refill. The refill is prepared using 5 mg of active ingredient per dose, as opposed to 0.5 mg.

1. What translation error occurred in Scenario 1?

2. What effect will the error in Scenario 1 have?

3. What translation error occurred in Scenario 2?

4. What effect will the error in Scenario 2 have?

5. Who is responsible for the mistake in Scenario 2? How could it most easily have been avoided?

6. What can you do to ensure that these types of errors are avoided?

_____

_____

_____

_____

ACTIVITY 5-2: Practice with Abbreviations

For each of the following, write the meaning next to the abbreviation.

1. p *after*
2. pm *afternoon*
3. N/V *nausea & vomiting*
4. ac *before meals*
5. po *by mouth*
6. DAW *dispense as written*
7. NS *normal saline*
8. bid *two per day*
9. u.d. *as directed*
10. qd *every day*

11. s *without*
12. AU *both ears*
13. prn *as needed*
14. qw *every week*
15. WA *while awake*
16. disp. *dispense*
17. fl. *fluid*
18. D5W *Dextrose 5% in water*
19. DM *Diabetes mellitus*
20. NKA *No known allergies*

Now, write the appropriate abbreviation after its meaning.

21. suppository *supp*
22. every day at bedtime *qhs*
23. microgram *mcg*
24. with *C*
25. right eye *OD*
26. intravenous *IV*
27. by mouth *PO*
28. left ear *AS*
29. otic *OT*
30. drops *gtts*

ACTIVITY 5-3: Defining Medical Terms

Using a medical dictionary, your text, or an online medical resource, define the following medical terms. Then, break the term into its word parts and define each word part as well.

1. gynecologist
   Definition: _Doctor who studies female reproductive system_
   Word parts: _gyno = woman   logist = specialist_

2. rhinoplasty
   Definition: _surgical repair of the nose_
   Word parts: _rhino = nose   plasty = surgical repair_

3. dermatologist
   Definition: _Doctor who studies the skin_
   Word parts: _derm = skin   logist = specialist_

4. arthritis
   Definition: _inflammation of the joints_
   Word parts: _arth = joint   itis = inflammation_

5. polyurea
   Definition: _increased urination_
   Word parts: _poly = many   urea = urine_

6. erythrocytes
   Definition: _Red Blood cells_
   Word parts: _erythro = red   cytes = cells_

7. leukocytes
   Definition: _White Blood cells_
   Word parts: _leuko = white   cytes = cells_

8. arteriosclerosis
   Definition: _Hardening of the arteries_
   Word parts: _arter = artery   sclerosis = hardening_

9. hematuria
   Definition: _Blood in the urine_
   Word parts: _hema = bood   uria = urine_

10. tachycardia
    Definition: _fast heartbeat_
    Word parts: _tachy = fast   cardia = heart_

LAB 5-1: Translating a Medical Record

Objective:

Reinforce your knowledge of terminology and abbreviations by completing this exercise based on a medical record entry.

Pre-Lab Information:

Review Chapter 5, "Terminology and Abbreviations," in your text.

Explanation:

It is important for pharmacy technicians to have a basic understanding of the language used in medicine. This exercise will help you gain experience by "translating" a medical record entry.

Activity:

Read the following pharmacist SOAP (Subjective, Objective, Assessment, Plan) note from a patient's pharmacist consultation and answer questions related to the content, using your knowledge of terminology and abbreviations.

S:	67 yo BF with Hx of arthritis, obesity, hyperlipidemia, hypertension. Several questions about medications and improving health status.	
O:	Type 2 DM *Diabetes Mellitus*	Morning BS 130–155+; does not test routinely, A1c 8.5% (6 mo ago)
	HTN *hypertension*	155/95 on ramipril 10 mg bid *2 times a day*
	Hyperlipidemia	TC 219, LDL 143, TRG 185 (6 mo ago) on simvastatin 20 mg once daily
	Obesity	59'90" / 230 lb, BMI 34 *acetaminophen as needed*
	RA *Rheumatoid Arthritis*	Knee and hip pain with exercise, APAP prn only
	SCr	1.6 (6 mo ago)
	Vitals	P 78, R 19 *Aspirin cardiovascular*
		Not taking ASA for CVD prevention *Blood sugar*
A:	Diabetes	Poor compliance diet/meal planning; poor understanding of BS testing; above goal of A1c, 7%
	HTN *hypertension*	Above goal of BP 125/80 with Tx *Treatment blood pressure*
	Hyperlipidemia	Above goal of LDL ≤ 100 with Tx *Treatment*
	Obesity	Above goal, 25 lb gain over last 6 mo, min exercise frequency; Initial goal 10% weight loss at 1–2 lb/wk (23 lb in 4 mo)
	RA *Rheumatoid Arthritis*	Still not well controlled

History

P:	Improve medication adherence and health outcomes.
	• HTN: Recommended changing ramipril 10 mg bid to lisinopril/HCTZ 20/12.5 bid
	• Hyperlipidemia: Recommended increasing simvastatin from 20 mg to 40 mg once daily
	• RA: Recommended diclofenac XR 100 mg once daily for RA
	• Cardiovascular health: Recommended adding lo-dose ASA daily
	• Provided and instructed pt with daily BS monitoring log
	• Provided and instructed pt with personal health tracking tool
	• Reviewed "ADA Dietary Guidelines" and shopping/meal planner guide
	• Suggested pt walk 30–60 min/day
	• Schedule for 90-day F/U appt.
	• Schedule for repeat of the following labs 2 weeks prior to 90-day FU appt: SCr, fasting lipid profile, A1c, BG

[Handwritten annotations: "Hypertension" next to HTN line, "2 times a day" above bid, "2 times a day" at top right, "extended release" above diclofenac XR, "Rheumatoid Arthritis" next to RA line, "aspirin" above ASA, "patient" above pt, "blood sugar" above BS, "Rheumatoid Arthritis" in left margin, "patient" annotations]

Duration of appt: 45 minutes

Pharmacist's signature: _____

Questions:

1. What does the abbreviation Hx mean?

   History

2. What does APAP prn mean?

   acetaminophen (Tylenol) as needed

3. In the "Objective" section, which drug (generic and brand name) did the patient take to control cholesterol?

   simvastatin (Zocor)

4. In the "Objective" section, which drug (generic and brand name) did the patient take to control blood pressure?

   ramipril

5. What does the abbreviation BS mean?

   Blood sugar

6. What does the abbreviation HTN mean?

   Hypertension

7. In the "Plan" section, what drug (generic and brand) did the pharmacist recommend changing for the patient's HTN?

lisinopril/HCTZ (Prinizide or Zestoretic)

8. In the "Plan" section, what does the abbreviation ASA mean?

aspirin

LAB 5-2: Translating a Prescription

Objective:

Reinforce your knowledge of terminology and abbreviations by completing this exercise based on a prescription.

Pre-Lab Information:

Review Chapter 5, "Terminology and Abbreviations," in your text.

Explanation:

It is critical for pharmacy technicians to have an understanding of the terminology and abbreviations used in pharmacy. This exercise will help you gain experience by "translating" the directions on prescriptions.

Activity:

Review and translate the following prescriptions, then either prepare an accurate prescription label for each prescription or write out the information requested below.

Rx #1

Towne Center Family Medicine
40 Towne Center Drive
Pleasantville, Texas 77248-0124
Phone 281-555-0134 Fax 281-555-0125

James L. Brook, MD BB1234563   Rebecca Smith, MD AS1234563   Walter Roberts, MD AR1234563
Sharon Ortiz, NP   Beth Matthews, NP   Terri King, NP

Name _*Cindy Redding*_   Age _____

Address _____   Date _*Aug 05*_

℞

Zoloft 50 mg

#30

T po qam

Refill __2__ times

Terri King
Signature

A generically equivalent drug product may be dispensed unless the practitioner hand writes the words
'Brand Necessary' or 'Brand Medically Necessary' on the face of the prescription.

6HUR133050

1. Patient name: _Cindy Redding_
2. Prescriber: _Terri King_
3. Drug name and strength: _Zoloft 50 mg_
4. Is generic substitution permitted? _yes_
5. Quantity to dispense: _30_
6. Directions: _Take by mouth every morning_
7. Refills authorized: _2_
8. Days Supply: _30_

Rx #2

Towne Center Family Medicine
40 Towne Center Drive
Pleasantville, Texas 77248-0124
Phone 281-555-0134 Fax 281-555-0125

James L. Brook, MD BB1234563   Rebecca Smith, MD AS1234563   Walter Roberts, MD AR1234563
Sharon Ortiz, NP   Beth Matthews, NP   Terri King, NP

Name _Felix Ortiz_____ Age _____

Address _____ Date _Jan 20_____

Rx

Glucophage 850mg

#30

T po qd c̄ food

Refill ___I___ times

Rebecca Smith
Signature

A generically equivalent drug product may be dispensed unless the practitioner hand writes the words
'Brand Necessary' or 'Brand Medically Necessary' on the face of the prescription.

6HUR133050

---

1. Patient name: _Felix Ortiz_
2. Prescriber: _Rebecca Smith_
3. Drug name and strength: _Glucophage 850 mg_
4. Is generic substitution permitted? _yes_
5. Quantity to dispense: _30_
6. Directions: _Take by mouth everyday with food_
7. Refills authorized: _1_
8. Days Supply: _30_

Rx #3

Towne Center Family Medicine
40 Towne Center Drive
Pleasantville, Texas 77248-0124
Phone 281-555-0134 Fax 281-555-0125

James L. Brook, MD BB1234563   Rebecca Smith, MD AS1234563   Walter Roberts, MD AR1234563
Sharon Ortiz, NP   Beth Matthews, NP   Terri King, NP

Name _Nancy Nguyen_   Age _____

Address _____   Date _Oct 12_

℞

Amoxil 500mg

#28

T po bid × 14d

Refill ___0___ times

J. L. Brook
Signature

A generically equivalent drug product may be dispensed unless the practitioner hand writes the words
'Brand Necessary' or 'Brand Medically Necessary' on the face of the prescription.

6HUR133050

---

1. Patient name: _Nancy Nguyen_
2. Prescriber: _James L. Brook_
3. Drug name and strength: _Amoxil 500mg_
4. Is generic substitution permitted? _yes_
5. Quantity to dispense: _28_
6. Directions: _Take by mouth twice a day for 14 days_
7. Refills authorized: _0_
8. Days Supply: _14_

LAB 5-3: Translating a Medication Order

Objective:

Reinforce your knowledge of terminology and abbreviations by completing this exercise based on a prescription.

Pre-Lab Information:

Review Chapter 5, "Terminology and Abbreviations," in your text.

Explanation:

It is critical for pharmacy technicians to have an understanding of the terminology and abbreviations used in pharmacy. This exercise will help you gain experience by "translating" the directions on medication orders.

Activity:

Review and translate the following medication orders, then either prepare an accurate prescription label for each prescription or write out the information requested below.

Medication Order #1

PHYSICIAN'S ORDER WORKSHEET

NOTE: *Person initiating entry should write legibly, date the form using (Mo/Day/Yr.), enter time, sign, and indicate their title.*

USE BALL POINT PEN (PRESS FIRMLY)

17325   220

04-06-1968

Dr. S. Turner

Date	Time	Treatment
5/15	18:30	Merrem IV 500mg q 8hr
		②

		Distribution:	
‖‖‖‖‖	**PHYSICIAN'S ORDER WORKSHEET**	(Original) Medical Record Copy (Plies 3, 2, & 1) Pharmacy	**T-5**

1. Patient name: _____
2. Prescriber: _Dr. S Turner_____
3. Drug name and strength: ___Merrem 500 mg_____
4. Is generic substitution permitted? __yes_____
5. Quantity to dispense: _____
6. Directions: _____IV every 8 hours_____
7. Refills authorized: _____
8. Days Supply: _____

Medication Order #2

PHYSICIAN'S ORDER WORKSHEET

NOTE: *Person initiating entry should write legibly, date the form using (Mo/Day/Yr.), enter time, sign, and indicate their title.*

USE BALL POINT PEN (PRESS FIRMLY)

034561   405 B

07-14-1987

Dr. F. Roberts

Date	Time	Treatment
9/4	10:15	Morphine inj 3mg
		②

PHYSICIAN'S ORDER WORKSHEET

Distribution:
(Original) Medical Record Copy
(Plies 3, 2, & 1) Pharmacy

T-5

1. Patient name: _____
2. Prescriber: ___Dr. F Roberts_____
3. Drug name and strength: ___Morphine 3 mg_____
4. Is generic substitution permitted? ___yes_____
5. Quantity to dispense: _____
6. Directions: ___Injection_____
7. Refills authorized: _____
8. Days Supply: _____

Medication Order #3

PHYSICIAN'S ORDER WORKSHEET

NOTE: *Person initiating entry should write legibly, date the form using (Mo/Day/Yr.), enter time, sign, and indicate their title.*

USE BALL POINT PEN (PRESS FIRMLY)

6702340   102

12-03-1949

Dr. R. Khan

Date	Time	Treatment
3/18	16.45	Zofran inj. 4mg
		②

PHYSICIAN'S ORDER WORKSHEET

Distribution:
(Original) Medical Record Copy
(Plies 3, 2, & 1) Pharmacy

T-5

1. Patient name: _____
2. Prescriber: Dr. R Khan
3. Drug name and strength: Zofran 4 mg
4. Is generic substitution permitted? yes
5. Quantity to dispense: _____
6. Directions: Injection
7. Refills authorized: _____
8. Days Supply: _____

CHAPTER 6
Dosage Formulations and Routes of Administration

After completing Chapter 6 from the textbook, you should be able to:	Related Activity in the Workbook/Lab Manual
1. Explain drug nomenclature.	Review Questions
2. Identify various dosage formulations.	Review Questions, PTCB Exam Practice Questions
3. Identify the advantages and disadvantages of solid and liquid medication dosage formulations.	Review Questions, PTCB Exam Practice Questions
4. Explain the differences between solutions, emulsions, and suspensions.	Review Questions, PTCB Exam Practice Questions
5. Explain the difference between ointments and creams.	Review Questions, PTCB Exam Practice Questions
6. Identify the various routes of administration and give examples of each.	Review Questions, PTCB Exam Practice Questions
7. Give examples of common medications for various routes of administration.	Review Questions
8. Identify the advantages and disadvantages of each route of administration.	Review Questions
9. Identify the parenteral routes of administration.	Review Questions, PTCB Exam Practice Questions
10. Explain the difference between transdermal and topical routes of administration.	Review Questions, PTCB Exam Practice Questions
11. Explain the difference between sublingual and buccal routes of administration.	Review Questions, PTCB Exam Practice Questions
12. Identify the abbreviations for the common routes of administration and dosage formulations.	Review Questions

INTRODUCTION

As a pharmacy technician, one of your many responsibilities is to work with the pharmacist to prepare and dispense medications to patients. You need to know that drugs can come from one of three sources: natural, synthetic, or genetically engineered.

You also need to understand the concept of drug nomenclature and how to recognize a drug's chemical, generic, and trade/brand names. Finally, you must be familiar with the meaning of and use for each dosage form and route. Most of the dosage forms do imply a certain route that is to be used. However, many dosage forms may be administered via several different routes. For example, a tablet is commonly administered orally, but it can be administered vaginally as well. Liquid medications can also be administered in a variety of ways. If the prescription order is not clear as to the dosage form and route, the pharmacy staff and medical staff must work together to determine what is best for the patient and to avoid medication errors.

REVIEW QUESTIONS

Match the following.

1. __f__ anhydrous
2. __i__ aromatic
3. __l__ aqueous
4. __a__ dosage form
5. __r__ emollient
6. __n__ emulsion
7. __b__ formulary
8. __m__ HMO
9. __c__ homogenous
10. __q__ hydrophobic
11. __e__ nomenclature
12. __p__ occlusive
13. __h__ oleaginous
14. __o__ route of administration
15. __s__ synthesized
16. __j__ semi-synthetic
17. __s__ synthetic
18. __g__ viscous
19. __d__ volatile

a. actual form of the drug
b. listing of drugs approved for use
c. a group having all the same qualities
d. evaporates rapidly
e. set of names; way of naming
f. without water
g. thick; almost jelly-like
h. containing oil; has oil-like properties
i. having a fragrant aroma
j. a naturally occurring compound that has been chemically altered
k. drug produced in a laboratory to imitate a naturally occurring compound
l. contains water
m. health maintenance organization
n. liquid mixture of water and oil
o. how a drug is introduced into or on the body
p. closes off; keeps air away
q. repels water
r. softening and soothing to the skin
s. drugs that are not naturally occurring in the body

Choose the best answer.

20. Which is not one of the classifications of sources of drugs?
    a. genetically engineered
    b. synthetic
    c. natural
    (d.) manufactured

21. A disadvantage of solid-dose medications is:
    a. longer shelf life before expiration.
    b. dosing is more accurate.
    c. patients are able to self-administer.
    (d.) they take longer to be absorbed.

22. Creams are:
    (a.) semisolid.
    b. solid.
    c. semiliquid.
    d. jellyfied.

Match the following drugs with their sources.

23. __f__ morphine
24. __g__ aspirin
25. __e__ human growth hormone
26. __d__ vincristine
27. __c__ OxyContin
28. __b__ Pepsin
29. __a__ adrenaline
30. __h__ digoxin

a. synthesized epinephrine
b. the stomach of a cow
c. synthetic opium
d. periwinkle
e. pituitary gland
f. opium poppy plant
g. white willow bark
h. foxglove

Fill in the blanks.

31. A drug is __semi-synthetic__ if it is a naturally occurring substance that has been chemically altered.
32. __Effverscent preparations__ release carbon dioxide when they come into contact with liquid.
33. Collodions are alcoholic solutions that contain __pyroxylin__.
34. Oleaginous ointments are __emollients__ used to soothe and cool the skin or mucous membranes.
35. Emulsions are comprised of __oil__ and __water__.

PHARMACY CALCULATION PROBLEMS

Calculate the following.

10 mg/Kg twice daily

$\dfrac{10mg}{Kg} \left| \dfrac{1Kg}{2.2lbs} \right| 45 lbs$

1. Levetiracetam is usually initiated at 20 mg/kg/day in two divided doses for a pediatric patient. Determine the dose in milligrams for a boy who weighs 45 pounds.

200 mg

2. Levetiracetam comes in a 100 mg/mL oral solution. How many milliliters will you need per dose for the patient in question #1?

$\dfrac{200mg}{} \left| \dfrac{1mL}{100mg} \right. = 2\ mL$

3. If a patient is receiving ondansetron 4 mg IVP tid prn, what is the maximum daily dosage the patient will receive in milligrams?

4 × 3 = 12 mg

4. If an acetaminophen 80 mg suppository is prescribed q6–8 hr prn, what is the maximum number of suppositories the patient can receive in a day? 4

5. What amount of active ingredient is contained in 60 gm of a 2.5% cream?

$$(60)(.025) = 1.5\,gm$$

PTCB EXAM PRACTICE QUESTIONS

1. The best known example of a sublingual tablet formulation is:
   a. hydrochlorothiazide.
   b. nitroglycerin.
   c. digoxin.
   d. codeine.

2. Which would *not* be caused by particulate material in an intravenous injection?
   a. air emboli
   b. thrombus
   c. phlebitis
   d. necrosis

3. Emulsions are likely to be used in which route of administration?
   a. oral
   b. buccal
   c. topical
   d. sublingual

4. Which ophthalmic formulation will maintain the drug in contact with the eye the longest?
   a. solution
   b. gel
   c. suspension
   d. ointment

5. Which is the most common and uncomplicated route of administration?
   a. buccal
   b. intravenous
   c. oral
   d. topical

CHAPTER 7
Referencing and Drug Information Resources

After completing Chapter 7 from the textbook, you should be able to:	Related Activity in the Workbook/Lab Manual
1. Explain the need for referencing and drug information resources.	Review Questions, PTCB Exam Practice Questions
2. Outline and describe the proper steps for referencing drug information resources.	Review Questions
3. Explain how package insert monographs are used for referencing.	Review Questions, PTCB Exam Practice Questions
4. List and describe the most commonly used printed drug reference books in pharmacies.	Review Questions, PTCB Exam Practice Questions
5. List and describe the most commonly used electronic and web-based references in pharmacies.	Review Questions
6. Outline and describe the proper steps for evaluating the credibility of a website for use as a reference.	Review Questions
7. List and describe the most commonly used journals and magazines in pharmacies	Review Questions

INTRODUCTION

Pharmacy practice relies on accurate and timely information, and new, revised, and updated information occurs at a frequent pace within health care sciences. Physicians, nurses, pharmacists, pharmacy technicians, and other health care professionals must stay constantly informed on the latest drugs, therapeutic indications, dosing standards, and clinical evidence. Pharmacy professionals, in particular, must stay well informed as both patients and health care professionals, such as doctors and nurses, often turn to the pharmacist for answers to their medication-related questions. The pharmacist commonly handles these inquiries through the process of referencing. As a pharmacy technician, therefore, mastering the ability to reference drug information resources is critical. Although in many cases the information will be able to be communicated only by the pharmacist, a pharmacy technician can play a vital role in helping the pharmacist look up the needed information. In other cases, pharmacy technicians will rely on the ability to reference drug information resources for their roles in pharmacy practice.

REVIEW QUESTIONS

Match the following.

1. __e__ referencing
2. __a__ drug information resources
3. __g__ off-label usage
4. __b__ drug classification
5. __d__ therapeutic indication
6. __c__ index
7. __f__ apps

a. any source providing credible, evidence-based, and evaluated drug information.

b. grouping drugs together based on similar chemical structures, mechanisms of action, or pharmacologic effects.

c. an alphabetical listing of names or subjects with page references for ease of use.

d. the specific disease or condition a drug is intended to treat.

e. using drug information resources to find evidence-based information.

f. applications, can refer to use on computers, smartphones, tablets, etc.

g. the practice, regulated by the FDA, of physicians prescribing approved medications for use other than their intended indication.

Choose the best answer.

8. Off-label usage is regulated by the _____.
   - a. DEA
   - b. FDA
   - c. SBOP
   - d. USP

9. _____ refers to a specific disease or condition a drug is intended to treat.
   - a. Drug classification
   - b. Drug indication
   - c. Therapeutic classification
   - d. Therapeutic indication

10. Which reference book contains average wholesale prices (AWP) for prescription drugs?
    - a. *AHFS-DI*
    - b. *Facts and Comparisons*
    - c. *RED BOOK*
    - d. *USP-NF*

11. The _____ contains detailed information on more than 1,000 of the most prescribed drugs, but it is designed primarily for use in physician offices.
    - a. *AHFS-DI*
    - b. *FDA Orange Book*
    - c. *PDR*
    - d. *USP-NF*

12. _____ is part of the U.S. National Library of Medicine.
    - a. Medline
    - b. MEDMARX
    - c. Micromedex
    - d. none of the above

13. The *Handbook on Injectable Drugs* contains all of the following information on parenteral drugs, except:
    - a. compatibility.
    - b. pricing.
    - c. sizes.
    - d. strengths.

14. Determining the appropriate reference source is the _____ step in referencing.
    a. first
    b. second
    c. third
    d. fourth

15. Skyscape is an example of a _____ reference source:
    a. book-based
    b. journal-based
    c. website-based
    d. all of the above

Identify which of the following reference sources contain drug monograph information.

16. _B_ PDR
17. _A_ *Handbook on Injectable Drugs*
18. _B_ *Remington*
19. _B_ Medline
20. _A_ USP-NF
21. _B_ *Goodman & Gilman's*
22. _B_ AJHP
23. _B_ *Orange Book*
24. _B_ RED BOOK
25. _A_ *Facts and Comparisons*

a. contains drug monograph information

b. does NOT contain drug monograph information

Fill in the blanks.

26. __Medmarx__ is the largest registry of adverse drug events in the United States.
27. __Indentidex__ is the Micromedex product that assists in the identification of unknown drugs by imprint code or slang term.
28. *Drug Topics*, *Pharmacy Times*, and *U.S. Pharmacist* are all published __12__ times per year.
29. __Drug Facts & Companions__ is the most commonly used drug information reference used in community pharmacies.
30. AHFS Drug Information is primarily used in __Health System__ pharmacies.

PHARMACY CALCULATION PROBLEMS

Calculate the following.

1. $1/8 + 1/4 =$ $\frac{3}{8}$ or .375

2. $3/5 - 1/10 =$ $\frac{1}{2}$ or .5

3. $4 \times 1/3 =$ $\frac{4}{3}$ or $1\frac{1}{3}$ or 1.33

4. $1/8 \div 2/3 =$ $\frac{3}{16}$

5. $5\ 3/7 \times 2\ 1/2$ $\frac{190}{14}$ or 13.57

$\frac{1}{8} + \frac{1}{4}$
$\frac{1}{8} + \frac{2}{8}) \times 2 = \frac{3}{8}$

$\times 2 (\frac{3}{6}\frac{5}{6} - \frac{1}{10}\frac{1}{10}) = \frac{5}{10} \div \frac{1}{2}$

$\frac{4}{1} \times \frac{1}{3} = \frac{4}{3}$ $3\overline{)\frac{4}{3}}^{1\frac{1}{3}}$

$\frac{1}{8} \div \frac{2}{3}$

$\frac{1}{8} \times \frac{3}{2} = \frac{3}{16}$

PTCB EXAM PRACTICE QUESTIONS

1. On a package insert, the _____ section lists the types of patients who should not use the medication.
   a. contraindications
   b. clinical pharmacology
   c. indications and usage
   d. warnings

2. Which of the following reference sources does not contain drug monographs?
   a. *American Drug Index*
   b. *Facts and Comparisons*
   c. *Geriatric Dosage Handbook*
   d. *Remington*

3. The _____ requires package inserts as part of the labeling of a drug.
   a. CDC
   b. DEA
   c. FDA
   d. USP

4. _____ allows facilities to anonymously and voluntarily report adverse drug events.
   a. Medline
   b. Medscape
   c. MEDMARX
   d. Micromedex

5. The _____ is published by the FDA.
   a. *American Drug Index*
   b. *Orange Book*
   c. *RED BOOK*
   d. *USP-NF*

CHAPTER 8
Retail Pharmacy

After completing Chapter 8 from the textbook, you should be able to:	Related Activity in the Workbook/Lab Manual
1. Explain the ambulatory pharmacy practice setting.	Review Questions
2. Describe the two main types of retail pharmacies.	Review Questions
3. List the various staff positions in retail pharmacies.	Review Questions, Activity 8-4
4. Describe the typical work environment of a retail pharmacy.	Review Questions
5. Discuss the two agencies that regulate retail pharmacy practice.	Review Questions, PTCB Exam Practice Questions
6. List the legal requirements of a prescription medication order.	Review Questions, PTCB Exam Practice Questions, Activity 8-3, Lab 8-1
7. Describe the different ways prescriptions arrive at a retail pharmacy.	Review Questions, Activity 8-1
8. List the steps required for a prescription to be filled.	Review Questions, PTCB Exam Practice Questions, Activity 8-1
9. Discuss the various job duties of technicians in retail pharmacies.	Review Questions, Activity 8-1, Activity 8-3, Activity 8-4, Lab 8-1, Lab 8-2
10. Discuss the importance of confidentiality for personal health information.	Review Questions, PTCB Exam Practice Questions, Activity 8-2

INTRODUCTION

The two main types of pharmacy practice are ambulatory and institutional. An institutional pharmacy is located on the site of the patients' residence; pharmacies within hospitals, nursing homes, hospices, and long-term care facilities are examples. Most other pharmacies fall into the category of ambulatory. Examples of ambulatory settings, which are usually called *community-based* or *retail pharmacies*, are privately owned, chain, and franchise pharmacies, as well as clinics. Retail pharmacy is the largest category of pharmacy in the United States. These types of pharmacies serve the community in which they are located.

The staff at a retail pharmacy includes the pharmacist in charge (PIC), pharmacy manager, staff pharmacists, pharmacy technicians, and, in many cases, pharmacy clerks. It is a fast-paced work environment where pharmacy professionals interact with patients face to face. Pharmacy technicians have numerous job responsibilities, from taking care of inventory orders, rotations, returns, and billing to counting, measuring, filling, and labeling. In the retail environment, you may also help patients find over-the-counter (OTC) medications or lead them to the pharmacist for counseling, to name only a few of your daily tasks. In ambulatory pharmacy, every day is another opportunity to serve the community.

REVIEW QUESTIONS

Match each of the following.

1. __c__ chain pharmacy
2. __a__ franchise pharmacy
3. __b__ neighborhood pharmacy
4. __d__ outpatient pharmacy

a. owned by an individual, with several different owner-operated locations
b. privately owned, relatively small in size, pharmacy
c. corporately owned, more than four pharmacies
d. affiliated with a health care system, hospital, clinic, or ambulatory care facility

Fill in the blanks.

5. The process of transmitting a prescription electronically to the appropriate insurance carrier for approval is called __adjudication__.
6. The code DAW, when written by the prescriber, means __Dispense as written__.
7. An electronic record stored in the pharmacy computer system detailing the patient's personal and billing information, prescription records, and medical conditions is known as a/an __patient profile__
8. When the patient resides where the medication is kept, the pharmacy there is described as a/an __instutional__ pharmacy.
9. The agency that registers and regulates pharmacies, pharmacists, and pharmacy technicians, as well as the practice of pharmacy, is known as the __SBOP__.
10. The __CMS__ conducts inspections to ensure compliance with its guidelines and also approves reimbursement for Medicare and Medicaid.

True or False?

11. Retail pharmacy practice allows for a more hands-on approach.
    (T)   F

12. The term "Pharm.D." is used to designate a Director of Pharmacy.
    T   (F)

13. Pregnancy tests can be obtained only with a prescription.
    T   (F)

14. Any OTC product may be kept behind the counter if the pharmacist chooses.
    (T)   F

Choose the best answer.

15. Which of the following is not an approved prescriber?

   a. DDS   c. DVM

   b. PA   d. RN

16. Which of the following is a valid DEA number for Dr. Rebecca Carey?

   a. AC5932764   c. BC3791250

   b. BC8162753   d. AC79131591

17. A C-III prescription may be refilled:

   a. six times.   c. for six months from the date it was written.

   b. zero times.   d. for one year from the date it was first filled.

18. Which of the following is not required on a prescription?

   a. route of administration   c. strength of drug

   b. patient's age   d. prescriber's signature

19. The prescriber wrote Mr. Mallory's prescription for Synthroid® on 12/14/2008 with prn refills. Mr. Mallory had the prescription filled for the first time on 03/09/2009. He may continue receiving monthly refills until:

   a. 12/14/2009.   c. 03/09/2010.

   b. 12/14/2008.   d. 03/09/2009.

20. The second group of numbers in an NDC code signifies:

   a. package size.   c. drug, strength, and form.

   b. manufacturer.   d. cost (AWP).

21. Once a medication has left the pharmacy counter, it may:

   a. not be returned for resale.   c. not be returned for resale or refund.

   b. not be returned for a refund.   d. be refunded and/or resold if the pharmacist allows.

22. Most pharmacies and insurance providers require a prescription to be _ used before it may be refilled.

   a. 50%   c. 75%

   b. 90%   d. 100%

23. Most states restrict controlled medications with refills:

   a. to a maximum of one transfer.

   b. to zero transfers; controlled substances may not be refilled.

   c. so that all refills written by the prescriber may be transferred.

   d. to a maximum of three refills that are transferred.

24. It is not a technician's responsibility to:
    a. verify the information in a patient's profile.
    b. counsel a patient on the use of a medication.
    c. double-count a controlled medication for accuracy.
    d. contact an insurance provider on behalf of a patient.

25. When Mrs. Rigby asked to have her Lunesta® prescription transferred from across town, the technician should:
    a. explain to her that controlled medications cannot be transferred.
    b. inform her that the sending pharmacy has to call.
    c. check her profile to see if the prescription had been transferred before and if there are any refills remaining.
    d. apprise her that it may take up to 24 hours to complete the transfer.

PHARMACY CALCULATION PROBLEMS

Calculate the following.

$5 \times 6 = 30$ $30\overline{)120}$ by mouth every 4 hrs as needed

1. The directions for a prescription cough medicine states: Take 5 mL po q4h prn. If the patient takes the maximum daily amount, how long will a 120 mL bottle last?

   4 days

2. If the sig on the prescription states "2 tabs po q hs," how many tablets will you need to dispense in order to last for 28 days?   by mouth every bedtime

   56 tablets

3. If a patient is taking tetracycline 500 mg caps po bid, how many capsules are needed for a 30-day supply?   by mouth 2 times a day

   60 capsules

4. Jill is compounding a prescription that requires $\frac{3}{4}$ oz. of hydrocortisone 1% cream, $\frac{1}{4}$ oz. nystatin cream, and $\frac{1}{4}$ oz. of clotrimazole 1% cream. How many ounces will be in the finished product?

   1.25 oz

5. The directions for a prescription antibiotic state: Give 5 mL tid. Disp: 150 mL. What is the correct days supply for this prescription?   3 times a day

   $5 \times 3 = 15$ 10 days

PTCB EXAM PRACTICE QUESTIONS

1. Which organization oversees the practice of community pharmacies in the United States?
   a. FDA
   b. DEA
   c. SBOP
   d. APHA

2. In the following number, NDC 51285-601-05, the first set (51285) represents which of the following?
   a. drug name
   b. manufacturer
   c. dosage form
   d. capsule size

3. How many times can you refill a prescription for Viagra®?
   a. As many times as indicated by the prescriber.
   (b.) As many times as indicated by the prescriber within one year from the date the prescription was written.
   c. Six times within six months.
   d. None.

4. Which law provides for protection of patient confidentiality?
   (a.) HIPAA
   b. TJC
   c. OSHA
   d. CSA

5. A technician receives a prescription for a controlled substance. The prescription is from out of state and the technician is unfamiliar with the physician and the customer. The DEA number for the physician is AG8642123. Based on the physician's DEA number, is this a fraudulent prescription?

$$\text{No}$$

$$\begin{array}{r} 8 \\ + 4 \\ \hline 12 \\ + 1 \\ \hline 13 \end{array}$$

$$\begin{array}{r} 6 \\ + 2 \\ \hline 8 \\ + 2 \\ \hline 10 \times 2 = 20 \end{array}$$

$$\begin{array}{r} 20 \\ + 13 \\ \hline 33 \end{array}$$

ACTIVITY 8-1: Prescription Translation Worksheet

Review each of the following three prescriptions, then translate the information contained in each one.

Rx #1

Towne Center Family Medicine
40 Towne Center Drive
Pleasantville, Texas 77248-0124
Phone 281-555-0134 Fax 281-555-0125

| James L. Brook, MD BB1234563 | Rebecca Smith, MD AS1234563 | Walter Roberts, MD AR1234563 |
| Sharon Ortiz, NP | Beth Matthews, NP | Terri King, NP |

Name _Melvin Brooks_____ Age_____

Address_____ Date _Nov 21_____

R

Isordol 10 mg

#60

Tpo bid

Refill _____ times

(signature)

Signature

A generically equivalent drug product may be dispensed unless the practitioner hand writes the words
'Brand Necessary' or 'Brand Medically Necessary' on the face of the prescription.   6HUR133050

---

1. Patient name: _Melvin Brookers_____
2. Prescriber: _Sharon Ortiz for James Brook_____
3. Drug name and strength: _Isordol 10 mg_____
4. Is generic substitution permitted? _yes_____
5. Quantity to dispense: _60_____
6. Directions/ SIG: _Take by mouth 2 times a day__
7. Refills authorized: _zero_____

Rx #2

Towne Center Family Medicine
40 Towne Center Drive
Pleasantville, Texas 77248-0124
Phone 281-555-0134 Fax 281-555-0125

James L. Brook, MD BB1234563   Rebecca Smith, MD AS1234563   Walter Roberts, MD AR1234563
Sharon Ortiz, NP   Beth Matthews, NP   Terri King, NP

Name _____*Beth Andrews*_____ Age _____

Address _____ Date _*03/12*_____

℞

         Allegra 60mg

                #60

        T po Bid

Refill ___*2*___ times

_____ *Signature*

A generically equivalent drug product may be dispensed unless the practitioner hand writes the words
'Brand Necessary' or 'Brand Medically Necessary' on the face of the prescription.

                                                  6HUR133050

---

1. Patient name: ____*Beth Andrews*_____
2. Prescriber: ____*James Brook*_____
3. Drug name and strength: ____*Allegra 60mg*_____
4. Is generic substitution permitted? ____*yes*_____
5. Quantity to dispense: ____*60*_____
6. Directions/ SIG: ____*Take by mouth 2 times a day*____
7. Refills authorized: ____*2*_____

Rx #3

Towne Center Family Medicine
40 Towne Center Drive
Pleasantville, Texas 77248-0124
Phone 281-555-0134 Fax 281-555-0125

James L. Brook, MD BB1234563   Rebecca Smith, MD AS1234563   Walter Roberts, MD AR1234563
Sharon Ortiz, NP   Beth Matthews, NP   Terri King, NP

Name _Stephanie Ruiz_   Age _____

Address _____   Date _March 12_

℞

Azelex 30%

#1

U UD

Refill __3__ times

Becky Smith
Signature

A generically equivalent drug product may be dispensed unless the practitioner hand writes the words
'Brand Necessary' or 'Brand Medically Necessary' on the face of the prescription.

6HUR133050

1. Patient name: _Stephanie Ruiz_
2. Prescriber: _Rebecca Smith_
3. Drug name and strength: _Azelex 30g_
4. Is generic substitution permitted? _yes_
5. Quantity to dispense: _1_
6. Directions/ SIG: _use as directed_
7. Refills authorized: _3_

ACTIVITY 8-2: Case Study—Privacy/HIPAA

Instructions: Read the following scenario and then answer the critical thinking questions.

A remodel of the work space at the retail pharmacy in which you work has finally begun. Many people were involved in the design planning, including various construction personnel. However, no one from the pharmacy itself was included on the planning committee. Weeks pass, and it appears that the newly remodeled pharmacy will allow a more efficient use of space.

The remodel is completed on a Friday, and everyone returns to work on Monday excited to see the new space. Almost immediately, everyone notices that the redesigned space lacks an adequate area for patient counseling. HIPAA mandates that every pharmacy have a patient counseling area.

The pharmacy does not close down while this space is added, but instead remains open for business, and pharmacy personnel are asked to "work around" the inconvenience. You are told that the counseling area will be in place after two more weeks of construction. In the meantime, it seems almost impossible to find a private space to counsel patients.

1. What are some creative ways in which the pharmacy could assure patient privacy during counseling until construction is complete?

_____

_____

_____

_____

2. What effect might this inconvenience have on the pharmacy workload, in terms of time?

_____

_____

_____

_____

3. Describe what a HIPAA-compliant counseling area, which protects patient privacy, might look like or include.

_____

_____

_____

_____

Research: Research more information about HIPAA-compliant counseling areas for pharmacy. Does any of the information you find surprise you? How does the information you discover compare with the reality of the pharmacy you personally use?

ACTIVITY 8-3: Case Study—Biases

Instructions: Read the following scenario and then answer the critical thinking questions.

A gangly, unkempt, middle-aged man with a slightly offensive odor presents a prescription at your pharmacy for hydrocodone bitartrate 5 mg/acetaminophen 500 mg #120 to be taken twice daily as needed for pain. He attempts to rush you through the process, talking excessively and stating that he should be getting more than what was prescribed. His actions make you suspicious, in that he appears nervous, is constantly looking around, and becomes increasingly agitated with each question you ask, such as his address and phone number. It appears that the amount of tablets may have been altered, but you are not quite certain, as this provider's writing is not very legible.

The man becomes more and more uncooperative as you try to gain the information you need to process the prescription, but finally you have everything you need. You have been trained to notice things that may raise questions as to the validity of prescriptions and feel that this may be one such situation. You bring this to the attention of the pharmacist in charge, who in turn calls to verify the prescription. It turns out that the prescription is legitimate and the patient has some mental health issues.

1. What were some factors in this scene that made the technician suspect that this might be a fraudulent prescription?

   _____

   _____

   _____

   _____

2. Can you identify any communication barriers present with this type of patient?

   _____

   _____

   _____

   _____

3. Do you think that the way the patient was dressed or acted contributed to the assessment that his might be a fraudulent prescription?

   _____

   _____

   _____

   _____

ACTIVITY 8-4: Case Study—Patient Requests Recommendations

Instructions: Read the following scenario and then answer the critical thinking questions.

Mrs. Hornbuckle, with her 4-year-old daughter in tow, approaches the pharmacy counter and requests some assistance in locating the Children's Tylenol Liquid. You are the only person available, and state that it is located on aisle 6 toward the back of the store; you then offer to show her to the area. Mrs. Hornbuckle accepts your offer and the three of you head to aisle 6.

You point out the Children's Tylenol Liquid section, but before you can walk away, Mrs. Hornbuckle begins asking questions about the wide array of Tylenol liquid preparations. She states that her daughter has a really bad cough and wants to know which one works best, the grape- or the cherry-flavored. Meanwhile, she is picking up boxes and reading the information on the back.

You explain that a pharmacist could answer any questions she may have about the medicines. With a frustrated sigh, she says, "Forget it," and starts to walk out in a huff, obviously upset that you were not able to answer the questions yourself.

1. Why might Mrs. Hornbuckle have felt that you could (and should) have answered her questions about medications?

   _____
   _____
   _____
   _____

2. Do you think pharmacy technicians should identify themselves as such, or would it matter to the general public, who may not know the difference between pharmacy technicians and pharmacists?

   _____
   _____
   _____
   _____

3. How would you explain to a patient/customer, in an understanding way, your limited authority as a pharmacy technician?

   _____
   _____
   _____
   _____

LAB 8-1: Checking a Prescription for Completeness

Objective:

To interpret some sample prescriptions, identify their key components, and then determine if the prescriptions contain all of the necessary information required for processing.

Pre-Lab Information:

Review Tables 5-4, 5-5, 5-6, and 5-7 from Chapter 5 of your textbook to re-familiarize yourself with various medical terms and abbreviations.

Explanation:

Many times a legitimate prescription lacks some of the information required for processing. This exercise will help you review the key components of a prescription, practice translating prescriptions, as well as for you to identify any imperative missing information required for processing.

Activity:

Four prescriptions have been dropped off at the pharmacy to be filled. The first step is to put the data from the prescriptions into the computer. Translate the prescription, note all key points that must be printed on the labels, and determine if the prescriptions contain all the information needed for processing.

Dr. L. MacCoy
1234 Enterprise Dr
San Francisco, CA 00000
800-555-1234

Name _Jill Johnson_ Age _____

Address _79 Holiday Rd_ Date _06/08/15_

Rx

Metoprolol tablets

#60

Sig: 1 po bid

Refill _5_ times

L. MacCoy
Signature

A generically equivalent drug product may be dispensed unless the practitioner hand writes the words
'Brand Necessary' or 'Brand Medically Necessary' on the face of the prescription.

6HUR133050

1. Does the information seem correct on the prescription for Jill Johnson? How would you translate
   the instructions for the prescription label? Is there any imperative missing information from this prescription?

   1 by mouth 2 times a day
   Missing the strength

```
                    Dr. Fillmore McGraw
                    100 Hollywood Blvd.
                    Los Angeles, CA 00000
                      (800) 123-4567



Name_Britanny Spires_____ Age_____

Address_6002 Hillside Place_____ Date_07/02/15_____

℞

        Xanax 0.25 mg tablet



        Sig: 1 po tid prn anxiety



Refill ___0___ times

            Fillmore McGraw
                    Signature

A generically equivalent drug product may be dispensed unless the practitioner hand writes the words
'Brand Necessary' or 'Brand Medically Necessary' on the face of the prescription.
                                              6HUR133050
```

2. Does the information seem correct on the prescription for Britanny Spires? How would you translate the instructions for the prescription label? Is there any imperative missing information from this prescription?

_____DEA number_____

_____1 by mouth 3 times a day as needed for anxiety_

_____

Elsie Kumar, MD
4605 Lakeshore Drive
Chicago, IL 00000
(819) 555-1111

Name _Sandy Deitz_____ Age_____

Address _123 Laramy Ct_____ Date _05/14/15_____

℞

Sig: Promethazine 25 mg

1 q4-6hr prn nausea

Refill ____0____ times

_Elsie Kumar, MD_____
Signature

A generically equivalent drug product may be dispensed unless the practitioner hand writes the words
'Brand Necessary' or 'Brand Medically Necessary' on the face of the prescription.   6HUR133050

3. Does the information seem correct on the prescription for Sandy Deitz? How would you translate
the instructions for the prescription label? Is there any imperative missing information from this
prescription? _route of administration_____

___1 every 4-6hrs as needed for nausea_____

_____

```
                    Timothy Stiles, DDS
                        65 Main St.
                    Davenport, IA 00000
                     (563) 111-2222




Name    Jeremy Jacobsen                          Age_____

Address    455 Brady Street              Date   7/25/15

℞


              Amoxicillin 500mg



              Sig: 1 po TID X 10 days




Refill_____O_____times
_____
                          Signature
```

A generically equivalent drug product may be dispensed unless the practitioner hand writes the words
'Brand Necessary' or 'Brand Medically Necessary' on the face of the prescription.   6HUR133050

---

4. Does the information seem correct on the prescription for Jeremy Jacobsen? How would you translate the instructions for the prescription label? How many capsules will be needed to fill this prescription? Is there any imperative missing information from this prescription?

Signature
30 capsules

LAB 8-2: Counting Oral Medication in a Community Pharmacy Setting

Objective:

To demonstrate the ability to count oral medications manually as well as gain experience with cleaning procedures in the pharmacy.

Pre-Lab Information:

- Review Chapter 8, "Retail Pharmacy," in the textbook.
- Gather the following supplies:
- Pill counting tray and spatula
- Large bag of M&Ms®, Skittles®, or other small-sized hard candy
- Prescription vials, plastic sandwich bags, or other containers for the "tablets"
- Isopropyl alcohol (70%)

Explanation:

This exercise will give you the opportunity to practice counting "tablets" manually. In the pharmacy, tablets are generally counted in increments of five, while using a pill counting tray and spatula on a clean, clutter-free counter. It requires ongoing practice for you to feel confident and efficient in counting tablets by fives. Until you gain experience, please remember to count tablets twice before giving them to the "pharmacist."

Option: You can complete this lab utilizing automated counting and dispensing equipment to gain experience in using this equipment.

Activity:

Part 1

For this first exercise, you will count 15 tablets.

1. Prepare a clean, clutter-free work surface, and then place a clean pill counting tray and spatula in front of you.
2. Pour a substantial amount of your "tablets" into the counting tray. Then open the lid of the pour compartment.
3. Begin counting the "tablets" in increments of five while using the counting spatula. Slide each group of five "tablets" into the pour compartment of your tray. Count by fives until you reach 15 tablets. Then close the lid of the pour compartment.
4. Return any unused "tablets" that remain in your counting tray to their original container or bag.
5. Select an appropriate-sized prescription vial and place it on the counter next to the counting tray.
6. Pour or "re-dispense" the "tablets" you counted into the vial.
7. Now pour the "tablets" you counted back into your counting tray and count them again to make sure you have 15.
8. Repeat step 6. Then place the appropriate-sized lid on the prescription vial.

Part 2

For this next exercise, you will use the materials from the previous activity to prepare the following "prescriptions" for "dispensing."

1. Ibuprofen [M&Ms] 800 mg   30 tablets

   Sig: 1 tab tid × 10 days
   3 times a day for 10 days
   Count the correct number of "tablets" required to fill this prescription.

2. M&Mcycline 320 mg tabs   20 tablets

   Sig: 1 tab qid × 5 days
   4 times a day for 5 days
   Count the correct number of "tablets" required to fill this prescription.

3. M&Mnisone 20 mg tabs   6   2   16 tablets
                              8
   Sig: 1 tab qid × 2 days; 1 tab tid × 2 days; then 1 tab daily × 2 days
   4 times a day   3 times a day
   Count the correct number of "tablets" required to fill this prescription.

Feel free to continue counting until all of the "tablets" are "re-dispensed."

Part 3

To complete this lab activity, please clean your materials and work area using a disinfectant solution of water and 70% isopropyl alcohol. Spray the solution on the counting tray and spatula, then wipe them both with a paper towel and return them to the shelf or appropriate storage location. Then, spray the counter with the solution and wipe the counter down.

CHAPTER 9
Health-System Pharmacy

After completing Chapter 9 from the textbook, you should be able to:	Related Activity in the Workbook/Lab Manual
1. Describe the health-system pharmacy practice setting.	Review Questions, PTCB Exam Practice Questions
2. Describe the advantages of a unit-dose system.	Review Questions, PTCB Exam Practice Questions
3. List the necessary components of a medication order.	Review Questions, Activity 9-1, Lab 9-1
4. Compare the duties of a technician with those of a pharmacist in accepting a medication order in a health-system setting.	Review Questions, Activity 9-1
5. Compare centralized and decentralized unit-dose systems.	Review Questions
6. Compare the duties of a technician with those of a pharmacist in filling a medication order in a health-system setting.	Review Questions, Activity 9-1, Lab 9-1
7. Define the tasks pharmacy technicians perform in health-system settings.	Review Questions, Activity 9-1, Lab 9-1

INTRODUCTION

A health-system pharmacy, also called an *institutional pharmacy*, is designed to serve patients who live onsite. Examples of facilities that might include an institutional pharmacy are long-term care facilities, nursing homes, hospitals, correctional facilities, and hospices. Regardless of the type of facility, the on-site pharmacy is responsible for all patients' medications; pharmacy staff must ensure that drug therapies are appropriate, effective, and safe. The health-system pharmacist also identifies, resolves, and prevents medication-related problems. As a pharmacy technician working in this setting, you must understand the policies and procedures of your institution, as well as state and federal laws. In addition to filling prescriptions and medication orders, you might also work with several distribution systems, repackage bulk medications for floors and patient care areas, use unit-dose and automatic dispensing systems, and handle sterile products.

REVIEW QUESTIONS

Match each of the following.

1. __g__ blister packs
2. __f__ decentralized pharmacy system
3. __h__ centralized pharmacy system
4. __a__ emergency medication orders
5. __k__ floor stock
6. __d__ POE system
7. __j__ unit dose
8. __b__ STAT order
9. __e__ standing order
10. __c__ patient prescription stock system
11. __i__ PRN order

a. a specific order required to respond to a medical emergency

b. medication order that takes priority over other orders and requests

c. orders are reviewed, prepared, verified, and delivered to the patient

d. allows prescribers to enter orders directly into the pharmacy computer system

e. scheduled order to be administered throughout the day

f. consists of central, inpatient, outpatient, and satellite pharmacies

g. unit-dose packages

h. all pharmacy-related services are performed in one location

i. order used only as necessary or needed

j. medication order is filled for no more than a 24-hour period

k. medications stored on the same floor where patients' rooms are, for patient distribution

Choose the best answer.

12. A licensed individual who is trained to examine patients, diagnose illnesses, and prescribe/administer medication is a:
    - (a.) doctor of medicine (MD).
    - b. doctor of osteopathy (DO).
    - c. licensed nursing assistant (LNA).
    - d. licensed practical nurse (LPN).

13. An individual who is licensed to provide basic care, such as administering medication under the supervision of an RN, is a:
    - a. doctor of medicine (MD).
    - b. doctor of osteopathy (DO).
    - c. licensed nursing assistant (LNA).
    - (d.) licensed practical nurse (LPN).

14. An individual who is registered to assist physicians with specific procedures, administer medication, and provide patient care is a:
    - a. licensed practical nurse (LPN).
    - b. licensed nursing assistant (LNA).
    - (c.) registered nurse (RN).
    - d. nurse practitioner (NP).

15. An individual who is certified to assist RNs and LPNs in providing patient care, but is not permitted to administer medication, is a:
    - a. licensed practical nurse (LPN).
    - (b.) licensed nursing assistant (LNA).
    - c. registered nurse (RN).
    - d. nurse practitioner (NP).

16. An individual who is licensed to work closely with a physician in providing patient care, typically under the supervision of a physician, is a:
    - a. licensed practical nurse (LPN).
    - b. licensed nursing assistant (LNA).
    - c. registered nurse (RN).
    - (d.) nurse practitioner (NP).

17. A licensed individual, who is trained to coordinate patient care under the supervision of a medical or osteopathic doctor, is a:
    a. licensed practical nurse (LPN).
    b. licensed nursing assistant (LNA).
    c. physician's assistant (PA).
    d. nurse practitioner (NP).

18. A pharmacy that provides services to onsite patients 24 hours a day, 365 days each year, is called a:
    a. mail-order pharmacy.
    b. health-system pharmacy.
    c. community pharmacy.
    d. all of the above.

19. The American Hospital Association (AHA) categorizes hospitals as community-based, federal government, psychiatric, long-term care, or institutional hospital units. Which represent 85% of the total number of registered hospitals?
    a. community-based
    b. federal government
    c. long-term care
    d. psychiatric

Match the following organizations/agencies/regulations to their area of influence.

20. __c__ HIPAA   a. laboratories
21. __d__ OBRA   b. children
22. __f__ CMS   c. privacy
23. __b__ SCHIP   d. counseling
24. __e__ DPH   e. regulates hospitals
25. __a__ CLIA   f. Medicare/Medicaid

PHARMACY CALCULATION PROBLEMS

Calculate the following.

1. A hospitalized patient needs a 24-hour supply of sucralfate 1 gm tablets. How many tablets will be dispensed if the patient is administered it as a qid dose?

   4 times a day   4

2. A patient on the infectious disease floor takes 10 mL of levofloxacin syrup bid. If the product is only available as a 5 mL unit-dose oral syringe, how many syringes will the technician prepare for a 24-hour supply?

   2 times a day
   10 × 2 = 20

   4 syringes

3. A technician is checking floor stock on one of the nursing units. She notices that the floor has five acetaminophen 325 mg tablets left, but their par level is 20. How many tablets should the technician restock?

   15 tablets

4. While checking a crash cart tray that was recently used for a code, Bill finds that there are two epinephrine syringes left in the tray. When the tray is fully stocked, it contains 12 epinephrine syringes. How many syringes should be restocked in the tray?

10 syringes

5. Karen is repackaging cyanocobalamin 1,000 mcg tablets into unit dosages on February 16, 2014. The manufacturer's expiration date for the product is December 2015. What expiration date should Karen assign to the repackaged medication?

Feb. 16, 2015

PTCB EXAM PRACTICE QUESTIONS

1. Which of the following health care practitioners is not considered a prescriber?
   a. medical doctor (MD)
   b. physician assistant (PA)
   c. nurse practitioner (NP)
   d. certified nursing assistant (CNA)

2. A unit dose is a:
   a. package that contains all non-controlled medications for a given day.
   b. package that contains all medications for a given day.
   c. controlled substance.
   d. package that contains the amount of given day medication for one dose.

3. Which of the following allows a patient to receive medications on an as-needed basis?
   a. STAT order
   b. standing order
   c. parenteral
   d. PRN order

4. Nurses track medication administration on a/an:
   a. PCU.
   b. PRN.
   c. STAT.
   d. MAR.

5. In the health-system setting, needles and other items that can cut or puncture the skin should be thrown away in:
   a. MSDS.
   b. designated sharps containers.
   c. red garbage bags.
   d. regular garbage cans.

ACTIVITY 9-1: Medication Order Translation Worksheet

Review and translate each of the medication orders provided below.

Medication Order #1

PHYSICIAN'S ORDER WORKSHEET

NOTE: *Person initiating entry should write legibly, date the form using (Mo/Day/Yr.), enter time, sign, and indicate their title.*

USE BALL POINT PEN (PRESS FIRMLY)

```
45671001        311A
Eckels, Ruby G.
04-10-1943

Dr. C. Thomsen
```

Date	Time	Treatment
10/18	4:30	Dilaudid 0.5 mg IV inject q 3h prn pain
		②

PHYSICIAN'S ORDER WORKSHEET

Distribution:
(Original) Medical Record Copy
(Plies 3, 2, & 1) Pharmacy

T-5

1. Patient name: _Ruby G. Eckels_
2. Prescriber: _Dr. C. Thomsen_
3. Drug name and strength: _Dilaudid 0.5mg_
4. Directions/SIG: _IV injection every 3 hours as needed for pain_

Medication Order #2

PHYSICIAN'S ORDER WORKSHEET

NOTE: *Person initiating entry should write legibly, date the form
using (Mo/Day/Yr.), enter time, sign, and indicate their title.*

USE BALL POINT PEN (PRESS FIRMLY)

132445855   210
Sanchez, Roberto L.
10-01-1940

Dr. L. Hubbard

Date	Time	Treatment
7/14	10:50	Levaquin 500 mg IV infusion over 6hr
		②

▐▐▌▐	**PHYSICIAN'S ORDER WORKSHEET**	Distribution: (Original) Medical Record Copy (Plies 3, 2, & 1) Pharmacy **T-5**

1. Patient name: ___Roberto L. Sanchez___
2. Prescriber: ___Dr. L Hubbard___
3. Drug name and strength: ___Levaquin 500mg___
4. Directions/SIG: ___IV infusion over 6 hours___

Medication Order #3

PHYSICIAN'S ORDER WORKSHEET

NOTE: *Person initiating entry should write legibly, date the form using (Mo/Day/Yr.), enter time, sign, and indicate their title.*

USE BALL POINT PEN (PRESS FIRMLY)

```
82347665        835 A
George, Sarah M.
02-17-1961

Dr. L. Montgomery
```

Date	Time	Treatment
4/10	13:00	Ibuprofen 600 mg po q 6hr
		②

PHYSICIAN'S ORDER WORKSHEET Distribution: (Original) Medical Record Copy (Plies 3, 2, & 1) Pharmacy   **T-5**

1. Patient name: _Sarah M. George_
2. Prescriber: _Dr. L Montgomery_
3. Drug name and strength: _Ibuprofen 600mg_
4. Directions/SIG: _By mouth every 6 hours_

Medication Order #4

PHYSICIAN'S ORDER WORKSHEET

NOTE: *Person initiating entry should write legibly, date the form using (Mo/Day/Yr.), enter time, sign, and indicate their title.*

USE BALL POINT PEN (PRESS FIRMLY)

```
782467199        1410 B
Smith, Cody M.
11-18-1975

Dr. L. Halberdier
```

Date	Time	Treatment
8/14	13:15	Ranitidine 150 mg Infusion over 24 hr
		②

PHYSICIAN'S ORDER WORKSHEET

Distribution:
(Original) Medical Record Copy
(Plies 3, 2, & 1) Pharmacy

T-5

1. Patient name: _Cody M. Smith_
2. Prescriber: _Dr. L Halberdier_
3. Drug name and strength: _Ranitidine 150mg_
4. Directions/SIG: _Infusion over 24 hour_

LAB 9-1: Filling a Medication Order

Objective:

To follow the proper procedure for filling a medication order.

Pre-Lab Information:

Review Chapter 9, "Health-System Pharmacy," in your textbook.

Explanation:

The medication order form is a multipurpose tool for communication among various members of the health care team who are working within a health system. In addition to the listed prescribed medications, this form can be used by the physician for ordering lab values, dietary considerations, X-rays, or other medical procedures. It is imperative that all pharmacy personnel be able to properly distinguish and interpret medication orders.

Hospitals may use a physical, hard-copy medication order form. Alternatives to a hard-copy medication order form are: a physician order entry system (POE) or a computerized physician order entry system (CPOE). The CPOE is a computerized system in which orders are entered electronically into the hospital's networked system.

Activity:

Review each of the following medication orders. Please enter each of them into the pharmacy computer system to generate the appropriate labels. Then fill the medications, and label the prescriptions for the pharmacist to review.

If you do not have access to a pharmacy computer system, you may use the blank label that appears at the end of this lab.

PHYSICIAN'S ORDER WORKSHEET

NOTE: *Person initiating entry should write legibly, date the form using (Mo/Day/Yr.), enter time, sign, and indicate their title.*

USE BALL POINT PEN (PRESS FIRMLY)

```
63450091            105
Randall, Kristen F.
09-28-63

Dr. R. Manini
```

Date	Time	Treatment
3/30	10:30	Restoril 15mg po qhs prn sleep
		②

PHYSICIAN'S ORDER WORKSHEET

Distribution:
(Original) Medical Record Copy
(Plies 3, 2, & 1) Pharmacy

T-5

Medication Order # 2

PHYSICIAN'S ORDER WORKSHEET

NOTE: *Person initiating entry should write legibly, date the form using (Mo/Day/Yr.), enter time, sign, and indicate their title.*

USE BALL POINT PEN (PRESS FIRMLY)

51298556	620 B
Nguyen, Kim T.	
05-05-1971	

Dr. K. Tran

Date	Time	Treatment
9/8	8:30	√ICODIN 5/500 PO PRN PAIN
		②

PHYSICIAN'S ORDER WORKSHEET

Distribution:
(Original) Medical Record Copy
(Plies 3, 2, & 1) Pharmacy

T-5

Medication Order #3

PHYSICIAN'S ORDER WORKSHEET

NOTE: *Person initiating entry should write legibly, date the form using (Mo/Day/Yr.), enter time, sign, and indicate their title.*

USE BALL POINT PEN (PRESS FIRMLY)

Date	Time	Treatment
4/10	11:20	Diflucan 200 mg IV over 4 hrs
		②

PHYSICIAN'S ORDER WORKSHEET

Distribution:
(Original) Medical Record Copy
(Plies 3, 2, & 1) Pharmacy

T-5

Use the following label template to perform this lab if you do not have access to a computer.

```
Hometown Pharmacy, 325 Main St., Shelbyville, TX 72349, phone 321-555-8765

Prescription #:

Patient:

Prescriber:

Prescription:

Quantity:

Directions:

SIG:

Date Filled:

Refills Remaining:
```

Discussion Questions:

1. What was the most challenging aspect of this lab for you? Why?

_____

_____

_____

2. Did you enter and fill each prescription accurately and correctly? If not, what mistakes did you make? How will you avoid making such errors in the future?

_____

_____

_____

LAB 9-2: Unit-Dosing and Repackaging

Objective:

To become familiar with the process and procedures of unit-dosing and repackaging in inpatient settings.

Pre-Lab Information:

• Review Chapter 9, "Health-System Pharmacy" in your textbook.

Explanation:

As nursing homes and long-term care facilities, as well as closed-door pharmacies, often fill for their patients a unit-dose supply of medications, the technician is relied upon to repackage the orders for each patient.

Activity:

Review each of the following orders for the two "patients." Fill each of the orders using a 30-day blister card. This will be for a cold-seal tray. Make sure to notate the expiration date and lot number of each medication.

Patient #1: James Kicks

PHYSICIAN'S ORDER WORKSHEET

James Kicks

NOTE: *Person initiating entry should write legibly, date the form using (Mo/Day/Yr.), enter time, sign, and indicate their title.*

USE BALL POINT PEN (PRESS FIRMLY)

Date	Time	Treatment
		Truvada \t, qd
		Isentress \t, bid
		Multivitamin \t, qd

PHYSICIAN'S ORDER WORKSHEET

Distribution:
(Original) Medical Record Copy
(Plies 3, 2, & 1) Pharmacy

T-5

Patient #2: Karen Sweets

PHYSICIAN'S ORDER WORKSHEET

Karen Sweets

NOTE: *Person initiating entry should write legibly, date the form using (Mo/Day/Yr.), enter time, sign, and indicate their title.*

USE BALL POINT PEN (PRESS FIRMLY)

Date	Time	Treatment
		warfarin 2.5 mg 1t, qd, M,W,F, Sun
		warfarin 5 mg 1t, qd, Tues, Thur. Sat
		②

 PHYSICIAN'S ORDER WORKSHEET

Distribution:
(Original) Medical Record Copy
(Plies 3, 2, & 1) Pharmacy

T-5

CHAPTER 10
Technology in the Pharmacy

After completing Chapter 10 from the textbook, you should be able to:	Related Activity in the Workbook/Lab Manual
1. List the hardware and software components used in pharmacy computers and summarize their purpose.	Review Questions, PTCB Exam Practice Questions
2. Describe and discuss the use of automation and robotics in community pharmacies.	Review Questions, PTCB Exam Practice Questions
3. Describe and discuss the use of automation and robotics in health-system pharmacies.	Review Questions
4. Define and explain telepharmacy practice.	Review Questions
5. Summarize the impact of patient confidentiality regulations on the use of technology in the pharmacy.	Review Questions

INTRODUCTION

Over the past few decades, technology has revolutionized the practice of pharmacy. Today, virtually every pharmacy uses computers, automated systems, and other technology platforms for its operations and management of pharmaceutical care. Technology is used in both community and health-system pharmacies. As a pharmacy technician, it is important for you to have a basic understanding of the different technologies that are available and being used in pharmacies. These include basic tools, such as computers, printers, modems, and scanners, as well as more advanced tools, such as automatic counters, dispensing systems, bar coding, and even robots. Although you will certainly learn a lot on the job, if you enter the workplace computer literate and familiar with some basic concepts, you will be comfortable managing technological changes as they arise.

REVIEW QUESTIONS

Match the following.

1. _____ hardware
2. _____ hard drive
3. _____ database
4. _____ CPU
5. _____ applications
6. _____ input devices
7. _____ keyboard
8. _____ modem
9. _____ software
10. _____ ROM
11. _____ RAM
12. _____ operating system
13. _____ EHRs
14. _____ telepharmacy

a. connects computers via phone lines or cable
b. lists of information ordered in specific ways
c. hardware that allows information to be entered
d. primary software/program of a computer system
e. uses advanced telecommunications technology
f. brain of the computer system
g. permanent memory for essential operations
h. mechanical and electrical components of a computer
i. primary input device of a computer
j. temporary memory used for inputting
k. software/programs that perform specific functions
l. main storage device
m. programs and applications that control computers
n. electronic accessible patient records

True or False?

15. Electronic counters are a threat to pharmacy technician jobs.
    T   F

16. The FDA mandates that all prescription medications contain a bar code.
    T   F

17. A faxed prescription is considered a legal document in most states.
    T   F

18. Patient profiling is a violation of federal discrimination laws.
    T   F

19. Pharmacists and technicians may now research a patient's EHR.
    T   F

Fill in the blank.

20. Using telecommunications technology, pharmacists can provide care to patients in medically under-served areas at a distance. This is called _____.

PHARMACY CALCULATION PROBLEMS

Calculate the following.

1. A patient's medical order reads: "cefazolin 1,000 mg IVPB q8hr 3 days." How many grams of cefazolin will the patient receive in total?

   every 8 hrs for 3 days

   1 day = 3000 mg
   8 x 3 = 24

   3,000 x 3 = 9,000 mg
   9 g

2. A patient is going to receive 1,500 mg of vancomycin IVPB daily in three divided doses. How many milligrams will the patient receive in each dose?

   $$\frac{1,500}{3}$$

   500 mg

3. A technician runs a report and finds that an automated dispensing unit in the ER has only two vials of ondansetron left. The maximum par level for that medication is 20 vials. That item also has a minimum par set of five vials. How many vials should the technician restock?

   18

4. A patient needs 25 mg hydroxyzine IV push. The vial contains 50 mg in each mL. How many milliliters will the patient need?

   $$\frac{25 mg}{} \mid \frac{1 mL}{50 mg} = .5 mL$$

5. A patient is receiving 100 mL of NACl IV every hour. How long will a 1,000 mL IV bag last?

   $$\frac{1,000}{1000} = 10 \text{ hours}$$

PTCB EXAM PRACTICE QUESTIONS

1. What part of a computer is responsible for interpreting commands and running software applications?
   a. JAZ
   b. RAM
   c. CPU
   d. ROM

2. E-prescribing greatly reduces:
   a. illegible physician handwriting.
   b. forgeries.
   c. medication errors.
   d. all of the above.

3. Which of the following examples of pharmacy technology has not been associated with improved patient safety?
   a. computerized patient profiles
   b. automated dispensing systems
   c. central processing unit
   d. prescription filling robot

4. What information is contained in the bar code mandated by the FDA?
   a. NDC code
   b. DEA number
   c. Social Security number
   d. AWP

5. Which of the following is considered a hardware output device?
   a. keyboard
   b. mouse
   c. printer
   d. scanner

CHAPTER 11
Inventory Management

After completing Chapter 11 from the textbook, you should be able to:	Related Activity in the Workbook/Lab Manual
1. List and describe the various purchasing systems used in pharmacies.	Review Questions, PTCB Exam Practice Questions
2. List and describe the various methods of purchasing available in pharmacies.	Review Questions, PTCB Exam Practice Questions
3. Define and describe prescription formularies.	Review Questions, PTCB Exam Practice Questions
4. Describe and perform the steps necessary for placing orders.	Review Questions, PTCB Exam Practice Questions
5. Describe and perform the steps necessary for receiving orders.	Review Questions, PTCB Exam Practice Questions, Activity 11-1
6. List the atypical products to consider with inventory management.	Review Questions, PTCB Exam Practice Questions
7. List the reasons for back-ordered products and outline appropriate methods to communicate changes in product availability.	Review Questions, PTCB Exam Practice Questions, Activity 11-2
8. Classify the reasons for product returns and describe the process of making returns.	Review Questions, PTCB Exam Practice Questions, Activity 11-1
9. List and explain the three classifications of drug recalls.	Review Questions, PTCB Exam Practice Questions
10. Describe the process of handling expired drugs.	Review Questions, PTCB Exam Practice Questions

11. Identify the problems with having excessive inventory.	Reveiw Questions, PTCB Exam Practice Questions
12. Describe the issue of drug theft and diversion.	Review Questions, PTCB Exam Practice Questions, Activity 11-1

INTRODUCTION

One of the most common duties you will perform as a pharmacy technician is inventory management.

A pharmacy cannot dispense prescriptions if the proper medications are not in stock. A pharmacy obtains its inventory through a purchasing system, either as a member of a group purchasing system (GPO) or independently. The inventory is often based on an organization's formulary or the formularies approved by insurance carriers. A pharmacy's inventory must be closely and regularly monitored to ensure that adequate stock is available, to remove expired drugs, and to comply with any product recalls.

Although the management of inventory varies by facility, as a pharmacy technician, you will be available to assist the pharmacist by handling these responsibilities and allowing the pharmacist to focus on more clinical aspects of pharmaceutical care provision.

REVIEW QUESTIONS

Fill in the blanks.

1. A _____ is a collective purchasing system in which a pharmacy joins a GPO, which contracts with pharmaceutical manufacturers on behalf of its members.

2. A purchasing system in which the pharmacy is responsible for establishing contracts directly with each pharmaceutical manufacturer is a/an _____.

3. A procedure for obtaining medications, devices, and products for an organization is known as a/an _____.

4. The process through which a drug manufacturer or the FDA requires that specific drugs be returned to the manufacturer because of a specific concern is known as a/an _____.

5. A _____ enables the pharmacy to purchase a large number of products, from various manufacturers, from a single source.

Choose the best answer.

6. Formularies are used by:
   a. institutional pharmacies.
   b. insurance companies.
   c. ambulatory pharmacies.
   d. all of the above.

7. Inventory should be checked for "outdates":
   a. weekly.
   b. monthly.
   c. yearly.
   d. whenever there is time.

8. OTC products may be recalled by the:
   a. FDA.
   b. DEA.
   c. AFT.
   d. FTC.

9. The P&T Committee is composed of:
   a. physicians.
   b. pharmacists.
   c. nurses.
   d. all of the above.

10. Evaluating the costs of medications will vary greatly depending on:
    a. its NDC number.
    b. the wholesaler.
    c. if the drug is a brand or a generic.
    d. contracted prices between the manufacturer and the pharmacy.

Match the following.

11. _____ Class I Recall   a. someone has or could die from using a drug

12. _____ Class II Recall   b. a drug has been mislabeled or is noncompliant

13. _____ Class III Recall   c. a drug could cause harm, but is not deadly

PHARMACY CALCULATION PROBLEMS

Calculate the following.

1. The pharmacy's automated order system indicates that there are 240 hydrochlorothiazide 25 mg tablets left in inventory. If the system is programmed to reorder when the order point falls below 200, how many bottles of 100 tablets will the system order?

   0

2. The pharmacy's automated order system indicates that there are seven vials of Humulin R insulin left. How many vials will the system order if the reorder point falls below 10?

   3 vials

3. A small, independent pharmacy has a manual ordering system with maximum/minimum levels (in bottles) written on the shelf under the drug. If the maximum/minimum levels for nabumetone 500 mg are 4/2, and there is one bottle on the shelf, how many bottles should be reordered?

   1 - 3 bottles

4. A customer is picking up three prescriptions and owes a co-pay of $7.50 on each one. If she hands the pharmacy clerk $30, how much change should the customer receive?

   7.5 X 3 = 22.5   30 - 22.5 = $7.50

5. A pharmacy is running a special on cold medicines: buy two and get the third for 50% off. If a customer purchases three cold medicines that are all regularly $5.99 each, how much is the total cost to the customer?

   5.99 X 2 = 11.98   5.99 X .5 = 2.995

+11.98
  2.995
$14.98

PTCB EXAM PRACTICE QUESTIONS

1. A listing of the goods or items that a business will use in its normal operation is called a/an:
   a. purchasing.
   b. inventory.
   c. open formulary.
   d. closed formulary.

2. The goal of inventory management is:
   a. to ensure that drugs are available when they are needed.
   b. to maintain MSDS.
   c. to develop closed formularies.
   d. to increase use of wholesalers.

3. What do we call the minimum and maximum stock levels that are used to determine when to reorder a drug and how much to order?
   a. reorder points
   b. automatic ordering
   c. POS
   d. turnovers

4. Medications that are dropped on the floor should be:
   a. re-dispensed to the patient.
   b. swept up right away and packaged.
   c. put back into the original container.
   d. taken home by the technician for store credit or proper disposal.

5. Counterfeit medications should be reported to:
   a. the FDA.
   b. supervisors.
   c. appropriate authorities.
   d. all of the above

ACTIVITY 11-1: Case Study—DEA Forms and Shipment Do Not Match

Instructions: Read the following scenario and then answer the critical thinking questions.

In your pharmacy, controlled medications are ordered by the vault technician. The process specifies that the vault technician fills out the DEA 222 forms and has the head pharmacist sign them. Upon arrival, two people check in the freight, matching up the shipment to the order. For many months, the two who have checked in the freight each time are the exact same pharmacist and pharmacy technician. This is acceptable because they are not the same persons who do the ordering.

One day, the pharmacy technician who checks in orders is absent and you are asked to help receive a shipment. You have the forms, and you and the pharmacist begin opening the totes. You work without incident until you get to the third tote and notice that the red locking tie is not sealed. You point it out to the pharmacist, who brushes it off, stating that it probably got caught on something. The pharmacist is also rushing you along because he has prescriptions to check. Continuing to match up the medications to the order form, you realize that you are short one #30-count bottle of Oxycontin® 10 mg. A recount brings about the same results.

You expect the pharmacist to be concerned, but he is not. He just keeps pushing you to "get on with it" and says that he will figure it out later. You are very uncomfortable with this direction; however, this is your head pharmacist giving the order.

1. What is the right thing to do here?

   _____
   _____
   _____
   _____

2. What are some possible explanations for the one missing bottle?

   _____
   _____
   _____
   _____

3. Can and should the ordering/checking-in process be altered to better prevent such situations?

_____

_____

_____

4. Is there any reason why you should not do what the pharmacist directs you to do here?

_____

_____

_____

_____

ACTIVITY 11-2: Case Study—Out-of-Stock Item

Instructions: Read the following scenario and then answer the critical thinking questions.

It is late on a Saturday evening and the rural southwestern hospital where you work is the only medical facility open to the public. A middle-aged female comes into the emergency room after she has reported a sexual assault to the authorities. The physician on duty prescribes a post-exposure prophylaxis (PEP) regimen for the patient. PEP is a course of antiretroviral medications (ARVs) which are taken within 72 hours after the possible and potential exposure to human immunodeficiency virus (HIV). The regimen includes: one zidovudine 300 mg/ lamivudine 150 mg tablet and one tablet of tenofovir 300 mg. These medications, when taken within 72 hours after the potential exposure to HIV, may help keep the patient from converting to an HIV+ status.

For some reason, either through poor supply or high demand, you discover that your pharmacy is completely out of tenofovir. You are left with the task of obtaining tenofovir as soon as possible for this patient. There are only two independent pharmacies in the rural town where the hospital is located, and neither will be open on Sunday, leaving you unable to obtain a supply for at least two days. The nearest town is a two-and-a-half-hour drive away. What do you do?

1. What options do you have for obtaining the medication quickly?

_____

_____

_____

2. Where do you think you can find this medication in the time allowed?

_____

_____

_____

3. Detail how you would go about obtaining this medication, from time of contact to time of possession. How long does it actually take?

_____

_____

_____

Insurance and Third-Party Billing

After completing Chapter 12 from the textbook, you should be able to:	Related Activity in the Workbook/Lab Manual
1. Define and describe drug utilization reviews (evaluations).	Review Questions, PTCB Exam Practice Questions
2. List and describe the various types of insurance.	Review Questions, PTCB Exam Practice Questions
3. Describe and differentiate Medicare and Medicaid.	Review Questions, PTCB Exam Practice Questions
4. Recognize and define terms commonly used in insurance billing.	Review Questions, PTCB Exam Practice Questions
5. Describe and perform the steps required in collecting data for insurance purposes.	Review Questions, PTCB Exam Practice Questions
6. Describe and perform the steps necessary to transmit a prescription for insurance.	Review Questions, PTCB Exam Practice Questions, Activity 12-1
7. List and explain common insurance billing errors and their solutions.	Review Questions, PTCB Exam Practice Questions
8. Define fraud as it pertains to insurance billing.	Review Questions, PTCB Exam Practice Questions

INTRODUCTION

To operate effectively, the pharmacy must be reimbursed by insurance carriers in a timely fashion. Insurance billing requires a comprehensive knowledge of billing terms, codes, and policies, such as DAW codes, authorized days supply, and formularies. As a pharmacy technician, you can help prevent many insurance claim rejections by ensuring that all information is correctly entered into the pharmacy's computer system before a claim is submitted.

Although the process of insurance and third-party billing can vary by facility, as a pharmacy technician, you will be available to assist the pharmacist by handling these responsibilities and allowing the pharmacist to focus on more clinical aspects of pharmaceutical care provision.

REVIEW QUESTIONS

Fill in the blanks.

1. A request for reimbursement, from a health care provider to an insurance provider, for products or services rendered is known as a/an _____.

2. The portion of the cost of a service or product that a patient pays out of pocket each time the service or product is provided is called the _____.

3. _____ is the notation used by prescribers to instruct the pharmacy to use the exact drug written (usually a brand-name drug).

4. _____ is the number of days a dispensed quantity of medication will last.

5. A set amount that a client pays up front before insurance coverage applies is known as the _____.

6. A federally funded, state-administered insurance program for low-income and disadvantaged persons is _____.

7. The federally funded and administered health insurance program is called _____.

8. A company hired by the insurer to process claims is a/an _____.

9. HIPAA formed the Healthcare Fraud and Abuse Control Program to catch and prosecute any _____.

10. DUR stands for _____.

PHARMACY CALCULATION PROBLEMS

Calculate the following.

1. A physician orders amoxicillin 250 mg tid ×10 d. Calculate the quantity to be dispensed and the days supply for this order.

2. The oncologist orders ondansetron 0.15 mg/kg 30 minutes prior to the first dose of chemotherapy for a patient who weighs 150 lbs. for a 15 minute infusion. After the chemotherapy treatment, two subsequent doses of ondansetron 0.15 mg/kg are going to be administered four and eight hours after the first dose of ondansetron. How much ondansetron will be administered for each dose and what is the total volume for the three doses?

3. The oncologist has ordered for the same patient in question two gemcitabine as a part of the patient's chemotherapy regimen. The order is for 1,000 mg/m^2 over 30 minutes on Days 1 and 8 of each 21-day cycle. Factoring in the patient's weight from question two, the patient's height is 5'7". What is the BSA for this patient and what is the volume for each dose?

4. A physician orders 8 oz. of Hycodan cough syrup, with directions of 1 tsp q 4–6h. What is the correct day's supply to be entered for insurance purposes?

5. What quantity should be dispensed for a 90-day supply of capsules to be taken qod?

PTCB EXAM PRACTICE QUESTIONS

1. What do we call the portion of the price of the medication that the patient is required to pay?
   a. co-insurance
   b. co-pay
   c. maximum allowable cost
   d. usual and customary price

2. The process of transmitting a prescription electronically to the proper insurance company or third-party biller for approval and billing is called:
   a. notification.
   b. adjudication.
   c. settlement.
   d. accreditation.

3. A form of insurance for employees who are injured while at work is called:
   a. Medicaid.
   b. Worker's Reimbursement.
   c. Worker's Compensation.
   d. Worker's Reparation.

4. HIPAA stands for:
   a. Health Insurance Probability and Accountability Act.
   b. Health Insurance Portability and Accountability Acts.
   c. Health Insurance Portability and Accountability Act.
   d. Health Institution Portability and Accountable Act.

5. A pharmacy system should provide support for the following activities performed in the pharmacy except for:
   a. inpatient order entry, management, and dispensing.
   b. manufacturing and compounding.
   c. management and dispensing.
   d. All of the above are acceptable activities.

ACTIVITY 12-1: Case Study—Refill Too Soon

One area of third-party billing, which can be confusing for both the patient and the pharmacy technician alike, is when there is an error message of "Too early to refill." The primary reason for this error message is when the patient has not taken at least 75% of his or her medication before the next refill can be processed. Other reasons for this error message are:

A: The patient is going on a vacation or traveling outside of the United States and they are requesting another refill on the medication(s).

B: The patient has lost or has had stolen a portion or all of their medication.

C: The day supply of the medication may not have been entered correctly by the pharmacy team.

In any of these cases, it is important for the technician to recognize the error message as well as be able to relate the error message and the reason behind the message to the patient in a clear, effective and professional manner. Vacation supplies overrides from the pharmacy benefit management company are a benefit to a patient. A lost or stolen override also from the pharmacy benefit management company may be provided to a patient, provided that the medication is not a Schedule II medication.

Activity:

Calculate the following prescriptions' days supply as it relates to the corresponding requested refill dates. Given that the patient will need to take 75% of the medication. Each prescription has two refills remaining for the patient to submit.

1: metoprolol 100 mg po bid. Original fill date is 10/1/12. Requested refill date is 10/25/12. Can the patient refill this medication?

_____

2: albuterol inhaler two puff q 4–6 hrs prn. Original fill date is 11/15/12. Requested refill date is 12/9/12. Can the patient refill this medication?

_____

3: A patient comes in for his refill of his maintenance medication escitalopram 5 mg. He states that he is going on a vacation and he will not have a sufficient amount of the medication. He will be out of the country before he can refill the medication again. Can the patient refill this medication?

_____

CHAPTER 13
Over-the-Counter (OTC) Products

After completing Chapter 13 from the textbook, you should be able to:	Related Activity in the Workbook/Lab Manual
1. Define and describe the FDA categories and regulations pertaining to OTC products.	Review Questions, PTCB Exam Practice Questions
2. Outline the process for prescription drugs to become approved for OTC classification.	Review Questions, PTCB Exam Practice Questions
3. List and describe common OTC analgesics and antipyretics.	Review Questions, PTCB Exam Practice Questions, Activity 13-1, Lab 13-1
4. List and describe common OTC respiratory agents.	Review Questions, PTCB Exam Practice Questions, Activity 13-1, Lab 13-1
5. List and describe common gastrointestinal system agents.	Review Questions, PTCB Exam Practice Questions, Activity 13-1, Lab 13-1
6. List and describe common OTC integumentary system agents.	Review Questions, PTCB Exam Practice Questions, Activity 13-1, Lab 13-1
7. List and describe common OTC central nervous system agents.	Review Questions, PTCB Exam Practice Questions, Activity 13-1, Lab 13-1
8. List and describe common OTC ophthalmic, otic, and oral agents.	Review Questions, PTCB Exam Practice Questions, Activity 13-1, Lab 13-1
9. List and describe common OTC contraceptive products.	Review Questions, PTCB Exam Practice Questions, Activity 13-1, Lab 13-1

10. List and describe common smoking cessation products.	Review Questions, PTCB Exam Practice Questions, Activity 13-1, Lab 13-1
11. List and describe common behind-the-counter (BTC) products.	Review Questions, PTCB Exam Practice Questions, Activity 13-1, Lab 13-1
12. List and describe common herbal and alternative treatments.	Review Questions, PTCB Exam Practice Questions, Activity 13-1, Lab 13-1
13. List and describe common vitamins and supplements.	Review Questions, PTCB Exam Practice Questions, Activity 13-1, Lab 13-1
14. List and describe common OTC medical devices and diagnostic agents.	Review Questions, PTCB Exam Practice Questions, Activity 13-1, Lab 13-1
15. List and describe common OTC fertility and pregnancy tests.	Review Questions, PTCB Exam Practice Questions
16. Describe the use of nebulizers.	Review Questions, PTCB Exam Practice Questions
17. List and describe common OTC test screening kits.	Review Questions, PTCB Exam Practice Questions
18. List and describe common OTC medical supplies.	Review Questions, PTCB Exam Practice Questions
19. Define and describe the pharmacy technician's role with OTC products, devices, and supplies.	Review Questions, PTCB Exam Practice Questions

INTRODUCTION

Pharmacy technicians who understand how over-the-counter (OTC) products effect prescription medications, or know how to educate patients on the use of medical devices, help to alleviate patient concerns and build avenues of trust. Although providing patients with the best possible route of care is important, the pharmacy technician must also remember what information is within their lawful scope of practice. It cannot be said enough; it is unlawful for pharmacy technicians to provide medical advice or medication information; whether it is prescription or OTC. If a technician has a patient who request information concerning OTC medications they should refer the patient to the pharmacist. Above all other things, concern for the patient's safety must be the pharmacy technician's main priority. A technician who not only understands this but also mimics it in their career will not only have a long career in pharmacy, but gain the respect of other health care professional.

REVIEW QUESTIONS

Fill in the blanks.

1. The drug manufacturer must first seek approval from the _____ and in order to do that they must prove the drug has potential benefit to the general public as well as a limited risk of safety.

2. In 1951 the _____ to the Food, Drug and Cosmetic Act of _____, created two distinct classes of drugs; prescription and nonprescription.

3. There are more than _____ nonprescription products on the U.S. market.

4. It takes a minimum of _____ and quite often longer, for the FDA to approve a drug switch to OTC status.

5. If at any time the FDA finds a nonprescription drug to be unsafe or without benefit to the average consumer, they may remove the drug from _____.

6. Ibuprofen and naproxen sodium belong to the _____ class of analgesics.

7. Antitussives are used to suppress _____ coughs.

8. The three most common dosage forms for OTC smoking cessation products are _____, _____ and _____.

9. Vitamin _____ and Vitamin _____ can have a negative effect on Coumadin.

10. Antacids, which are often used to treat heartburn, _____ stomach acid.

11. A(n) _____ is a machine used to vaporize medication into the air, in order to open up airways.

12. Antiemetics are used to treat _____ and _____.

13. A cough that is caused by a buildup of phlegm or mucus would be treated with a(n) _____.

14. "Lice season" typically peaks between the months of _____ and _____.

15. The FDA only permits sunscreens with an SPF of _____ or higher to be labeled as having the ability to aid in the prevention of skin cancer.

PHARMACY CALCULATION PROBLEMS

Calculate the following.

1. The volume of OTC cough syrup that the customer is purchasing is 120 mL. The directions for adults and children who are 12 years and older are; 2 teaspoons every 4 hours. How many days will this cough syrup last the patient?

2. A customer is asking you for two boxes of pseudoephedrine that he would like to purchase for personal use. Each tablet is 30 mg of pseudoephedrine. How many grams of pseudoephedrine are in each 24 count box? What is the total amount of pseudoephedrine for both boxes?

3. A patient brings in a prescription for nitroglycerin 1/150 g. How many milligrams does that equate to?

4. A customer brings in a prescription for guaifenesin AC 10 mg–200 mg/5 mL. The directions are; 2tsp po q4h not to exceed 60 mL per day for 5 days. What is the total volume needed to fill the order?

5. A customer is asking you about the multivitamins that are on sale this week. The retail price for a 60 count bottle is 14.99 with a 20% discount. How much will the discount be for the customer if he purchases three bottles?

PTCB EXAM PRACTICE QUESTIONS

1. A patient asks you if he or she can take low dose aspirin while on warfarin therapy. Your response is:
   a. no that is a fatal interaction.
   b. that should be fine to do.
   c. let me have the pharmacist speak with you.
   d. the pharmacist is busy right now.

2. Which of the following medications does not contain acetaminophen:
   a. percodan.
   b. Excedrin.
   c. hydrocodone/APAP.
   d. fioricet.

3. The most recently approved class of OTC product to combat acid reflux is:
   a. H2 antagonists.
   b. antacids.
   c. PPIs.
   d. acid reducers.

4. NSAID stands for:
   a. Nonsteroidal anti-irritation drug.
   b. Nonsteroidal anti-inflammation drug.
   c. Non-sedating anti-inflammatory drug.
   d. Nonsteroidal anti-inflammatory drug.

5. Claritin is to loratadine as Allegra is to:
   a. fluticasone.
   b. fexofenadine.
   c. fluoxetine.
   d. furosemide.

ACTIVITY 13-1: Classifying OTC Products

Instructions: Match the various classifications of OTC products from the lists below.

Set 1:

1. cetirizine _____
2. calcium carbonate _____
3. naproxen sodium _____
4. dextromethorphan _____
5. omeprazole _____

A. NSAID
B. PPI
C. Antitussive
D. Antihistamine
E. Antacid

Set 2:

1. aspirin _____
2. loratadine _____
3. pseudoephedrine _____
4. ibuprofen _____
5. simethacone _____

A. Antihistamine
B. Salicylate
C. Decongestant
D. Antiflatulent
E. NSAID

LAB 13-1: Assisting Patients with OTC Products

Objective:

Exhibiting good customer service skills as well as memory recall.

Pre-Lab Information:

Review Chapter 13, "Over-the-Counter (OTC) Products," in the textbook.

Explanation:

There are numerous OTC products for customers to choose for various ailments. These products are at times readily available after a manufacturer has promoted it through successful marketing strategies. However, even with today's fast-paced environment of advertising techniques and mediums a product may not be as available as the media and manufacturer intended.

Any pseudoephedrine-containing product is now a BTC product. The sales of these products are facilitated and monitored by the pharmacy team.

Activity:

In this activity select a team of two, which will include a "technician" and a "patient." Decide upon which team member will take on each of the roles in this activity/scenarios.

Scenario 1

A customer comes in to purchase the latest product for his acid reflux symptoms. He approaches the counter and asks you if you currently have the product in stock as it has been advertised for the past week. Your shipment from the wholesaler had come in yesterday, and it did not include the product the customer is requesting. What should you do to help the customer?

_____

_____

_____

_____

Scenario 2

A customer comes in looking disheveled to both you and the pharmacy team. As she approaches the counter she asks you for four boxes of plain pseudoephedrine. You then tell the customer that only two boxes can be sold to her. She becomes frustrated and irritated by what you have just told her about the limitation. She then states that she will take two boxes and be on her way. As you leave the counter to retrieve the boxes, she becomes agitated and slams her hand on the counter. What should you do to help the customer?

_____

_____

_____

_____

CHAPTER 14
Introduction to Compounding

After completing Chapter 14 from the textbook, you should be able to:	Related Activity in the Workbook/Lab Manual
1. Explain the purpose and reason for compounding prescriptions.	Review Questions
2. Discuss the basic procedures involved in compounding.	Review Questions, PTCB Exam Practice Questions
3. List and describe the equipment, supplies, and facilities required for compounding.	Review Questions, PTCB Exam Practice Questions, Activity 14-1, Activity 14-2
4. List the major dosage forms used in compounding.	Review Questions, PTCB Exam Practice Questions
5. Discuss the considerations involved in flavoring a compounded prescription.	Review Questions, PTCB Exam Practice Questions, Activity 14-1, Activity 14-2

INTRODUCTION

Pharmaceutical *compounding* is the practice of extemporaneously preparing medications to meet the unique need of an individual patient according to the specific order of a physician or prescriber. Compounded medications may be either sterile or nonsterile and include suspensions, capsules, suppositories, topically applied medications, intravenous admixtures, and parenteral nutrition solutions.

Extemporaneous compounding is a special service provided by a number of community-based pharmacies. To assist the pharmacist in compounding medications, you will require additional training, skills, and practice. However, this unique area of pharmacy practice offers a number of advanced professional opportunities for those who pursue these skills.

REVIEW QUESTIONS

Match the following.

1. _____ comminuting
2. _____ compounding
3. _____ emulsion
4. _____ excipient
5. _____ geometric dilution
6. _____ suspension
7. _____ trituration

a. contains insoluble particles uniformly dispersed throughout the vehicle

b. another word for trituration

c. contains two immiscible liquids

d. any substance added to a prescription to make it a suitable consistency or to form the drug

e. reducing particle size of a substance by grinding

f. starts with smallest ingredient amount and doubles the portion by adding other ingredients

g. extemporaneously preparing medications to meet the unique need of an individual patient

Choose the best answer.

8. Which of the following is not a compounding resource?
   a. *United States Pharmacopoeia*
   b. Merck book of brand and generic drugs
   c. *Veterinary Drug Handbook*
   d. *Remington's Pharmaceutical Sciences*

9. Which of the following compounding steps should be completed before the others?
   a. Collecting all of the necessary ingredients.
   b. Writing up a compounding worksheet.
   c. Weighing each ingredient.
   d. Obtaining the formula from the pharmacist.

10. Which of the following is more appropriate for melting bases?
    a. a magnetic stirring plate
    b. a heat gun
    c. a hotplate
    d. an electronic mortar and pestle

11. When using geometric dilution, one should start with the:
    a. ingredient needed in the smallest amount.
    b. ingredient needed in the largest amount.
    c. equal amounts of each ingredient.
    d. the liquid or binding base.

12. Assuming that only the following dosage forms were suitable, which is the desirable choice for animal patients?
    a. cream
    b. ointment
    c. transdermal gel
    d. injection

Match the following.

13. _____ capsule
14. _____ emulsion
15. _____ stick
16. _____ troche
17. _____ cream
18. _____ suspension
19. _____ paste
20. _____ ointment

a. topical application of anesthetics or antivirals

b. dissipates into the skin when applied

c. liquid preparation that contains insoluble particles

d. oral dosage form, used for more than 100 years

e. oral form that disintegrates over time

f. liquid/semisolid form that can be taken orally or applied topically

g. stiff, viscous ointment

h. semisolid preparation that stays on top of skin

True or False?

21. Otic preparations may be used in the eye.

    T   F

22. The most common form of compounded transdermal gel therapy is a two-phase vehicle made from pluronic lecithin organogel.

    T   F

23. Using the proper coloring and flavoring in medications is important for patient compliance.

    T   F

24. One of the five basic flavoring techniques is physiological.

    T   F

25. Aseptic, or sterile, technique should be used in all extemporaneous compounding procedures.

    T   F

PHARMACY CALCULATION PROBLEMS

Calculate the following.

1. Tom is compounding a prescription that calls for 15 g betamethasone 0.05% cream, 15 g diphenhydramine cream, then qs ad 60 g with aquaphilic ointment. How much aquaphilic ointment will he need to add to this compound?

2. A prescription was brought to the pharmacy for a product that is not commercially available. It calls for clindamycin 4,500 mg qs ad 120 mL with lubricating lotion. If the clindamycin is available in 300 mg capsules, how many capsules should be opened for use in this compound?

3. How many sucralfate 1 g tablets will you need for an oral suspension that calls for 20 g sucralfate as the active ingredient?

4. A pharmacy received a faxed order from a veterinarian for celecoxib 25 mg chicken dog treats, #100. If the celecoxib comes in 100 mg capsules, how many capsules should be mixed in the chicken base to make 100 treats?

5. A special compound requires equal parts zinc oxide 20% ointment, nystatin ointment, and hydrocortisone 0.5% ointment. If the prescription calls for 60 g, how many grams of each ointment will be needed?

PTCB EXAM PRACTICE QUESTIONS

1. A two-phase system consisting of a finely divided solid dispersed in a liquid is a/an:
   a. suspension.
   b. emulsion.
   c. solution.
   d. trituration.

2. What is the on-demand preparation of a drug product according to a physician's prescription?
   a. IVPB
   b. extemporaneous compounding
   c. trituration
   d. spatulation

3. The fine grinding of a powder is called:
   a. extemporaneous compounding.
   b. suspension.
   c. emulsion.
   d. trituration.

4. Clear liquids in which the drug is completely dissolved are called:
   a. sublimations.
   b. suspensions.
   c. solutions.
   d. emulsions.

5. A system containing two immiscible liquids with one dispersed in the other is called a/an:
   a. emulsion.
   b. suspension.
   c. syrup.
   d. solution.

ACTIVITY 14-1: Case Study—Childproof Containers

Instructions: Read the following scenario and then answer the critical thinking questions.

Mrs. Gaynor has been on estrogen therapy for a short time now and is beginning to feel much better. Her premenopausal hot flashes and night sweats have subsided. She receives an 8 oz. jar of a custom-compounded estrogen cream made specifically for her. She uses it daily and keeps the jar under a sink in the bathroom.

While her prepubescent grandson is visiting, he becomes curious and applies some of the cream. He thinks it must be something special because of the claims made on the jar about feeling much better. The grandson continues to do this, without anyone's knowledge, as he visits on a weekly basis. Meanwhile, Mrs. Gaynor is receiving more frequent refills through the compounding pharmacy.

Soon the grandson develops gynecomastia (the development of abnormally large mammary glands that can sometimes secrete milk). A doctor's visit confirms that the grandson has been exposed to large amounts of estrogen and enlists the family's help in finding the source.

1. What steps could the compounding pharmacy take to help prevent this situation?

   _____

   _____

   _____

   _____

2. What steps could the grandmother take to help prevent easy access by the grandson?

_____

_____

_____

_____

3. From the information provided, what signs or "flags" were present to indicate that there might be a problem?

_____

_____

_____

_____

ACTIVITY 14-2: Case Study—Medication Flavoring

Instructions: Read the following scenario and then answer the critical thinking questions.

An adult parent comes into the pharmacy with an already reconstituted prescription for amoxicillin suspension for her four-year-old daughter. After an unsuccessful attempt to administer the medication to her daughter earlier in the day, and prior to her coming back now, she first called the pharmacy to see if there was any option for the pharmacist to make the medication taste better in order for the daughter to take another dose.

You explain to the parent that there are three flavoring agents available to make the medication palatable for the patient.

1. What steps could the pharmacist or pharmacy technician have taken prior to the parent coming in a second time? What should the technician do the next time a prescription for a suspension that is prescribed for a child is going to be filled?

_____

_____

_____

_____

2. What steps could the parent have taken to prevent a second trip to the pharmacy?

_____

_____

_____

_____

3. What are the flavoring agents that the technician could suggest to make suspensions more palatable?

_____

_____

_____

_____

Introduction to Sterile Products

After completing Chapter 15 from the textbook, you should be able to:	Related Activity in the Workbook/Lab Manual
1. Outline and describe the key regulations and guidelines pertaining to sterile product preparations.	Review Questions, PTCB Exam Practice Questions
2. Identify and list the equipment and supplies used in preparing sterile products.	Review Questions, PTCB Exam Practice Questions, Activity 15-1, Lab 15-1, Lab 15-2, Lab 15-3, Lab 15-4
3. Demonstrate proper cleaning of laminar flow hoods.	Review Questions, PTCB Exam Practice Questions
4. List the routes of administration associated with sterile products.	Review Questions, PTCB Exam Practice Questions, Activity 15-1, Lab 15-1, Lab 15-2, Lab 15-3, Lab 15-4
5. List and describe key characteristics of sterile products.	Review Questions, PTCB Exam Practice Questions, Activity 15-1, Lab 15-3, Lab 15-4
6. Discuss special concerns regarding total parenteral nutrition (TPN).	Review Questions, PTCB Exam Practice Questions
7. Discuss special concerns regarding chemotherapy and cytotoxic drugs.	Review Questions, PTCB Exam Practice Questions
8. Demonstrate proper garbing procedures.	Review Questions, PTCB Exam Practice Questions
9. Demonstrate proper hand-washing techniques.	Review Questions, PTCB Exam Practice Questions
10. Demonstrate how to withdraw from a vial.	Review Questions, PTCB Exam Practice Questions, Lab 15-1
11. Demonstrate how to reconstitute a powder vial.	Review Questions, PTCB Exam Practice Questions
12. Demonstrate how to remove fluid from an ampule.	Review Questions, PTCB Exam Practice Questions, Lab 15-1

INTRODUCTION

Sterile compounding is the preparation of compounded medications using aseptic technique, or the process of performing a procedure under controlled conditions in a manner that minimizes the chance of contamination of the preparation. Following proper aseptic techniques ensures that all compounded products remain free of bacteria, fungi, pyrogens, infectives, and other microorganisms. To ensure sterility, these products are prepared in laminar flow hoods, including horizontal flow hoods and biological safety cabinets, which contain a high-efficiency particulate air (HEPA) filter.

Patients generally receive sterile products parenterally through various administration sites, such as veins (IV) and muscle tissue (IM). Other sterile products include total parenteral nutrition (TPN), as well as ophthalmic and otic preparations.

Sterile product preparation can be a complex, high-risk process in the health care setting. As a pharmacy technician with proper training, you can play an integral role in the procurement, storage, preparation, and distribution of sterile products.

REVIEW QUESTIONS

Match the following.

1. _____ antineoplastics
2. _____ intradermal
3. _____ infusion
4. _____ pH
5. _____ buffer capacity
6. _____ intramuscular
7. _____ isotonic
8. _____ precipitate
9. _____ intrathecal

a. a relatively large volume of solution given at a constant rate

b. parenteral injection into a muscle

c. containing the same tonicity as red blood cells

d. parenteral injection into the spine

e. medications to prevent the growth of malignant cells

f. parenteral injection into the skin

g. solid that forms within a solution

h. ability of a solution to resist a change in pH when either an acidic or an alkaline substance is added to the solution

i. the degree of acidity of a solution

Choose the best answer.

10. A bevel is:
    a. an angle cut to measure cc/mL.
    b. a rounded-edge needle.
    c. the sharp pointed end of a needle.
    d. the only part of a needle that can be touched.

11. Medication class which is used to treat cancer is called:
    a. antitoxin.
    b. chemotherapy.
    c. radiation.
    d. cytoblast.

12. Class 100 environment is:
    a. a classification of an airflow unit.
    b. a dimensional measurement of the floor plan.
    c. an airflow of 100 psi.
    d. the best level of sterility available.

13. HEPA refers to:
    a. patient privacy rights.
    b. a large insurance group.
    c. a type of air filter.
    d. the government group that inspects air filters.

Identify and indicate the parts of a needle.

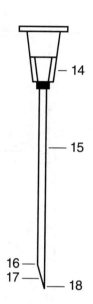

14. _____
15. _____
16. _____
17. _____
18. _____

Identify and indicate the parts of a syringe.

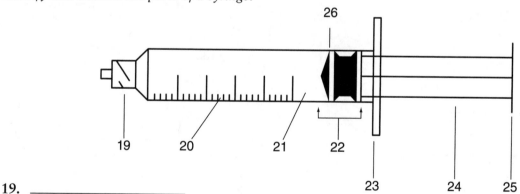

19. _____
20. _____
21. _____
22. _____
23. _____
24. _____
25. _____
26. _____

Identify and indicate the parts of an IV bag system.

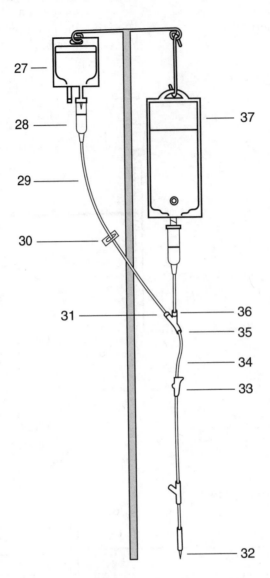

27. _____
28. _____
29. _____
30. _____
31. _____
32. _____
33. _____
34. _____
35. _____
36. _____
37. _____

PHARMACY CALCULATION PROBLEMS

Calculate the following.

1. A medical order states that a patient is to receive 500 mL of 0.9% sodium chloride IV over two hours. How fast is the IV running in mL/hr?

$$\frac{500\,mL}{2\,hrs} = 250\,mL/hr$$

2. A technician prepares a sterile compound that contains 100 mg/mL of active drug. How many mL are required for a dose of 800 mg?

$$\frac{800\,mg}{} \cdot \frac{mL}{100\,mg} = 8\,mL$$

3. If a bulk bottle of IV multivitamins contains 50 mL, how many 10 mL doses can be obtained from the bottle?

5 doses

4. After reconstitution, ceftriaxone for IM injection contains 350 mg/mL. How many milligrams are in 2.5 milliliters?

$$\frac{350\,mg}{mL} \cdot 2.5\,mL = 875\,mg$$

5. A 1,000 mL bag of 5% dextrose with 20 mEq KCl is infusing at 125 mL/hr. How many hours will the bag last before it must be replaced?

$$\frac{1000\,mL}{} \cdot \frac{hr}{125\,mL} = 8\,hr$$

PTCB EXAM PRACTICE QUESTIONS

1. When using a horizontal laminar airflow hood, how far should the technician work inside the hood?
   a. at least 2 inches
   b. at least 4 inches
   c. at least 6 inches
   d. at least 8 inches

2. In a laminar airflow hood, the air flows in how many direction(s)?
   a. four
   b. three
   c. two
   d. one

3. In horizontal laminar airflow hoods, the air blows in which direction?
   a. down toward the work area
   b. away from the operator
   c. toward the operator
   d. up toward the HEPA filter

4. Large-volume parenterals (LVPs) usually have what kind of infusion rates?
   a. intermittent
   b. rapid
   c. slow
   d. instantaneous

5. Vertical airflow hoods have what characteristic?
   a. vertical airflow down toward the product
   b. horizontal airflow away from the operator
   c. vertical airflow up toward the HEPA filter
   d. horizontal airflow toward the operator

ACTIVITY 15-1: Case Study—Identifying Errors in Aseptic Technique

Read the following scenario and identify at least 10 aseptic errors that the pharmacy technician made. Describe ways to improve her technique.

As a student, you are assigned to observe the aseptic technique of the IV room technician. Mindy is scheduled to work in the IV room this morning, but she stayed up too late the night before and had to rush to get to work on time. Before leaving home, she quickly put on some makeup to cover up the circles under her eyes. After punching in late, she began by washing her hands for 10 seconds, missing the dirt she had under her fingernails. After drying her hands with a paper towel, she threw the towel away and then shut off the faucet with her right hand. Next, she put on her gloves, a face mask, and a gown.

Once gowned, Mindy began cleaning the laminar airflow hood with blue window cleaner, using paper towels. She randomly wiped down the hood in circular patterns, and then began preparations for compounding some IV orders. She piled several syringes and needles in the hood, as well as several vials of various medications for the prescriptions that had to be prepared.

At this point, Mindy told you she needed a cup of coffee to perk herself up, so she excused herself to grab some coffee in the break area. A few minutes later, she returned to the clean room with the coffee. She resumed preparing the IVs, selecting several small-volume bags that she would need for the medications. She put those in the hood next to the syringes and began removing the caps to the vials. She assembled a needle and syringe, pulled out the appropriate volume from one of the vials, and immediately injected it into a small-volume bag. It was at this point that you recognized she would need more aseptic training.

Critical Thinking Questions:

1. List at least 10 aseptic errors made in this scenario, then describe the correct solutions to the errors.

   Mistake 1: _____

   Correct Procedure: _____

   _____

   _____

   _____

   Mistake 2: _____

   Correct Procedure: _____

   _____

   _____

   _____

   Mistake 3: _____

   Correct Procedure: _____

   _____

   _____

   _____

   Mistake 4: _____

   Correct Procedure: _____

   _____

   _____

   _____

Mistake 5: _____
Correct Procedure: _____
_____
_____
_____

Mistake 6: _____
Correct Procedure: _____
_____
_____
_____

Mistake 7: _____
Correct Procedure: _____
_____
_____
_____

Mistake 8: _____
Correct Procedure: _____
_____
_____
_____

Mistake 9: _____
Correct Procedure: _____
_____
_____
_____

Mistake 10: _____
Correct Procedure: _____
_____
_____
_____

2. How could this pharmacy technician's negligent technique result in serious harm to a patient?
_____
_____
_____
_____
_____

LAB 15-1: Withdrawing Medication from a Vial or Glass Ampule

Objective:

Demonstrate the techniques involved in withdrawing medications from vials or glass ampules.

Pre-Lab Information:

- Review Chapter 15 in your textbook for review of aseptic compounding, needles, and syringes.
- Gather the following materials:
  - sterile vials and ampules of 0.9% sodium chloride
  - 10 mL syringes
  - 18 gauge, 1 1/2 inch needles
  - filter needles
  - gloves
  - alcohol swabs

Explanation:

You will learn the proper aseptic techniques for withdrawing medication from vials and glass ampules. If your instructor is unable to provide a lab component, your local hospital pharmacy may provide a demonstration for students upon request.

Activity:

Your instructor will take you through the proper procedures for withdrawing medication from vials and glass ampules. You will then have the opportunity to practice some of these techniques in class. If a laminar airflow hood is not available, you will need to use a little imagination regarding aseptic technique and the standards of USP 797.

Key points for working with vials:

1. Always observe the 6-inch rule and critical areas while you are working with sterile products in a laminar airflow hood.

2. Always disinfect the top of the vial with an alcohol swab. One single swipe in one direction should be adequate to disinfect the vial and its stopper. Wait a moment for the alcohol to evaporate before entering the vial with a needle.

3. Attach a needle to a syringe of appropriate size. Before entering the vial, always draw some air into the syringe, to a volume that is slightly less than what you want to withdraw from the vial. This extra air will be pushed into the vial before withdrawing the contents to help equalize the air pressure and make the withdrawal of the solution easier to accomplish.

4. Use care when entering the vial's stopper with the needle. Using too large a needle or the wrong entry technique could result in "coring" of the stopper. Coring could lead to small fragments of the rubber stopper in the medication vial. Adding too much air to the vial could also cause some of the medication to accidentally spray out or aspirate, reducing the required volume available for use as well as potentially contaminating the hood.

5. With the bevel of the needle facing upward, enter the vial's stopper by using a 60- to 90-degree angle entrance point. Press the needle into the middle of the stopper until it has completely broken the seal. Be careful not to interrupt any of the airflow between the hood and the entry point shared between the vial and the needle. This next process can be challenging for the beginner. Carefully reverse the vial and syringe while the needle is still inside the vial, to an upside-down position while maintaining aseptic technique. Gently push some of the air from the syringe into the vial. The syringe will usually start to withdraw some of the fluid on its own filling the syringe. Repeat the process until all the air is out of the syringe and you have withdrawn the correct amount of fluid.

6. The syringe is now ready either to be capped or to be added to an IV bag for an infusion.

Key points for working with glass ampules:

1. Always observe the 6-inch rule and critical areas while you are working with sterile products in a laminar airflow hood.

2. Always disinfect the narrow portion of the ampule with an alcohol swab.

3. Make sure that no liquid is trapped in the neck of the ampule. Gently tapping the top of the ampule with a finger usually will release any remaining liquid from the neck and allowing it to settle in the bottom of the ampule.

4. Break the ampule open at the weakest part around the neck, usually indicated by a dot or a stripe. Be sure to break it open toward the sides of the hood and not toward the back of the hood or toward yourself. Glass fragments can damage the HEPA filter.

5. When withdrawing a medication from a glass ampule, you must use a filter needle in order to filter out any glass particles and also any potential microbial contaminants that may have gotten into the medication. You do not need to withdraw air into the syringe before withdrawing medication from an ampule, because there is no longer a vacuum once you have broken open the ampule.

6. Using a filter needle attached to an appropriate syringe, tilt the ampule slightly in order to withdraw the amount of medication desired. You may need to adjust the volume in the syringe and repeat until you have the correct amount. Be careful not to push any air into the ampule container. Doing so may produce an aspirate and contaminate the airflow hood. If there is any excess liquid in the syringe carefully dispose of it onto a gauze pad or slowly push it back into the ampule.

7. If the contents of the syringe are to be added to an IV bag, you must first change to a new, nonfiltered standard needle. If you keep the same needle, all of the glass particles you may have trapped will be pushed into the IV bag along with the medication and potential microbial contaminants, negating the filtering process.

8. Alternatively, some technicians prefer to draw the medication from the ampule with a regular needle, and then change to a filter needle before injecting the medication into an IV bag. Either method will prevents glass particles from entering into the syringe or the IV bag.

Questions:

1. Why do you need to pull air into the syringe before withdrawing medication from a vial?

_____

_____

_____

2. Why do you need to swab off the top of a vial or a glass ampule with alcohol?

_____

_____

_____

3. Why is it important to use a filter needle when working with glass ampules?

_____

_____

_____

4. Why should you break open a glass ampule toward the sides of the hood instead of toward the back of the hood or toward yourself?

_____

_____

_____

5. Why do you not need to pull air into the syringe before withdrawing medication from a glass ampule?

_____

_____

_____

LAB 15-2: Transferring Liquid into an IV Bag

Objective:

Understand the technique involved in transferring liquid medication from a syringe into an IV bag so that you are able to apply the technique in a pharmacy setting.

Pre-Lab Information:

Review Chapter 15 in your textbook for information regarding aseptic technique and IV medications.

Explanation:

Many IV medications have to be further diluted before they are administered to patients. This process, also known as *sterile compounding*, is most often done with one or more syringes and an IV bag containing an isotonic fluid. In this activity, you will learn the proper aseptic technique for transferring solutions from a syringe into the IV bag, identify which port on the IV bag is used for the transfer, and learn how to add multiple products to the same bag.

Activity:

When compounding sterile products, follow these simple guidelines:

1. Read the prescription label to determine which products you need to use.

2. Select the correct IV bag and size (example: dextrose 5%, 100 mL) and the correct medication that will be transferred to this bag (example: diltiazem 125 mg/25 mL).

3. Remove the outer packaging and wipe down the entire bag with alcohol (in a clean room, parts of these processes may be done by a coworker).

4. Place the disinfected bag on a hanger in the laminar airflow hood.

5. Strip off the seal to the center port of the IV bag and disinfect the port with an alcohol swab. (The port is usually in the middle with a blue seal, but certain IV bags have more than one port for pharmacy use).

6. Prepare the medication for transfer to the IV bag. If it comes in a sterile powder, first follow the directions for reconstitution; then draw the appropriate amount of medication into a syringe, using aseptic technique.

7. Taking care to observe the critical areas of the hood and the 6-inch rule, insert the needle (which is still attached to the syringe of medication from step 6) straight into the center of the port. You will need to pass the needle through the outer core and through an inner membrane. Try to keep the needle straight so as not to puncture the side of the port or the bag. A puncture will void the sterility of all the products involved and you will have to start over with new supplies.

8. Once the needle has passed the inner membrane, gently push the fluid from the syringe into the bag; then carefully pull out the needle and the syringe.

9. If your pharmacist has not double-checked your work at this point, some pharmacies allow you to pull the empty syringe back with air to the volume that you placed in the bag, to indicate how much drug you used.

10. After your work has been checked by a pharmacist, place a cap or seal over the port you just used (this step may be omitted depending on the pharmacy). Remove the IV from the hook, gently shake the bag to distribute the drug, and then label the bag appropriately.

11. If multiple drugs are used in the same bag, gently shake the IV bag between medications to avoid possible precipitation. "Banana bags," which got their nickname from their yellow color, are a multivitamin/mineral infusion and are a good example of a prescription for which you would use more than one drug in a bag.

These step-by-step instructions can be used to prepare most sterile products that require further dilution in an IV bag. You or your instructor may be able to get permission from a local hospital to demonstrate these techniques or allow you to practice.

Questions:

1. What might happen if a punctured bag accidentally made it out of the pharmacy and were hung for a patient?

_____

_____

_____

_____

2. What might happen if you added several products to an IV bag without mixing in between additions?

_____

_____

_____

_____

3. Why is it so important to practice aseptic technique when preparing IV medications?

_____

_____

_____

_____

4. While you are performing a fluid transfer, you accidently lose your grip on the syringe and it falls onto the hood. You discover that the needle has touched the surface of the hood. What should you do?

_____

_____

_____

_____

LAB 15-3: Cefazolin

Order:

Patient: Judy Chambers Weight: 110 lb

Rx: cefazolin 1 g in 250 mL bag; dilute to 200 mg/mL

Supplies Needed

(1) Training Powder-Y Vial (cefazolin 1 g)

(1) Training Vial 50 mL (diluent)

(2) 5 cc Syringes

(1) IV Bag, 250 mL NaCl 0.9%

(3) Alcohol Swabs

Calculations

To dilute to 200 mg/mL – add 4.5 cc of diluent.

Stock	Needed
200 mg	1,000 mg
1 mL	X

5 mL of the reconstituted cefazolin is needed.

Procedure

1. Prepare yourself with proper garb and proper hand-washing technique.
2. Ensure the laminar flow hood has been running for 30 minutes and is cleaned.
3. Bring all necessary supplies into the flow hood. Open and clean appropriate items.
4. Open the syringe and draw up 5 cc of air.
5. Insert the syringe into the Training Diluent MDV and add the 5 cc of air.
6. Draw up 5 cc of diluent into the syringe and remove.
7. Insert the syringe into the Training Powder Y Vial and add the 5 cc of diluent using the milking technique.
8. Reconstitute the Training Powder Y by gently mixing the contents.
9. Withdraw 5 cc of the reconstituted cefazolin and add to the IV bag.
10. Inspect and label the IV bag.

LAB 15-4: Intropin

Order:

Patient: Susan Jones Weight: 147 lb
Rx: Intropin 400 mg in 1,000 mL bag

Supplies Needed

(1) Training Ampule (Intropin 160 mg/mL)

(1) 3 cc Syringe

(1) IV Bag, 1,000 mL NaCl 0.9%

(1) Filter Needle

(3) Alcohol Swabs

Calculations

Stock	Needed
160 mg	400 mg
1 mL	X

2.5 mL of the stock Intropin is needed.

Procedure

1. Prepare yourself with proper garb and proper hand-washing technique.
2. Ensure the laminar flow hood has been running for 30 minutes and is cleaned.
3. Bring all necessary supplies into the flow hood. Open and clean appropriate items.
4. Insert the syringe into the Training Ampule and draw up 2.5 cc of the Intropin.
5. Replace the needle with a filter needle.
6. Insert the syringe into the IV bag and add the Intropin.
7. Inspect and label the IV bag.

CHAPTER 16
Basic Math Skills

After completing Chapter 16 from the textbook, you should be able to:	Related Activity in the Workbook/Lab Manual
1. Determine the value of a decimal.	Review Questions, Pharmacy Calculation Problems, PTCB Exam Practice Questions
2. Add, subtract, multiply, and divide decimals.	Review Questions, Pharmacy Calculation Problems, PTCB Exam Practice Questions, Activity 16-1
3. Recognize and interpret Roman numerals.	Review Questions, Pharmacy Calculation Problems, PTCB Exam Practice Questions
4. Change Roman numerals to Arabic numerals.	Review Questions, Pharmacy Calculation Problems, PTCB Exam Practice Questions
5. Change Arabic numerals to Roman numerals.	Review Questions, Pharmacy Calculation Problems, PTCB Exam Practice Questions
6. Describe the different types of common fractions.	Review Questions, Activity 16-4
7. Add, subtract, multiply, and divide fractions.	Review Questions, Pharmacy Calculation Problems, PTCB Exam Practice Questions, Activity 16-2
8. Define a ratio.	Review Questions, Activity 16-4
9. Define a proportion.	Review Questions, Activity 16-4
10. Solve math problems by using ratios and proportions.	Review Questions, Pharmacy Calculation Problems, PTCB Exam Practice Questions, Activity 16-3

INTRODUCTION

Knowledge of basic arithmetic is essential for today's pharmacy technician. You need basic math skills to understand and perform drug preparations. Nearly every aspect of drug dispensing requires a consideration of numbers. All advanced pharmacy calculations, which are explained throughout this text, rely on a solid understanding of basic math principles. Remember that Chapter 16 in your textbook is designed to serve as a review of these general principles and as an assessment of your basic math skills; the activities in this workbook/lab manual will provide you with additional review.

REVIEW QUESTIONS

Match the following.

1. _____ common fractions
2. _____ complex fractions
3. _____ cross-multiplication
4. _____ decimal fractions
5. _____ denominator
6. _____ fraction line
7. _____ improper fraction
8. _____ numerator
9. _____ proper fraction
10. _____ proportion
11. _____ ratio
12. _____ Roman numerals
13. _____ simple fractions

a. bottom value of a fraction; the number below the fraction line

b. setting up two ratios or fractions in relationship to each other as a proportion and solving for the unknown variable (X)

c. a symbol representing the division of two values; separates the numerator and denominator of a fraction

d. fractions written with a numerator separated by a fraction line from and positioned above a denominator

e. fraction in which both the numerator and the denominator are themselves fractions

f. fractions written as a whole number with a zero and a decimal point in front of the value

g. a fraction in which the value of the numerator is smaller than the value of the denominator

h. letters and symbols used to represent numbers

i. top value of a fraction; the number above the fraction line

j. expresses the relationship of two numbers, separated by a colon (:) between the numbers

k. proper fraction, with both the numerator and denominator reduced to lowest terms

l. fraction in which the value of the numerator is larger than the value of the denominator

m. two or more equivalent ratios or fractions that both represent the same value

Choose the best answer.

14. Which of these decimals has the highest value?
    - a. 0.21
    - b. 0.35
    - c. 0.31
    - d. 0.42

15. Which of these decimals has the highest value?
    - a. 1.37
    - b. 1.43
    - c. 1.89
    - d. 1.25

16. Add the following decimals: 14.25 + 36.75 =
    - a. 55
    - b. 51
    - c. 21.5
    - d. 60

17. Which of these decimals has the lowest value?
    - a. 12.4
    - b. 12.006
    - c. 12.03
    - d. 12.891

18. Which of these decimals has the lowest value?
    - a. 0.15
    - b. 0.16
    - c. 0.016
    - d. 0.22

19. Subtract the following decimals: 104.9 − 55.9 =
    - a. 48
    - b. 160.8
    - c. 49
    - d. 49.9

Multiply the following decimals.

20. $8.63 \times 0.24 =$ _____

21. $6.583 \times 2.26 =$ _____

22. $5.53 \times 4.986 =$ _____

Divide the following decimals.

23. 0.98 / 40.3 = _____

24. 5.54 / 0.4 = _____

25. 6.04 / 0.66 = _____

Change these Roman numerals to Arabic.

26. XC _____

27. CL _____

28. XXI _____

29. LX _____

30. XXX _____

PHARMACY CALCULATION PROBLEMS

Calculate the following.

1. Add the following fractions: $\dfrac{2}{4} + \dfrac{1}{8} + \dfrac{3}{16} =$

2. Solve for X: $\dfrac{100}{2} = \dfrac{3}{X}$

3. Solve for X: $500 \text{ mg}/1 \text{ mL} = \dfrac{X}{5} \text{ mL}$

4. Solve for X: $1{,}000 \text{ mcg}/1 \text{ mL} = \dfrac{X}{2} \text{ mL}$

5. A physician writes an order for XL tablets. The patient's SIG states for the patient: 1 tab po × 10d. What will the day supply be for as it relates to the quantity being dispensed?

PTCB EXAM PRACTICE QUESTIONS

1. How many capsules will be taken in three days if a prescription order reads tetracycline 250 mg/capsule, one capsule qid?
   a. 16
   b. 12
   c. 3
   d. 6

2. Express 33.3% as a decimal:
   a. 33.3
   b. 0.333
   c. 3.33
   d. 333

3. What is 20% of 30?
   a. 6
   b. 60
   c. 3
   d. 300

4. Express 55 as a Roman numeral:
   a. LIXV
   b. XLV
   c. XXXXIX
   d. LV

5. Round 145.1155 to the nearest hundredth:
   a. 145.1
   b. 145.11
   c. 145.12
   d. 145.116

ACTIVITY 16-1: Case Study—How Much?

Instructions: Read the following scenario and then answer the critical thinking questions.

Ms. Kipsky is an elderly woman who is on a very tight budget. She has worked at the local fabric store on a part-time status since her children have all moved out of the home. In addition to this part-time job, she receives an overdue child support check that assists with her finances until the next payday. Luckily, she does not have any major health conditions or concerns that would require her to be on medication. She is very glad about her not having any major health conditions or concerns because she would not be able to afford medications along with her bills and the monthly bus fare that she spends on traveling to work every day.

It is deep into the winter season in the small town Ms. Kipsky works in. She comes into the independent pharmacy where you work and brings in a prescription that the health care team at the free clinic gave to her for an infection. They prescribed to her: amoxicillin 500 mg capsules and she is to take one capsule q8h until gone (for 10 days).

Unfortunately for Ms. Kipsky, her next payday is the following Friday and today is only Saturday. She brings the prescription to the pharmacy to be filled and asks you about the cost. You calculate the amount for her as $30.

1. Ms. Kipsky is uninsured and is paying cash. She asks you how much of the medication she will be able to purchase if she can only pay for 15 capsules right now.

   _____

   _____

   _____

2. Ms. Kipsky checks her purse and finds that she has only $5.00. She wants to know how many capsules that the $5.00 will buy. (Use the formula based on $30 for the entire prescription amount.)

   _____

   _____

   _____

3. She next asks you, how many capsules can she purchase for $10?

   _____

   _____

   _____

ACTIVITY 16-2: Case Study—A Tapering Dose

Instructions: Read the following scenario, and then answer the critical thinking questions.

Mr. Mindes is a regular customer at your retail pharmacy. His medication profile seems to be a who's who of allergy medicines. Your pharmacy typically begins to see Mr. Mindes in early spring when the rain slows down and the flowers start to bloom. He has tried a variety of medications to help relieve allergy symptoms, such as fexofenadine, chlorpheniramine, and loratadine. He also has a nasal spray that keeps his sinuses clear during allergy attacks.

In spite of Mr. Mindes's preparation for each spring's natural bounties, this year he finds that he has actually acquired an infection that makes it tough for him to breathe. He has an uncomfortable case of bronchitis. His provider is prescribing a course of prednisone to help reduce the inflammation in his lungs.

The prescription is as follows: five tablets daily for five days, then four tablets daily for five days, then three tablets daily for five days, then two tablets daily for five days, and then one tablet daily for six days.

1. What is the total number of tablets needed to fill the complete prescription?

   _____

   _____

2. At exactly halfway through his course of prednisone treatment, how many tablets will Mr. Mindes have left in the bottle?

   _____

   _____

3. With three days to the end of his treatment and last dose, how many tablets are left in his prescription bottle?

   _____

   _____

ACTIVITY 16-3: Case Study—Cream Compound

Instructions: Read the following scenario and then answer the critical thinking questions.

Sebastian, a very nice elderly man, has an irritating and unpleasant skin condition. For the past year, he has been uncomfortable with major constant itching and raised bumps that will not go away. Over the past year, he has tried a multitude of moisturizers, none of which seems to help keep his skin from getting the raised bumps that make him itch constantly.

Sebastian has put up with the skin condition for almost a year. His primary care physician (PCP) explained to Sebastian that it was not a condition such as psoriasis or eczema. Sebastian has tried a variety of home remedies and herbal concoctions to make the skin condition go away, but the skin condition is persistent. The active areas of his skin condition remains on his lower arms near the elbows.

Sebastian had an appointment with his PCP earlier in the day. He explained to his PCP that the rash has gotten a bit worse on his arms and that he is experiencing more uncomfortable itching. The PCP decides to try a compound of two ingredients that she thinks might help alleviate the itching and add more moisture to the skin. Sebastian brings the prescription to your pharmacy to have it filled. The prescription is for 60% of ingredient A and 40% of ingredient B. The total amount is 155 g.

1. How many grams of each ingredient will be used to make the compound?

   _____

   _____

   _____

   _____

2. If Sebastian wants to pick up only 80% of his prescription today, how many grams will he be receiving?

_____

_____

3. After you explain to Sebastian how much 80% of his prescription will cost him, he tells you that he only wants 50% of the prescription to be filled. How many grams will that be?

_____

_____

4. After you compound 50% of the prescription, Sebastian now has 3.5 refills on his prescription. After he is able to pay for the full amount of the prescription, he would like to know when he can pick up all of the remaining refills and how many grams of the cream will he be paying for.

_____

_____

ACTIVITY 16-4: Math Definitions

Match the math term in the left-hand column with its definition in the right-hand column.

Term	Definition
1. _____ proportion	a. can be expressed as one number that is set on a fraction line above another number
2. _____ common fraction	b. the value of the numerator is smaller than the value of the denominator
3. _____ improper fraction	c. expresses the relationship of two numbers
4. _____ simple fraction	d. two or more equivalent ratios or fractions that both represent the same value
5. _____ proper fraction	e. the value of the numerator is larger than the value of the denominator
6. _____ ratio	f. cannot be reduced to any lower terms

CHAPTER 17
Measurement Systems

After completing Chapter 17 from the textbook, you should be able to:	Related Activity in the Workbook/Lab Manual
1. List the three fundamental systems of measurement.	Review Questions, Pharmacy Calculation Problems, PTCB Exam Practice Questions
2. List the three primary units of the metric system.	Review Questions, Pharmacy Calculation Problems, PTCB Exam Practice Questions
3. Define the various prefixes used in the metric system.	Review Questions, Pharmacy Calculation Problems, PTCB Exam Practice Questions
4. Recognize abbreviations used in measurements.	Review Questions, Pharmacy Calculation Problems, PTCB Exam Practice Questions, Activity 17-1, Activity 17-2, Activity 17-3
5. Explain the use of International Units and milliequivalents.	Review Questions, Pharmacy Calculation Problems, PTCB Exam Practice Questions
6. Convert measurements between the household system and the metric system.	Review Questions, Pharmacy Calculation Problems, PTCB Exam Practice Questions
7. Convert measurements between the apothecary system and the metric system.	Review Questions, Pharmacy Calculation Problems, PTCB Exam Practice Questions
8. Perform temperature conversions.	Review Questions, Pharmacy Calculation Problems, PTCB Exam Practice Questions, Activity 17-3

INTRODUCTION

Three fundamental systems of measurement are used to calculate dosages: the metric, apothecary, and household systems. Most prescriptions are written using the metric system. Regardless of your practice setting as a pharmacy technician, you must understand each system and how to convert from one system to another. With practice, the conversions you need to calculate dosages will become second nature to you. Until that time, use the charts and formulas from Chapter 17 as a guide. Remember that although miscalculating a conversion may seem to be a minor issue, it could have irrevocable effects on a patient's health.

REVIEW QUESTIONS

Match the following.

1. _____ apothecary system
2. _____ avoirdupois system
3. _____ household system
4. _____ International Units
5. _____ metric system
6. _____ Celsius
7. _____ Fahrenheit
8. _____ grain
9. _____ milliequivalent
10. _____ gram
11. _____ liter
12. _____ meter

a. measures a drug in terms of its action not its physical weight
b. metric unit of length; (m), (cm), (mm)
c. the number of grams of a drug in 1 mL of a normal solution
d. metric unit of volume; (L), (mL)
e. international temperature unit
f. metric unit of weight; (kg), (g), (mg), (mcg)
g. more accurate than the household and apothecary systems
h. system based on 1 lb being equivalent to 16 oz.
i. old English system of measurement
j. American measurement of temperature
k. American measurement for weight
l. primary unit of weight in the apothecary system

Choose the best answer.

13. If you are denoting two-tenths of a milligram, you would write:
    a. 2/10 mg.
    b. 0.2 mg.
    c. 2 mg.
    d. .2 mg.

14. 4 g is equivalent to:
    a. 4,000 mg.
    b. 40,000 mg.
    c. 400 mg.
    d. 40 mg.

15. 8 oz. is equivalent to how many milliliters?
    a. 16 mL
    b. 24 mL
    c. 240 mL
    d. 160 mL

16. There are 16 oz. in a pint. How many milliliters is that?
    a. 480 mL
    b. 48 mL
    c. 4.8 mL
    d. 4,800 mL

17. If Mary is to take 3 teaspoonfuls twice a day for 10 days, how many milliliters will be dispensed?
    a. 30,000 mL
    b. 3,000 mL
    c. 300 mL
    d. 30 mL

Match the following.

18. _____ mg   **a.** microgram
19. _____ mL   **b.** milligram
20. _____ g   **c.** milliliter
21. _____ mcg   **d.** gram

PHARMACY CALCULATION PROBLEMS

Calculate the following.

I drop in left eye every day

1. An optometrist orders the medication latanoprost ophthalmic solution. The SIG is written as 1 gtt os qd. The bottle you have in stock is 2.5 mL. What is the total day supply for the order?

$$\frac{2.5mL}{} \bigg| \frac{20\,gtt}{1mL} \bigg| \frac{1\,day}{1\,gtt} = \boxed{50\ day\ supply}$$

2. Metronidazole IV comes in a 500 mg/100 mL concentration. If the patient received 100 mL for eight doses, how many grams of metronidazole were given in total?

$$\frac{500\,mg}{100mL} \bigg| \frac{800mL}{} \bigg| \frac{1\,g}{1000mg} = \boxed{4\,g}$$

by mouth 4 times a day

3. A prescription is written for 8 fl. oz. of guaifenesin a.c. syrup. If the patient is to take 10 mL po qid, what is the total day supply for the order? *before meals*

$$\frac{8\,fl\,oz}{} \bigg| \frac{30mL}{1\,oz} \bigg| \frac{1\,day}{40mL} = \boxed{6\ days}$$

4. A patient is to take 1 g valacyclovir po bid for five days. If the medication comes in 500 mg tablets, how many tablets will the patient need? *by mouth 2 times a day*

$2 \times 5 = 10$
$1\,g \times 10 = 10\,g$ $\cdot 500\,mg = 0.5\,g$ $\dfrac{10\,g}{0.5\,g} = \boxed{20\ tablets}$

5. A 3 L TPN is ordered for a patient in ICU. The pump is to be programmed for 120 mL/hr. How many hours will the TPN last?

$$\frac{3000\,mL}{} \bigg| \frac{hr}{120\,mL} = \boxed{25\,hr}$$

PTCB EXAM PRACTICE QUESTIONS

1. A prescription is written for a hydrocortisone 5% in zinc oxide compound. The total quantity to be dispensed is 50 g. On stock you have 50 mg of hydrocortisone tablets. *5% Zn O*

    How many hydrocortisone 50 mg tablets will you need to triturate for this compound? $\dfrac{5g}{100g} = \dfrac{X}{50g}$
    a. ½ tablet   *1 tablet = 50 m g*   c. 5 tablets
    b. 2.5 tablets $\dfrac{2500mg}{50mg} = 50\ tablets$ **d.** 50 tablets $X = 2.5\,g$ $2500\,mg$

2. KCl 30 mEq is to be given in 250 mL of IV fluid. Available vials contain 40 mEq/20 mL. What is the volume you require to fill the order? $\dfrac{30mEq}{X} = \dfrac{40mEq}{20mL}$
    a. 1.5 mL   c. 60 mL
    b. 15 mL   d. 6 mL $X = 15\,mL$

3. You receive an order for 0.5 g of Tigan IM. You have a 5 mL vial labeled 100 mg/mL. What is the volume you will need to fill the order?
    a. 2 mL   c. 0.5 mL
    b. 5 mL   d. 0.02 mL

$$C = \frac{F-32}{1.8}$$

4. You check the pharmacy refrigerator and it is 40 °F. What is the temperature in degrees Celsius?
   a. 4 °C
   b. −4 °C
   c. 104 °C
   d. 72 °C

5. How many milligrams of phenobarbital are in one tablet of 2 grain phenobarbital?
   a. 65 mg
   b. 6.5 mg
   c. 13 mg
   d. 130 mg

$$\frac{2\,gr \mid 65\,mg}{\mid 1\,gr} = 130\,mg$$

ACTIVITY 17-1: Case Study—Kilograms

Instructions: Read the following scenario and then answer the critical thinking questions.

Mrs. Sarnoto is probably one of the world's best mothers. In addition to her three biological children, she has adopted four boys. Her days are full of chores, activities, driving, and homework, but many people say Mrs. Sarnoto would not have it any other way.

Mrs. Sarnoto also takes care of all the children's health care needs, from vaccinations to outbreaks of poison oak exposure. For this reason, she is a frequent visitor at the retail pharmacy where you work. Over the past five years alone, she has probably purchased at least half of the products in the pharmacy.

As luck would have it, five of the seven children have come down with a terrible bronchial infection. Everyone in the household is miserable, including Mrs. Sarnoto, who is also sick. She knows she has to be the strong one, though, and heads to the pharmacy to fill the amoxicillin prescriptions she has gotten for the family. Each person weighs a different amount, and the amoxicillin prescription doses are based on weight in the following formula: 40 mg/kg/day in divided doses every eight hours. The amoxicillin you have available in the pharmacy is 250 mg/5 mL.

1. One of the children weighs 28 lb. How much amoxicillin suspension (in milliliters) will this child receive for a seven-day course of treatment?

   _____
   _____
   _____
   _____

2. One of the children weighs 83 lb. How much amoxicillin suspension (in milliliters) will this child receive for each dose?

   _____
   _____
   _____

3. Mrs. Sarnoto has been prescribed amoxicillin capsules 500 mg three times daily, but she has a sore throat and wants the suspension. How much suspension (in milliliters) does she need to complete a 10-day course of treatment?

   _____
   _____
   _____
   _____

4. Mrs. Sarnoto had to travel 3 km to get to the pharmacy. How many miles is her round trip?

_____

_____

_____

_____

ACTIVITY 17-2: Case Study—Milliliters

Instructions: Read the following scenario and then answer the critical thinking questions.

Carlene is the most experienced IV pharmacy technician at the Children's Hospital on the hill. She has been making IVs of all types for more than 11 years. She is in charge of all the specialty formulations that require precise measuring of multiple ingredients. Carlene takes great pride in what she does and shares all the little tricks she knows with the other pharmacy technicians who mix IVs. She has found a way to manipulate fluids when measuring so that they come out with exactly the same volume the doctor has ordered, regardless of the IV contents. Some of the tricks she has learned include ways to use milliliters and liter measurements interchangeably, taking into account displacement of added items.

1. From a 2.5 L volume, Carlene removes 325 mL. What is the final volume in milliliters?

_____

_____

_____

_____

2. Carlene adds 6,700 mL to a volume of 2 L. How many total liters are there?

_____

_____

_____

_____

3. A formulation of 3.2 L requires Carlene to remove 1,600 mL of fluid. How many milliliters are left after this?

_____

_____

_____

_____

ACTIVITY 17-3: Case Study—Drug Storage

Instructions: Read the following scenario and then answer the critical thinking questions.

Note: False medication names are used in this case study.

Sam is an inventory pharmacy technician at one of the biggest compounding pharmacies in his home town. He is in charge of medication purchasing, rotation, budget, and destruction, to name just a few of his tasks. The medication inventory in the pharmacy is very large. The pharmacy has an inventory of more than 10,000 classifications of medications in their various dosage forms.

Many of the medications that are used for compounding in Sam's pharmacy are in raw and bulk forms. Proper storage of the bulk medications is very important in order to prevent the breakdown of the active components in each medication. With the volume of inventory Sam has to manage, it is challenging to recall the storage instructions for each medication or product. Sam periodically refers to the reference texts and tools in each section of the pharmacy.

In addition to counting all of the medications and products, Sam uses this time to ensure that all of the medications are stored within their optimum temperature ranges. For some of the medications, the manufacturers periodically issue updates on storage instructions and, where the medications should normally be stored when not in use.

1. The product ectium is a fine powder that must be kept in a temperature-controlled environment of 40–48 °F per the manufacturer's storage requirements. What is this temperature in degrees Celsius? Where is the ectium normally stored when not in use?

   _____

   _____

   _____

   _____

2. Another product, silicutitum, is composed of small 4 cm balls that will melt if it is stored at a temperature of above 55 °F, per the manufacturer's storage requirements. What is this temperature in degrees Celsius? Where is the silicutitum normally stored when not in use?

   _____

   _____

   _____

   _____

3. A liquid known as pasitoxel will release a vapor if it is stored in an area at a temperature above 3.333 °C per the manufacturer's storage requirements and warnings. What is this temperature in degrees Fahrenheit? Where is the pasitoxel normally stored when not in use?

   _____

   _____

   _____

   _____

4. The lab where the mixing takes place is kept at a steady 72 °F. When the staff needs to mix basculum, they have to drop the lab's temperature to 11.11 °C per the manufacturer's storage requirement. After the reduction in the lab's temperature occurs for mixing the basculum, what is the lab temperature in degrees Fahrenheit? Where is the basculum normally stored when not in use?

_____

_____

_____

_____

CHAPTER 18
Dosage Calculations

After completing Chapter 18 from the textbook, you should be able to:	Related Activity in the Workbook/Lab Manual
1. Calculate the correct number of doses in a prescription.	Review Questions, Pharmacy Calculation Problems, PTCB Exam Practice Questions, Activity 18-1, Activity 18-2
2. Determine the quantity to dispense for a prescription.	Review Questions, Pharmacy Calculation Problems, PTCB Exam Practice Questions, Activity 18-1, Activity 18-2, Activity 18-3
3. Calculate the amount of active ingredient in a prescription.	Review Questions, Pharmacy Calculation Problems, PTCB Exam Practice Questions
4. Determine the correct days supply for a prescription.	Review Questions, Pharmacy Calculation Problems, PTCB Exam Practice Questions, Activity 18-1, Activity 18-2
5. Perform multiple dosage calculations for a single prescription.	Review Questions, Pharmacy Calculation Problems, PTCB Exam Practice Questions, Activity 18-2, Activity 18-3
6. Calculate accurate dosages for pediatric patients.	Review Questions, Pharmacy Calculation Problems, PTCB Exam Practice Questions, Activity 18-1
7. Convert a patient's weight from pounds to kilograms.	Review Questions, Pharmacy Calculation Problems, PTCB Exam Practice Questions, Activity 18-1
8. Perform dosage calculations based upon mg/kg/day.	Review Questions, Pharmacy Calculation Problems, PTCB Exam Practice Questions

INTRODUCTION

Proper dosing of medications is important to ensure patient safety. Dosage calculations include calculating the number of doses and dispensing quantities and ingredient quantities. These calculations are performed in the pharmacy on a daily basis. As a pharmacy technician, you must have a full working knowledge of how to perform these calculations. To perform dosage calculations, you will draw upon the knowledge you have mastered in previous chapters in the textbook, such as setting up ratios and proportions, keeping like units consistent, and cross-multiplying to solve for an unknown.

REVIEW QUESTIONS

Match the following.

1. _____ Clark's Rule
2. _____ dispensing quantity
3. _____ dose
4. _____ Fried's Rule
5. _____ days supply

   a. pediatric dose based on age in months

   b. how long the amount of medication dispensed will last if taken as directed

   c. pediatric dose based on weight expressed in pounds

   d. total amount of medication to be dispensed

   e. amount of medication prescribed to be taken at one time

Write the correct sig codes.

6. every six hours _____
7. every day _____
8. four times daily _____
9. every other day _____
10. twice daily _____
11. every eight hours _____
12. as needed _____
13. every four hours _____
14. every 12 hours _____
15. every four to six hours _____
16. six times daily _____
17. three times daily _____
18. four to six times each day _____

Choose the best answer.

19. When calculating the quantity to be dispensed you should always:
    a. round up, so the patient gets enough medication.
    b. round down, so the patient will not overdose.
    c. dispense the exact quantity, including a tablet if necessary.
    d. not worry too much about quantity if the patient has refills.

20. A 5 mL bottle of eye drops will last for how long if the patient is using 1 gtt ou bid?
    a. 30   c. 20
    b. 25   d. 15

Fill in the blanks.

For questions 21–24:

Mr. Mestophel has a prescription for cephalexin 500 mg, #60, with the sig code "1 po bid ud."

21. The dose is _____ capsules.

22. The days supply is _____ days.

23. The daily dose is _____ mg.

24. The dispensing quantity is _____.

25. If Tyra's emergency inhaler contains 200 puffs and she uses 1 puff up to four times daily, how long should her inhaler normally last? _____

PHARMACY CALCULATION PROBLEMS

Calculate the following.

1. How many grams are in an 8 oz. bottle of levetiracetam 100 mg/mL oral solution?

$$\frac{8oz}{} \bigg| \frac{30ml}{1oz} = 240ml \qquad \frac{100mg}{mL} \bigg| \frac{240mL}{} \bigg| \frac{1g}{1000mg} = 24g$$

2. A patient is prescribed 2 teaspoonfuls of citalopram hydrobromide 2 mg/mL. How many micrograms are in each dose?

$$\frac{2\,tsp}{} \bigg| \frac{5mL}{1\,tsp} = 10mL \quad \frac{2mg}{mL} \bigg| \frac{10mL}{} \bigg| \frac{1000\mu g}{1mg} = 20,000\,\mu g$$

3. A patient is prescribed, 4 mg/kg/day of a medication. The patient weighs 165 lbs. What is the final strength that the patient will receive?

$$\frac{165\,lbs}{} \bigg| \frac{1kg}{2.2\,lbs} = 75\,kg$$

$$\frac{4mg}{kg} \bigg| \frac{75kg}{} = 300\,mg$$

4. A child needs a medication that does not have a pediatric formula available. The usual adult dosage for this medication is 800 mg. If the child weighs 60 lbs., how many milligrams would constitute a safe pediatric dose?

$$\left(\frac{60}{150}\right)(800) = 320$$

5. A patient weighing in at 220 lbs. is prescribed a medication that will be dosed at 10 mcg/kg/day in three divided doses. How many micrograms are in each of the doses?

$$\frac{220lbs}{} \bigg| \frac{1kg}{2.2\,lbs} = 100\,kg \qquad \frac{10mcg}{kg} \bigg| \frac{100kg}{} = \frac{1000}{3} = 333.33\,mcg$$

PTCB EXAM PRACTICE QUESTIONS

1. A prescription reads: Amoxicillin 250 mg/10 mL, 1 tsp bid 10d. How many milliliters will you need to dispense?
   a. 50 mL
   (b.) 100 mL
   c. 150 mL
   d. 200 mL

   every 12 hrs

2. The doctor orders vancomycin 10 mg/kg q12h IV for a toddler. The toddler weighs approximately 55 lbs. What is the strength that the toddler will receive per dose?
   a. 1,210 mg
   b. 250 mg
   c. 550 mg
   (d.) 500 mg

   $$\frac{55lbs}{} \bigg| \frac{1kg}{2.2\,lbs} = 25\,kg$$

$$\frac{10mg}{kg} \bigg| \frac{25kg}{} = 250\,mg \times 2 = 500\,mg$$

3. Calculate a single dose, in milliliters, for a 22-lb. child receiving gentamicin 2 mg/kg of body weight IVPB q8h. Gentamicin is available in 20 mg/2 mL concentration.
   - (a.) 2 mL
   - b. 10 mL
   - c. 15 mL
   - d. 20 mL

4. You have received a prescription for diphenhydramine 12.5 mg/5 mL, dispense 240 mL. The patient is to take 50 mg tid. What is the day's supply for this prescription?
   - a. 60 days
   - (b.) 12 days
   - c. 20 days
   - d. 15 days

5. A parent of a five-year-old child weighing 47 lbs. needs to give an oral dose of Tylenol elixir. The literature states that the dose for a child of this age and weight should not exceed 70 mg/kg/day. This daily maximum is to be divided into six doses. Tylenol elixir contains 125 mg/5 mL. How many teaspoonfuls would the parent give to the child for a single dose?
   - a. 1 tsp.
   - b. 1.25 tsp.
   - c. 1.5 tsp.
   - (d.) 2 tsp.

$$\frac{249.2\,mg \mid 5\,mL}{125\,mg} = 9.96\,mL$$

$$\frac{9.96\,mL \mid 1\,tsp}{5\,mL} = 2\,tsp$$

$$\frac{47\,lbs \mid 1\,Kg}{2.2\,lbs} = 21.36\,Kg$$

$$\frac{70\,mg \mid 21.36\,Kg}{Kg} = 1495\,mg$$

$$\frac{1495\,mg}{6} = 249.2\,mg$$

ACTIVITY 18-1: Case Study—Pediatric Dosing

Instructions: Read the following scenario and then answer the critical thinking questions.

Jimmy is an eight-year-old boy who weighs 55 lbs. and presents the typical symptoms of a cold. The primary symptoms he exhibits are a fever of 101 degrees and he is constantly tugging at his ears. The doctor has diagnosed Jimmy with acute otitis media and prescribes a seven-day course of amoxicillin capsules and acetaminophen tablets for fever. When Jimmy's mother hands the prescription to you, you notice that the doctor has forgotten to write in the dose for the amoxicillin.

1. What do the pharmacist and the technician need to know and do in order to dispense the correct doses and quantities of the amoxicillin and acetaminophen for Jimmy?

   _____

   _____

   _____

   _____

2. While turning the prescription in, the mother mentions that Jimmy's throat is very sore and he has had a hard time swallowing food and liquids. You realize that capsules and tablets will be too difficult for Jimmy to swallow. How is Jimmy going to take his medicine?

   _____

   _____

   _____

   _____

3. The ordered dose for the amoxicillin capsules turns out to be 500 mg three times daily (one capsule). If you were to dispense a suspension of 250 mg/5 mL, how much would Jimmy then receive per dose? How much would you need to dispense for the full seven days?

   _____

   _____

   _____

   _____

4. The ordered dose for the acetaminophen tablets is 250 mg for three days. However, the maximum total daily dose for a child less than 12 years old is 75 mg/kg/day, not to exceed 3,750 mg/day. What is the volume you would need to dispense if the order is now 10 mg/kg/dose every four to six hours as needed; do not exceed five doses in 24 hours?

_____

_____

_____

ACTIVITY 18-2: Case Study—Tablets

Instructions: Read the following scenario and then answer the critical thinking questions.

Ms. Kelsey, two-time award-winning journalist, has worked for the newspaper for more than 22 years. She absolutely loves her job because of the places it has taken her and the people she has met. Ms. Kelsey has interviewed so many different people that it truly has made her feel like she has lived a rewarding life.

Ms. Kelsey has taken one particular medication all through her life in tablet form. She has a form of asthma and this medication helps her breathe. In addition to this one tablet, she has a rescue inhaler. A few times in the past she has been treated with maintenance inhalers, but luckily does not have to be on them most of the time. The tablets seem to work very well. Occasionally, depending on age and situation, her doctor has increased or decreased the amount of medication in the tablets to prevent flare-ups.

1. In her 20s, Ms. Kelsey was instructed to take 3 tablets twice a day for 28 days at a time. How many tablets did she need to complete one course of treatment?

_____

_____

_____

_____

2. When she turned 30 years of age, Ms. Kelsey was instructed to take 3.5 tablets three times a day for 28 days. How many tablets did she need for one course of treatment?

_____

_____

_____

_____

3. Now that Ms. Kelsey is over 40 years of age, she is instructed to take 3.75 tablets twice a day for 34 days. How many tablets does she need to complete this course of treatment?

_____

_____

_____

_____

4. When Ms. Kelsey turns 50 years old, she will need to take 272 tablets over 32 days with twice-daily dosing. How many tablets will she be taking per dose?

_____

_____

_____

_____

ACTIVITY 18-3: Case Study—Cream

Instructions: Read the following scenario and then answer the critical thinking questions.

Note: False medication names are used in this case study.

Sharla is a very beautiful and active 16-year-old girl. She is captain of her high school cheerleading team, has played the lead role in three of the school's plays this year, and is taking classes for a future career in modeling. Sharla takes exceptionally good care of her body and skin from the inside out, so it was quite disturbing for her when one day she noticed that her slight acne had begun to worsen.

During her teenage years, Sharla has had periodic face and skin conditions resulting from sensitive skin. It turns out that she is very sensitive to detergents, soaps, lotions, and perfumes. It is very difficult for her to keep the rashes under control when she breaks the rules and wears perfume for special occasions such as school dances.

Sharla has received prescriptions from the compounding pharmacy for all types of perfume-free creams over the years. Almost all have helped, and she uses this pharmacy exclusively for all new formulations she is prescribed. She has received some prescriptions in heavy jars or small tubes depending on the area to be treated.

1. When Sharla had a round, mild rash on her bottom left cheek, she was prescribed listfal 34 g and palfite 16 g combined. How many milligrams is this?

   _____

   _____

   _____

   _____

2. When her legs were covered in a rash, Sharla was prescribed 12 lbs. of crexopen cream. How much is this in ounces?

   _____

   _____

   _____

   _____

3. For the mild hypersensitive reaction just under her ear, she was prescribed junisten 1.2 kg. How many ounces is this?

   _____

   _____

   _____

   _____

CHAPTER 19
Concentrations and Dilutions

After completing Chapter 19 from the textbook, you should be able to:	Related Activity in the Workbook/Lab Manual
1. Calculate weight/weight concentrations.	Review Questions, Pharmacy Calculation Problems, PTCB Exam Practice Questions
2. Calculate weight/volume concentrations.	Review Questions, Pharmacy Calculation Problems, PTCB Exam Practice Questions, Activity 19-1, Activity 19-2
3. Calculate volume/volume concentrations.	Review Questions, Pharmacy Calculation Problems, PTCB Exam Practice Questions, Activity 19-1
4. Calculate dilutions of stock solutions.	Review Questions, Pharmacy Calculation Problems, PTCB Exam Practice Questions

INTRODUCTION

Concentrations and dilutions, which can feel overwhelming and intimidating, are really no more than a series of simple ratios and proportions. Concentrations of many pharmaceutical preparations are expressed as a percent strength. Percent strength represents how many grams of active ingredient are in 100 mL. In the case of solids such as ointments, percent strength represents the number of grams of active ingredient contained in 100 g. Percent strength can be reduced to a fraction or to a decimal, which may be useful in solving these calculations. It is best to convert any ratio strengths to a percent. As a pharmacy technician, you will use concentrations and dilutions in a variety of pharmacy practice settings, so it is important that you master this skill.

REVIEW QUESTIONS

Match the following.

1. _____ concentration
2. _____ diluent
3. _____ percent strength
4. _____ % volume/volume
5. _____ % weight/volume
6. _____ % weight/weight

a. concentrations are those in which a liquid active ingredient is mixed with a liquid base
b. concentrations are those in which a solid active ingredient is mixed with a solid base
c. concentrations are those in which a solid active ingredient is mixed with a liquid base
d. the strength of active pharmaceutical ingredient in a medication
e. representation of the number of grams of active ingredient contained in 100 mL
f. a larger volume that you mix with the stock solution

True or False?

7. Grams and milliliters are used interchangeably in concentration problems, depending on whether you are working with solids in grams or liquids in milliliters, as they are considered equivalent measures.
   T   F

8. Concentration problems are classified into four categories.
   T   F

9. When mixing powders with liquids, the liquid (base) quantity is considered the total quantity, as the powder will either dissolve or suspend within the base liquid.
   T   F

Choose the best answer.

10. What is the first step when calculating a weight/weight concentration?
    a. add both the active and base quantities for the total quantity
    b. multiply the converted number by 100 to express the final
    c. set up a proportion with the amount of active ingredient listed over the total quantity, as grams over grams.
    d. convert the proportion to a decimal concentration as a percentage

11. How many 500 mg metronidazole tablets will be needed to compound the following prescription for a patient? "Metronidazole 3%, suspending agent 30%, simple syrup 40% qs ad H_2O to 150 mL."
    a. 9 tablets $.03\% \quad \dfrac{4500 mg}{500 mg} = 9$ c. 10 tablets $\dfrac{150 mL}{1 mL} \cdot .03 g = 4.5 g$
    b. 7 tablets   d. 18 tablets   4500 mg

12. You receive a prescription for "Amoxil 400 mg po tid × 10 days." Your pharmacy has in stock Amoxil oral suspension 250 mg/5 mL. What is the exact volume of medication you will need to correctly and completely fill the prescription for the patient?
    a. 150 mL   c. 240 mL
    b. 168 mL   d. 200 mL

$\dfrac{12000 mg}{250 mg} \cdot \dfrac{5 mL}{} = 240 mL$

$400 \times 3 = 1200 \times 10 = 12000 mg$

by mouth 3 times a day for 10 days

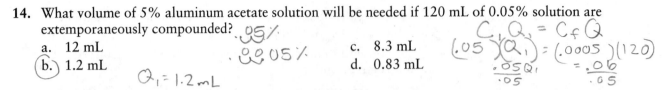

13. How many grams of 2% silver nitrate ointment will deliver 1 g of the active ingredient?
    a. 25 g
    c. 50 g
    b. 4 g
    d. 20 g

14. What volume of 5% aluminum acetate solution will be needed if 120 mL of 0.05% solution are extemporaneously compounded?
    a. 12 mL
    c. 8.3 mL
    b. 1.2 mL
    d. 0.83 mL

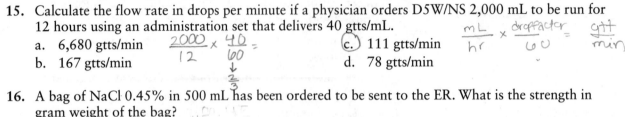

15. Calculate the flow rate in drops per minute if a physician orders D5W/NS 2,000 mL to be run for 12 hours using an administration set that delivers 40 gtts/mL.
    a. 6,680 gtts/min
    c. 111 gtts/min
    b. 167 gtts/min
    d. 78 gtts/min

16. A bag of NaCl 0.45% in 500 mL has been ordered to be sent to the ER. What is the strength in gram weight of the bag?
    a. 45 g
    c. 0.0009 g
    b. 1,111 g
    d. 0.45 g

17. From the following formula, calculate in grams the quantity of miconazole needed to prepare 12 kg of powder.

    zinc oxide 1 part

    calamine 2 parts

    miconazole 1.5 parts

    bismuth subgallate 3 parts

    talcum 8 parts
    a. 15.5 g
    c. 1,161 g
    b. 0.09 g
    d. 1,548 g

18. Calculate the flow rate for an IV of 1,000 mL to run in over eight hours with a set calibrated at 20 gtt/mL.
    a. 42 gtt/min
    c. 125.1 gtt/min
    b. 17.36 gtt/min
    d. 50 gtt/min

PHARMACY CALCULATION PROBLEMS

Calculate the following.

1. How many grams of a drug are contained in 250 mL of a 20% solution?

$$\frac{20 g}{100 mL} \mid \frac{250 mL}{} = 50 g$$

2. A technician has an order to compound metoclopramide suspension 5 mg/5 mL, qs ad 100 mL. In stock, the technician has metoclopramide 10 mg tablets. How many tablets will the technician need to triturate for this compound?

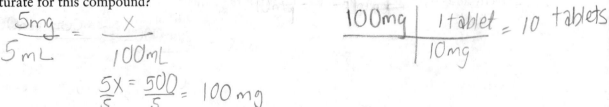

$$\frac{250g}{650mL} = \frac{X}{100mL} \quad (250)(100) = 650X$$

3. What is the percent strength of a solution that is made by adding 150 mL of sterile water to 500 mL of a 50% solution? $\frac{50g}{100mL} | 500mL = 250g \qquad 150mL + 500mL = 650mL$

   38%

4. If a technician is compounding a 5% hydrocortisone emulsion in 120 g of aquaphilic ointment, how many grams of hydrocortisone powder will the technician need to add to the compound?

   $.05 \times 120 = 6g$

5. How many grams of active ingredient are in 500 mL of a 1:20 solution?

   $\frac{1}{20} \rightarrow (.05)(500mL) = 25g$

PTCB EXAM PRACTICE QUESTIONS

1. You have 200 mL of a 30% solution. You dilute the solution to 600 mL. What is the percent strength of the final solution?
   - a. 60%
   - b. 30%
   - c. 12%
   - d. 10%

   $C_iQ_i = C_fQ_f$
   $(200)(.3) = C_f(600)$
   $C_f = .1 \rightarrow 10\%$

2. A solution of ampicillin contains 250 mg/mL. What is the percent strength of the solution?
   - a. 2.5%
   - b. 25%
   - c. 12.5%
   - d. 15.2%

   $\frac{250mg}{mL} | \frac{1g}{1000mg} \qquad .25mg$

3. What is the final volume when you dilute 50 mL of sorbitol 50% solution to a 20% solution?
   - a. 150 mL
   - b. 125 mL
   - c. 250 mL
   - d. 500 mL

   $C_iQ_i = C_fQ_f$
   $(50)(.5) = (.2)Q_f$
   $Q_f = 125mL$

4. Neostigmine is available in a 1:1000 concentration in a 20 mL vial. You have a prescription for 16 mg. How many milliliters are required?
   - a. 1.6 mL
   - b. 16 mL
   - c. 12.5 mL
   - d. 1.2 mL

   $\frac{1g}{1000mL} = \frac{.016g}{X} \qquad X = (.016)(1000)$

   $16mL$

   .016mg

   You will need 16mL from a 20mL vial

   .016g

5. Epinephrine is available as a 1:1000 w/v solution. If the patient dose is 0.2 mg IM, how many milliliters are needed?
   - a. 2 mL
   - b. 1 mL
   - c. 0.2 mL
   - d. 0.1 mL

   $\frac{1g}{1000mL} = \frac{.0002g}{X}$

   $0.00.2$

   $X = (.0002)(1000mL)$

ACTIVITY 19-1: Case Study—Dosing

Instructions: Read the following scenario, and then answer the critical thinking questions.

Wintertime brings a barrage of colds throughout the Hudson family. They are a very active family of Dad, Mom, two boys (11 and 14), and two girls (8 and 12). Each child participates in at least one winter sport, keeping them on the go. The children spend a lot of time riding to games with other families, and their parents think this makes it easier to pick up infections. Although they manage to avoid most ailments year round, three weeks in January of each year seem to bring an assortment of infection bugs to this household. This past winter was no exception.

When January rolled around, the infections hit this family like dominoes. The pattern is almost the same every year. Once everyone was sick at the same time, and everyone received treatments for different bacterial infections.

1. Dad received cefotetan in either 1 g or 2 g for IM injection. The 1 g vial would be mixed with 2 mL of sterile water and .5mL of powder and the 2 g would be mixed with 3 mL of sterile water and 1 mL of powder. What is the concentration of the 1 g and the 2 g cefotetan with these diluent amounts?

_____

_____

_____

_____

2. Mom is going to receive a Zithromax suspension 500 mg/day for one day, then 250 mg/day for four days. The concentration available to you is 200 mg/5 mL. How many teaspoonfuls does Mom receive per dose on day 1? How many on day 2?

_____

_____

_____

_____

3. The eight-year-old girl weighs 42 lbs. and will receive Unasyn at 300 mg/kg/day. How much is her dose per day?

_____

_____

_____

_____

4. The 14-year-old boy is going to receive ceftriaxone 2 g IV daily for three days, to be infused over 30 minutes. For a 2 g dose, 19.2 mL of sterile water were added to the vial and the medication was then injected into a 100 mL bag of NS. When reconstituting with 19.2 mg diluent with the medication (powder volume of 0.8 mL) the total volume will be 20 mL. How many milliliters per minute are infused if the total volume of the piggyback has to empty out over 30 minutes?

_____

_____

_____

_____

ACTIVITY 19-2: Case Study—Reconstitution

Instructions: Read the following scenario and then answer the critical thinking questions.

Jeremy is a recent graduate of the Pharmacy Technician Training program from the local community college. This is his first job as he is working in an independent closed-door pharmacy. Within six months of his hire date, he is already being trained to compound orders for small-volume parenteral admixtures in the sterile preparation area of the pharmacy. Training in this area begins with practicing reconstitution techniques for a month and then after specific competencies have been met per USP <797>, Jeremy will be compounding large-volume parenteral admixtures.

During each workday, Jeremy compounds about 30–50 small-volume parenteral admixtures that are less than 50 mL of total volume. The medications Jeremy works within this pharmacy use sterile water as the main diluent. Jeremy works with any number of powdered medications within vials, in which he is required to reconstitute to compound sterile admixtures.

1. Jeremy has a 1 g vial of vancomycin and adds 10 mL of sterile water. What is the final concentration of the vancomycin?

   _____

   _____

   _____

   _____

2. If Jeremy were to add 20 mL of sterile water to this vancomycin, what would be the final concentration?

   _____

   _____

   _____

   _____

3. What is the final concentration if Jeremy has 2 g of vancomycin and he added 20 mL of sterile water to this vial?

   _____

   _____

   _____

   _____

4. Jeremy has progressed with his skill sets so well that his supervisor would like for him to prepare a 500 mL bag of vancomycin. The order is prescribed for 500 mg vancomycin in 500 mL NaCl. As there is only the 1 g vial in stock, how much diluent will be needed to compound this medication?

   _____

   _____

   _____

ACTIVITY 19-3 Case Study—Concentration

Instructions: Read the following scenario and then answer the critical thinking questions.

Note: False medication names are used in this case study.

Renee is a clinical pharmacy technician at a mid-sized hospital with about 120 patient beds. This bed count includes a small 20-bed unit that is for patients who require a little longer stay for rehabilitation purposes. Typically these patients are a little older and less mobile than patients who are in the hospital for routine surgical needs. Many of these patients move on to some sort of assisted living situation, such as community apartment homes where part-time nursing care is available.

Part of the care the nurses provide to these patients is the administration of medications such as IV infusions, insulin shots (for the squeamish), and other types of injections (such as cyanocobalamin). Other nurses occasionally have to do careful calculation and administration of pain medications in suspension or injectable forms.

Part of Renee's job is to help provide the medications to the nursing unit for patient administration; this includes mixing of unit-dose preparations such as injectables or oral liquids. In addition, Renee helps double-check all the calculations as part of a safety check. Because she works in pharmacy, she also knows what drug forms and strengths are immediately available.

1. Bascoletine is available as 30 mg/mL in a 15 mL vial. How many total milligrams are available in this vial?

    _____

    _____

    _____

    _____

2. If the nurse withdrew one-quarter of the vial contents for a dose, how many milligrams would be in that dose?

    _____

    _____

    _____

    _____

3. The doctor prescribes the entire vial of medication from question 1, divided into five equal doses. How many milligrams and milliliters would each dose have?

    _____

    _____

    _____

4. Using the medication information from question 1, how many milligrams are in 5 mL?

    _____

    _____

    _____

    _____

CHAPTER 20
Alligations

After completing Chapter 20 from the textbook, you should be able to:	Related Activity in the Workbook/Lab Manual
1. Understand when to use the alligation principle for calculations.	Review Questions, Pharmacy Calculation Problems, PTCB Exam Practice Questions, Activity 20-1, Activity 20-2, Activity 20-3
2. Calculate and solve a variety of alligation-related problems.	Review Questions, Pharmacy Calculation Problems, PTCB Exam Practice Questions, Activity 20-1, Activity 20-2, Activity 20-3

INTRODUCTION

The alligation method is used in the pharmacy when it is necessary to mix two products that have different percent strengths of the same active ingredient. The strength of the final product will fall between the strengths of each original product. Although these calculations can be confusing at first, once you master the alligation grid, you should be able to perform these calculations easily.

REVIEW QUESTIONS

Fill in the blanks.

1. Solvents and diluents such as water, vanishing cream base, and white petrolatum are considered a percent strength of _____.

2. Liquids, including solutions, syrups, elixirs, and even lotions, are expressed in _____.

3. Solids are expressed in _____. Examples of solids are powders, creams, and ointments.

4. The alligation formula requires that you express the strength as a _____ when setting up the problem.

5. When writing percentages or using decimals, always use a leading _____.

6. 1 fl. oz. is equal to _____ mL but it is commonly rounded to _____ mL.

7. 1 avoirdupois oz. is equal to _____ g but it is commonly rounded to _____ g.

8. The _____ strength goes in the top left box of an alligation grid.

9. The _____ strength goes in the bottom left box of an alligation grid.

10. The _____ goes in the center box of an alligation grid.

11. The allegation grid is also referred to as the _____ - _____ - _____
    _____.

Use the alligation method to answer the following questions.

You have in stock 1 gallon of silver nitrate 1% solution that you can dilute with distilled water. How many milliliters of each solution will you need in order to make 2 L of silver nitrate 0.5% solution?

12. _____ mL of the 1% stock solution

13. _____ mL of distilled water

You have in stock, hydrocortisone 10% ointment and hydrocortisone 2% ointment. How many grams of each ointment will you need in order to prepare hydrocortisone 5% ointment 120 g?

14. _____ g of the 10% ointment

15. _____ g of the 2% ointment

Prepare 480 mL of a 1:30 solution using a 1:10 solution and a 1:50 solution.

16. _____ mL of the 1:50 solution

17. _____ mL of the 1:10 solution

18. How many grams of 10% ointment should you add to 20 g of 2% ointment to make 5% ointment?
    _____ g

19. How many milliliters of water should you add to 50 mL of betadine 0.25% solution to prepare a betadine 1:1000 solution? _____ mL

20. How many grams of lidocaine 2% ointment should you mix with 22.5 g of lidocaine 10% ointment to prepare 2 oz of lidocaine 5% ointment? _____ g

21. Convert 25% to a ratio strength. _____

22. 1:2 is what percentage strength? _____

Fill in the blanks.

23. 1:2 50% 0.50 _____

24. _____ 33% 0.33 $\frac{1}{3}$

25. 3:4 _____ 0.75 $\frac{3}{4}$

26. 1:1 100% _____ 1

27. 1:4 _____ 0.25 _____

PHARMACY CALCULATION PROBLEMS

Calculate the following.

1. A technician is going to compound 8 oz of zinc oxide 7.5% ointment. In stock, there is zinc oxide 20% ointment and petroleum jelly. How many grams of each medication will the technician need in order to make the compound?

2. A physician prescribes 3 L of a 4% solution. The pharmacy has a 12% solution and a 2% solution in stock. How many milliliters of each solution will be needed to make the final product?

3. You will need to prepare a 5% solution from the 15% solution and sterile water. The final volume of the solution will be 4 fl. oz. What are the volumes of each solution?

4. You will need 0.5 L of a 2.5% solution for a prescription. In stock there is a 1:5 solution and a 1:100 solution. How many milliliters of each solution will be required for this compound?

5. A doctor prescribes 30 g of a 20% ointment. In stock, there are a 15% ointment and a 30% ointment. How many grams of each available ointment will be required to prepare the ointment prescribed?

PTCB EXAM PRACTICE QUESTIONS

1. What volumes of a 50% dextrose solution and of water are needed to prepare 3 L of a 30% solution?
    a. 1,800 mL dextrose and 1,200 mL water
    b. 30 mL dextrose and 20 mL water
    c. 1,200 mL dextrose and 1,800 mL water
    d. 20 mL dextrose and 30 mL water

2. What volumes of a 15% solution of sodium chloride and of water should be used to prepare 1 L of a 0.9% solution of sodium chloride?
    a. 60 mL 15% and 940 mL water
    b. 940 mL 15% and 60 mL water
    c. 500 mL 15% and 500 mL water
    d. 200 mL 15% and 800 mL water

3. How many grams of 10% boric acid ointment should be mixed with petrolatum (0%) to prepare 700 g of a 5% boric acid ointment?
    a. 300 g petrolatum and 400 g 10%
    b. 200 g petrolatum and 500 g 10%
    c. 300 g 10% and 400 g petrolatum
    d. 350 g 10% and 350 g petrolatum

4. What volumes of a 50% dextrose solution and of a 10% dextrose solution are needed to prepare 4 L of a 20% solution?
    a. 3,000 mL 50% solution and 1,000 mL 10% solution
    b. 3,000 mL 10% solution and 1,000 mL 50% solution
    c. 3.0 mL 50% solution and 0.1 mL 10% solution
    d. 3.0 mL 10% solution and 0.1 mL 50% solution

ACTIVITY 20-1: Case Study—Cream

Instructions: Read the following scenario and then answer the critical thinking questions.

Jerry Rands is hypersensitive to numerous substances and frequently develops a small rash somewhere on his body. He is not even sure of all the things he is sensitive to! All he knows is that over the course of his lifetime, he has had a skin rash at least once a month somewhere on his body. He has been to the pharmacy to purchase anti-itch cream in many different brands and strengths. Jerry's doctor usually advises him to purchase the OTC or prescription-strength product known as hydrocortisone cream.

The time has come again when Jerry develops a small rash and asks the doctor which strength he will need to treat this one. Just like anybody else, Jerry has a small collection of these creams in his medicine cabinet that are still in date and available for use. The problem, however, lies in getting the correct strength when he has only certain amounts of certain strengths. It seems that he does not have enough of the strength the doctor ordered this time, so he wonders if he can mix them.

1. Jerry is to use hydrocortisone 1% cream. All he has available is 2.5% and 0.25%. How many grams of 2.5% hydrocortisone cream should be mixed with 240 g of 0.25% hydrocortisone cream to make 1% hydrocortisone cream?

   _____
   _____
   _____
   _____

2. The doctor tells Jerry to divide the total amount of cream calculated in question 1 into six even doses for application. How many grams are in each dose?

   _____
   _____
   _____
   _____

3. What is the total amount of 1% hydrocortisone cream Jerry mixed?

   _____
   _____
   _____
   _____

4. Jerry decides to divide the total amount of 1% hydrocortisone cream he has mixed into 2 oz jars. How many jars does he need?

   _____
   _____
   _____
   _____

ACTIVITY 20-2: Case Study—Gelcaps

Instructions: Read the following scenario and then answer the critical thinking questions.

Maryann works in a mid-sized veterinarian compounding pharmacy. Each day brings something new and creative. She may receive an order for suppositories for medium-size rodents or syringes filled with antibiotics for baby birds. Maryann's job requires her to have solid math skills and excellent aseptic technique.

Compounding is used to formulate prescriptions when no commercial strength is available—and animal pharmaceuticals are a very narrow field. Compounding medications for animals fill a void in a world where little is known about what works on a grand scale for a general species. More and more information appears every week for new formulations and animal behavior. With these updates occurring constantly, Maryann must stay on top of her education and training to remain an asset to her chosen field.

A major part of Maryann's compounding is the creation of various gelcaps for various medications. It is a very convenient form for most animals, and flavoring is easily added to this drug form under most conditions.

1. The following formula is to make a total of 50 gelcaps. How much of each ingredient is needed to make only 10 gelcaps?

   FORMULA
   caffeine   0.6 g
   aspirin   2 g
   inert ingredient   0.25 g

   _____

   _____

   _____

   _____

2. How much is needed to make 15 capsules?

   _____

   _____

   _____

   _____

3. What is the total number of grams of all 3 ingredients for 20 capsules?

   _____

   _____

   _____

   _____

ACTIVITY 20-3: Case Study—Bulk

Instructions: Read the following scenario and then answer the critical thinking questions.

Note: False names are used for the homeopathic substances in this case study.

A good part of the day at the homeopathic compounding pharmacy, where Lynette the lead pharmacy technician works, is spent mixing large batches of specialty gels for patients who require these compounds to effectively treat each of their specific conditions. A variety of herbs for compounding the gels is available to Lynette. Lynette has to wear all of the appropriate personal protective equipment, such as gloves, gowns, and masks due to the fact that the strength of some of these compounds can cause allergic/hypersensitive skin reactions.

Part of Lynette's duties includes the purchasing of the larger size containers, lids, and packaging tools. It is very common for Lynette to make a 2,000 g jar full of homeopathic gel for a patient's muscle aches and pains. All of the final compounds in this facility are composed of four different strengths.

1. Lynette is making histkatel crucious gel for a patient's muscle fatigue. The order is for a 10% final concentration. How many grams of 15% histkatel crucious gel should be mixed with 1,800 g of 6% histkatel crucious gel to make the 10% gel?

   _____

   _____

   _____

   _____

2. Convert the final volume of this compound to pounds.

   _____

   _____

   _____

   _____

3. Lynette is to repackage the bulk gel into 6 oz sealed jars. How many jars will she need?

   _____

   _____

   _____

   _____

CHAPTER 21
Parenteral Calculations

After completing Chapter 21 from the textbook, you should be able to:	Related Activity in the Workbook/Lab Manual
1. Illustrate the principle of basic dimensional analysis.	Review Questions, Pharmacy Calculation Problems, PTCB Exam Practice Questions, Activity 21-1
2. Calculate flow duration for parenteral products.	Review Questions, Pharmacy Calculation Problems, PTCB Exam Practice Questions, Activity 21-1
3. Calculate the volume per hour for parenteral orders.	Review Questions, Pharmacy Calculation Problems, PTCB Exam Practice Questions
4. Calculate the drug per hour for parenteral products.	Review Questions, Pharmacy Calculation Problems, PTCB Exam Practice Questions
5. Calculate drip rates in both drops per minute and milliliters per hour.	Review Questions, Pharmacy Calculation Problems, PTCB Exam Practice Questions
6. Calculate TPN milliequivalents.	Review Questions, Pharmacy Calculation Problems, PTCB Exam Practice Questions

INTRODUCTION

The preparation and administration of parenteral products, such as IVs, infusions, TPN, and chemotherapy, require the performance of specific calculations. It is common for individuals to become overwhelmed and confused when approaching complex pharmacy calculations. The truth is, however, that although many pharmacy calculations appear to be complex, they are in actuality very simple. Often described as the most difficult and challenging calculations used in pharmacy, parenteral calculations, drip rates, and TPN milliequivalents are all solved with basic fundamental math and arithmetic skills. The use of proportions, cross-multiplication, and dimensional analysis will aid you in performing virtually all parenteral calculations that you will need to solve as a pharmacy technician.

REVIEW QUESTIONS

Match the following.

1. drop factor
2. drops per minute
3. milligrams per hour
4. flow rates
5. flow rate duration
6. hypertonic solutions
7. isotonic solutions
8. hypotonic solutions
9. IV infusion
10. micro drip
11. total parenteral nutrition
12. milliliters per hour

a. solutions that have osmotic pressure equal to that of cell contents

b. length of time for which an IV will be administered, or how long an IV bag will last before it must be changed

c. amount of fluid, or solution, that will be administered to the patient intravenously per hour

d. term used to describe a number of common pharmacy calculations used in the preparation of IV infusions

e. dosage, or amount of medication in milligrams, that will be administered per hour of infusion

f. solution made to supply many of the body's basic nutritional needs via parenteral administration

g. compounded solution that provides fluids, specific medications, nutrients, electrolytes, and minerals to a patient

h. the volume of medication to be administered each minute

i. solutions that have greater osmotic pressure than cell contents

j. solutions that have a lower osmotic pressure than cell contents

k. an abbreviated form referring to a specific drip rate

l. most commonly used drip rate, 60 gtts/mL

Solve the following problems.

13. A physician orders a 2 L IV bag to be administered at a rate of 250 mL/hr. How long will this IV bag last? _____

14. A physician orders a 3 L IV to be administered at a rate of 500 mL/hr. How long will the IV last?

_____

15. A patient is set to start a 250 mL infusion of amoxicillin in lactated Ringers 5% at noon. The bag is to be administered at a rate of 100 mL/hr. At what time will the infusion be complete?

_____

16. A physician orders three 500 mL IV bags that are to be infused at a rate of 150 mL/hr. How long will these three bags last? _____

17. A physician orders three 2 L IV bags containing ciprofloxacin and NS that are set to be administered at a rate of 250 mL/hr at 1:00 p.m. When will all three bags be completely administered?

_____

18. A patient is to receive a 1,500 mL IV infused over five hours. What is the rate of infusion in milliliters per hour? _____

19. A physician orders 500 mL IV, containing 2 mg of Toradol, which is to be infused to the patient over 120 minutes. What is the rate of infusion in milliliters per hour? _____

20. A physician orders 500 mL of D5W containing 1 g of lidocaine hydrochloride that is to be infused to the patient over 250 minutes. What is the infusion rate in milliliters per hour? _____

PHARMACY CALCULATION QUESTIONS

Calculate the following.

1. How many hours will a 3 L bag of TPN last if it is scheduled to run for 100 mL/hr?

2. A bag of heparin IV with a concentration of 25,000 units/250 mL is ordered for a patient. How many units per hour will the patient receive if the solution is infusing at 50 mL/hr?

3. What will the flow rate be in milliliters per hour for vancomycin 1g/500 mL IV, if it is to be infused for 90 minutes?

4. What will the flow rate be in drops per minute for 150 mL of an antifungal medication that is to be administered over 60 minutes? The tubing is calibrated at 30 gtts/mL.

5. If a 1 L bag of D5NS with 20 mEq KCl is hung at 0700, when will the new bag be due if it is running at 125 mL/hr?

PTCB EXAM PRACTICE QUESTIONS

1. If an order for a 1 L bag of D5W is to be infused into a patient's arm for eight hours, what is the rate of infusion in milliliters per hour?
   a. 100 mL/hr
   b. 10 mL/hr
   c. 12.5 mL/hr
   d. 125 mL/hr

2. If an order for a 1,000 mL bag of normal saline is to run at 100 mL/hr, how long will the bag last?
   a. 8 hours
   b. 10 hours
   c. 12 hours
   d. 6 hours

3. If the infusion rate for an IV is 60 mL/hr and it is running for 4 ½ hours, how many milliliters will the patient receive?
   a. 13 mL
   b. 270 mL
   c. 240 mL
   d. 380 mL

4. How many drops per minute will a patient receive if the order for an IV infusion of 1,000 mL of 5% dextrose injection is run for six hours? The drip factor is 15 gtts/mL.
   a. 7 gtts/min
   b. 167 gtts/min
   c. 90 gtts/min
   d. 67 gtts/min

5. You receive an order for heparin IV to be infused at 1,000 units/hr. What will be the flow rate be in milliliters per hour for a 500 mL bag of D5W with 25,000 units of heparin?
   a. 20 mL/hr
   b. 10 mL/hr
   c. 8 mL/hr
   d. 1 mL/hr

ACTIVITY 21-1: Case Study—Iron Dextran

Instructions: Read the following scenario and then answer the critical thinking questions.

After arguing with his then-girlfriend of whom his family did not approve, Philip drove away from the house in an angry state. He is certain now that he was not in the right frame of mind to be driving that night. The car spun out of control on a fairly isolated road and hit a tree. Eventually, Philip made it out alive, but he spent 12 weeks in the hospital recuperating. He did not call his family as he probably should have, because the last time he spoke to them, things ended on bad terms. It has now been eight months since the accident, and Philip has not seen his family during that time. He is reuniting with them now to discuss the accident, because he had decided that it would help him heal emotionally.

Philip was lucky to have made it back to health. He suffered a concussion, a fractured arm, and multiple bruises. The doctors told him he lost a lot of blood, but he is not exactly sure from what part of his body or how much. Philip received excellent care at the major medical center where he recalls being on numerous medications. Now all his family members are sharing stories of various hospital stays, and the discussion turns to the medications they recall getting, especially the IVs that hung on the poles while they were inpatients. Philip recalls one, called iron dextran, being "really black."

1. The first dose of iron dextran that Philip received was a test dose of 25 mg in 100 mL NS infused over 20 minutes. What was the concentration of this piggyback?

2. What was the infusion rate per minute for this test dose of iron dextran?

3. Philip's total daily dose of iron dextran became 1 g, mixed in a 1 L bag of NS, and infused over eight hours. What was the rate per hour?

4. Using the same information as in question 3, how much iron dextran did Philip receive per hour?

CHAPTER 22
Business Math

After completing Chapter 22 from the textbook, you should be able to:	Related Activity in the Workbook/Lab Manual
1. Define and understand how to calculate cost, selling price, and markup.	Review Questions, Pharmacy Calculation Problems, PTCB Exam Practice Questions, Activity 22-1, Activity 22-2, Activity 22-3, Activity 22-4, Lab 22-1, Lab 22-2
2. Explain co-payments and average wholesale price (AWP).	Review Questions, Pharmacy Calculation Problems, PTCB Exam Practice Questions, Activity 22-1, Activity 22-2, Activity 22-3, Activity 22-4, Lab 22-1, Lab 22-2
3. Define and understand how to determine markup and markup percent.	Review Questions, Pharmacy Calculation Problems, PTCB Exam Practice Questions, Activity 22-1, Activity 22-2, Activity 22-3, Activity 22-4, Lab 22-1, Lab 22-2
4. Define and understand how to calculate gross profit and net profit.	Review Questions, Pharmacy Calculation Problems, PTCB Exam Practice Questions, Activity 22-1, Activity 22-2, Activity 22-3, Activity 22-4, Lab 22-1, Lab 22-2

INTRODUCTION

The goal of any business is to make a profit; pharmacy is no different. It is necessary to maintain enough profit in the business model to be able to take care of obligations such as rent and inventory expense and have a positive net income at the end of the fiscal year. Profits help pay salaries of employees, so it is important to keep a certain profit margin above supply costs so that the business can afford to keep and pay its employees.

REVIEW QUESTIONS

Fill in the blanks.

1. For every product sold in a pharmacy, it has three essential numbers—they're
   _____, _____, and _____.

2. Every product in a pharmacy, whether it is a bottle of prescription antibiotics or an over-the-counter (OTC) product, was purchased from a _____ or _____ for a _____ _____.

3. Whereas cost refers to the amount of money the pharmacy paid for a product, the selling price is the _____ the pharmacy receives for the sale of the product.

4. For prescription products, the _____ includes the amount to be paid by the third-party insurer and the patient's co-payment.

5. Calculating the amount an insurance company will contribute to the selling price of a product can be done so long as you are provided with the _____ and the _____.

PHARMACY CALCULATION PROBLEMS

Calculate the following.

1. What is the price that a bottle of vitamins be sold for if the acquisition cost is $7.99 and there is a $2.50 markup?

2. If a vial of insulin sells for $12.50 and a $2.10 markup is included, what is the invoice cost of the insulin?

3. If an erectile dysfunction device that costs $80.00 is marked up to $130.00, what is the markup percent?

4. If a prescription costs the pharmacy $17.95 and sells for $45.50, what is the amount of gross profit?

5. A bottle of OTC cough syrup sells for $10.95. The pharmacy paid $4.60 for the product and has $3.00 in associated overhead. What is the net profit?

PTCB EXAM PRACTICE QUESTIONS

1. All costs associated with a business is known as:
   a. overstock
   b. rent
   c. cost of goods sold
   d. overhead

2. What is the term that refers to the money left over after you pay invoice cost (cost of goods sold) and overhead?
   a. net income
   b. revenue
   c. net profit
   d. taxes

3. A 100 count bottle of atenolol 50 mg costs $29.99. The patient is prescribed 30 atenolol 1 tab qd and wants to pay cash for the medication. What is the amount the patient will pay?
   a. $9.01
   b. $8.99
   c. $2,999
   d. $899

4. Which of the following is an example of overhead?
   a. payroll
   b. inventory
   c. cost of goods
   d. markup

5. If an item that costs $80.00 is marked up to $120.00, what is the markup percent?
   a. 1.5%
   b. 5%
   c. 50%
   d. 12%

ACTIVITY 22-1: Case Study—Cost Concerns

Instructions: Read the following scenario and then answer the critical thinking questions.

A well-known patient comes into the pharmacy with a prescription for a medication. The medication is rather new on the market and has been advertised heavily in the media. The AWP from the manufacturer for this medication is approximately $500.00 for a 100 tablet count bottle. The dispensing fee for each prescription is $5.00. The patient has been prescribed a quantity of 60 tablets and the patient has an insurance plan with an open formulary. The prescribing physician has prescribed a few medications to the patient that is on the open formulary and the patient's co-pay is $25.00 for brand-name medications and $10.00 for generic medications. You process the prescription and adjudicate the claim as usual; however, the reject notice comes back as "NDC not covered."

While speaking to the pharmacist about this rejection notice, you both realize that there is no other medication on the market that is therapeutically equivalent to the one that this patient needs. As you speak with the patient about this situation, the patient tells you that "I guess I will have to pay cash." However, the patient is low on funds and would like to pay for a quarter of the quantity prescribed.

1. How much will the patient have to pay for the quarter of the prescribed quantity?

   _____

   _____

2. The patient has changed his mind and would like to pay for half of the prescribed quantity?

   _____

   _____

3. Is there an option or options that you could look into so that the patient does not have to pay cash for the medication? If so, what are they?

_____

_____

ACTIVITY 22-2: Case Study—Markups

Instructions: Read the following scenario and then answer the critical thinking questions.

The newest shipment of OTC products has arrived from your distribution center. The newest nonsedating antihistamine has just been approved by the FDA and is now available for consumers without a prescription in quantities of 7, 15, and 30 tablets. You have noticed that the pricing fees for each of the tablet counts are:

7 count—$10.99
15 count—$20.99
30 count—$41.98

The markup for these new products is $4.00

1. How much will each of the items be with the markup?

_____

_____

_____

2. What is the percent markup for the products

_____

_____

_____

3. What will be the gross profit for the products?

_____

_____

_____

ACTIVITY 22-3: Case Study—The Bottom Line

Instructions: Review the income statement below and calculate the net profit to secure the bottom line.

Income	100%
Cost of goods sold	67%
Overhead and expenses	25%

Net profit

ACTIVITY 22-4: Case Study—Reimbursement Rates

Instructions: Review the following examples and calculate the reimbursements for each example.

1. The AWP for a medication in a 100 tablet count bottle is $90.00—13% with a processing fee of $3.00.

   _____

   _____

2. The AWP for a medication in a 1,000 tablet count bottle is $110.99—15% with a processing fee of $2.50. The patient has been prescribed a quantity of 120 tablets.

   _____

   _____

3. The AWP for 480 mL of a cough syrup is $75.99 less 10% with a processing fee of $3.50. The patient has been prescribed a volume of 120 mL.

   _____

   _____

LAB 22-1: Product Pricing

Objective:

To understand that every inventory product must be priced accurately with operational calculations.

Pre-Lab Information:

Review Chapter 22, "Business Math," in the textbook.

Explanation:

The pharmacy technician is relied upon to accurately price all of the products in a pharmacy based upon a determined pricing from the manufacturer and the owners of the pharmacy.

Activity:

Calculate the cost of a blood glucose meter.

1. A blood glucose meter is sold for $99.99. The net profit on the strips is $25.00. The store's overhead per blood glucose meter is $6.00. What is the invoice cost for the meter?

_____

Calculate the selling price of a bottle of vitamins.

2. The invoice cost for a bottle of vitamins is $6.74. The net profit on the vitamins is $1.35. The store's overhead per bottle is $0.18. What is the selling price for a bottle of vitamins?

_____

Calculate the selling price of a pill container.

3. A pill container costs the pharmacy $0.86 to purchase. If the pharmacy marks up the pill container 25%, what is the selling price?

_____

LAB 22-2: Profitability

Objective:

To understand that each item in a pharmacy is intended to make a profit and bring an income to keep the business running smoothly.

Pre-Lab Information:

Review Chapter 22, "Business Math," in the textbook.

Explanation:

The pharmacy technician is expected to understand that each item in the pharmacy is intended to bring in a profit for salaries to remain active and stable for the team as a part of the overhead.

Activity:

Calculate and determine the gross and net profits with each of the examples below.

1. Determine the cost for a product with a selling price of $45.55, overhead of $5.50, and net profit of $9.00. _____

2. Determine the gross profit for a product with a selling price of $98.99, cost of $47.00, and overhead of $8.50. _____

3. Determine the selling price for a product with a cost of $10.59, overhead of $3.69, and net profit of $3.50. _____

CHAPTER 23
The Body and Drugs

After completing Chapter 23 from the textbook, you should be able to:	Related Activity in the Workbook/Lab Manual
1. Explain the differences between pharmacodynamics and pharmacokinetics.	Review Questions, PTCB Exam Practice Questions
2. Understand the ways in which cell receptors react to drugs.	Review Questions
3. Describe mechanism of action and identify and understand its key factor.	Review Questions
4. Explain how drugs are absorbed, distributed, metabolized, and cleared by the body.	Review Questions, PTCB Exam Practice Questions
5. Explain the difference between fat-soluble and water-soluble drugs and give examples of each.	Review Questions
6. Identify and explain the effect of bioavailability and its relationship to drug effectiveness.	Review Questions
7. Understand addiction and addictive behavior.	Review Questions, PTCB Exam Practice Questions
8. Describe the role of the pharmacy technician in identifying drug-abusing patients.	Review Questions
9. List and identify some drugs that interact with alcohol.	Review Questions

INTRODUCTION

Pharmacology is the study of drugs, including their composition, uses, application, and effects. Although the pharmacist is responsible for using his or her specialized knowledge to provide pharmaceutical care to patients, pharmacy technicians too must understand the basics of pharmacology. *Pharmacodynamics* is the study of how drugs produce their effects on the desired cells, and how the drug is then processed by the body. *Pharmacokinetics* is the study of how the body handles drugs, how drugs are changed from their original form into something that the body can use, and how they are eliminated from the body.

REVIEW QUESTIONS

Match the following.

1. _____ absorption
2. _____ agonist
3. _____ bioavailability
4. _____ clearance
5. _____ dependency
6. _____ excretion
7. _____ metabolism
8. _____ addiction
9. _____ tolerance
10. _____ metabolites
11. _____ half-life
12. _____ distribution
13. _____ antagonist

a. the state of being dependent

b. a drug that does not produce any noticeable effect when it binds to a specific receptor on the cell

c. specific type of drug that produces a certain, predicted action when it binds to the correct receptor

d. the movement of an absorbed drug from the bloodstream into body tissues

e. the process by which drugs are eliminated from the body

f. pattern of compulsive substance abuse characterized by a continued psychological and physiological craving or need for the substance and its effects

g. any substance produced by the metabolic process

h. the time required for plasma serum concentration levels of an absorbed and distributed drug to decrease by one-half

i. process of transforming drugs in the body

j. when a person requires (psychologically or physiologically) larger doses of a drug to achieve the same effect

k. the degree to which a drug becomes available to body tissue(s) after administration

l. how a drug enters the body

m. the time it takes a drug to be eliminated from the body

Choose the best answer.

14. Pharmacodynamics can be described as the study of:
    a. how drugs produce their effects.
    b. what the body does to a drug.
    c. the process of drug interactions.
    d. how drugs are made on the desired cells.

15. How a drug works and produces its effect is called:
    a. effective distribution.
    b. chemical process.
    c. mechanism of action.
    d. potency.

16. Site of action refers to:
    a. the part of the body where a drug is injected.
    b. when the drug produces certain actions.
    c. the location where a drug will exert its effect.
    d. how the drug acts in the body.

17. ED50 refers to the:
    a. amount of a drug that produces half the normal response.
    b. binding medium used in compounding.
    c. effective drug at 50%.
    d. top 50 most effective drugs.

18. Once a drug is at a serum concentration of less than 3%, it is considered:
    a. nontoxic.
    b. out of range.
    c. eliminated.
    d. ineffective.

19. Which is not a form of excretion?
    a. breath
    b. sweat
    c. urine
    d. odor

20. Pinocytosis is a:
    a. form of transportation of drugs into cells.
    b. a medicinally powerful plant.
    c. a rare type of gum disease.
    d. none of the above.

21. The abbreviation for consumable alcohol is:
    a. ACh.
    b. EOH.
    c. ETOH.
    d. ISO.

22. The rate of administration of a drug is determined by the:
    a. prescriber.
    b. research and development process.
    c. chemical nature of the drug.
    d. health of the patient.

23. Addiction has how many criteria:
    a. 4
    b. 8
    c. 7
    d. 9

24. Which of these drugs may produce increased heart rate when mixed with alcohol?
    a. hydrocodone
    b. alprazolam
    c. metformin
    d. warfarin

25. Pharmacokinetics is a term for the study of:
    a. receptors producing a specific effect.
    b. the time course of a drug in the body.
    c. the process of drug interactions.
    d. how drugs are made.

True or False?

26. Salts do not matter if the active ingredient is the same.
    T   F

27. The absorption of a drug governs the bioavailability of that drug.
    T   F

28. Addiction is the same as chemical dependency.
    T   F

29. Pharmacokinetics involves absorption, distribution, metabolism, and elimination of a drug.
    T   F

30. Damaging consequences is not a characteristic of addiction.
    T   F

PHARMACY CALCULATION PROBLEMS

Calculate the following.

1. The physician ordered 500 mg tablets of a medication for a patient. The medication comes in a 250 mg tablet form. The patient was told to take the medication orally twice a day for 15 days. How many tablets are needed to fill this order?

2. A man has brought in a prescription for ranitidine 300 mg. The physician did not indicate Dispense As Written (DAW) on the prescription, but the customer insists on getting the brand-name drug. The insurance company will charge him the price of the co-pay, plus the difference in price between the generic and the brand. This is known as *difference pricing*. Calculate the cost to the customer if the generic price is $11.25 and the brand price is $27.95. His usual co-pay is $10.

   Hint: co-pay + (brand price − generic price) = cost

3. A customer wants to pay difference pricing for a prescription for nabumetone 500 mg. The price of the brand-name drug is $85.49, and the price of the generic drug is $17.99. His or her usual co-pay is $15. What will the insurance company charge the customer using difference pricing?

4. A pharmacy sets its retail prices as a 30% markup of cost. If a 100-count bottle of acetaminophen 325 mg costs the pharmacy $1.49, what will be the retail price for this item?

5. Conversion: 98 °F = _____ °C

PTCB EXAM PRACTICE QUESTIONS

1. Dopamine is a:
   a. hormone.
   b. catecholamine.
   c. neurotransmitter.
   d. all of the above.

2. Which organ is responsible for a drug's metabolism?
   a. kidney
   b. intestines
   c. lungs
   d. liver

3. All of the following drugs may be used to assist patients with smoking cessation *except*:
   a. nicotine patch.
   b. Chantix.
   c. Dilantin.
   d. Wellbutrin.

4. Which organ is responsible for the majority of a drug's excretion?
   a. kidney
   b. intestines
   c. lungs
   d. liver

5. Opiates fall under which schedule or category of controlled substances?
   a. C-I
   b. C-II
   c. C-III
   d. C-V

CHAPTER 24
The Skin

After completing Chapter 24 from the textbook, you should be able to:	Related Activity in the Workbook/Lab Manual
1. List, identify, and diagram the basic anatomical structure of the skin.	Review Questions, PTCB Exam Practice Questions
2. Explain the function or physiology of the skin.	Review Questions, PTCB Exam Practice Questions
3. List and define common diseases affecting the skin.	Review Questions, PTCB Exam Practice Questions

INTRODUCTION

The skin is the largest organ of the body. It consists of three main layers: the epidermis, the dermis, and the subcutaneous layer. Important functions of the skin include serving as a barrier to foreign organisms and debris, managing the regulation of body temperature, excreting salts and excess water, and acting as a "shock absorber" to protect the underlying organs. Unfortunately, the skin plays host to a wide variety of more than 1,000 medical conditions and diseases, ranging from minor irritations to severe infections. Although creams and ointments are widely used to treat skin conditions, treatment options also include oral and injectable medications. As a pharmacy technician, it is important for you to understand the basic anatomy and physiology of the skin and the conditions that affect it so that you have greater insight into how the drugs used to treat these conditions work.

REVIEW QUESTIONS

Match the following.

1. _____ acne
2. _____ sebum
3. _____ carcinoma
4. _____ pathogenic
5. _____ rosacea
6. _____ mitigate
7. _____ eczema
8. _____ bacteriostatic
9. _____ infection
10. _____ pigmentation
11. _____ bactericidal
12. _____ psoriasis
13. _____ rash
14. _____ parasite

a. oily substance produced by the sebaceous glands in the skin

b. an organism that lives on or inside another organism

c. a skin condition characterized by redness and inflammation

d. disease-causing microorganisms

e. kills microorganisms

f. inhibits the growth and/or reproduction of microorganisms

g. inflammatory skin condition characterized by itching, redness, blistering, and oozing

h. a bacterial infection accompanied by an overproduction of sebum

i. invasion of pathogens into the body; an infection occurs when a pathogenic microbe is able to multiply in the tissues (colonize)

j. malignant tumor

k. to lessen or decrease severity

l. a facial skin disorder accompanied by chronic redness and inflammation

m. color

n. a noncontagious, chronic immune disorder in which specific immune cells become overactive and release excessive amounts of proteins called cytokines

True or False?

15. The skin is the largest organ of the body.

    T   F

16. The outermost layer of the skin is the dermis.

    T   F

17. Cellulitis is caused by a fungus.

    T   F

18. Ringworm is an example of a bacterial infection.

    T   F

Choose the best answer.

19. Normal body temperature regulated by the skin is:
    a. 98.6 °F.   c. 69.8 °C.
    b. 89.6 °F.   d. 98.6 °C.

20. Skin infections are not caused by which of the following?
    a. bacteria   c. fungi
    b. cancer   d. viruses

21. The most severe burn would be classified as:
    a. first degree.
    b. second degree.
    c. third degree.
    d. fourth degree.

22. The second most common skin cancer is:
    a. malignant melanoma.
    b. actinic keratosis.
    c. basal cell carcinoma.
    d. squamous cell cancer.

Fill in the blanks.

23. An acute, deep infection of the connective tissue is called _____.

24. Small red bumps and intense itching caused by mites is known as _____.

Match the following ulcer descriptions with their classifications.

25. _____ Stage I   a. lesion extending through skin to the bone
26. _____ Stage II   b. crater-like lesion extending through tissue
27. _____ Stage III   c. reddening of unbroken skin
28. _____ Stage IV   d. abrasion or blister

PHARMACY CALCULATION PROBLEMS

Calculate the following.

1. A prescription reads: "Clindamycin 2% in aquaphilic ointment; 60 g. Apply to affected body part twice daily." The pharmacy stocks clindamycin 150 mg capsules. How many capsules will be needed to prepare this compound?

2. A physician has requested a compound for lidocaine 3% in 120 mL calamine lotion. How many milligrams of lidocaine powder must be added to the calamine lotion for the compound?

3. A compound is to contain equal parts nystatin cream, clotrimazole 1% cream, and triamcinolone 0.05% cream. How many grams of each product will be required to make 4 oz?

4. A physician wants to dilute 100 mL of a 10% topical solution to a 4% solution with sterile water. How many milliliters of sterile water will you need?

5. Conversion: 144 lbs = _____ kg

PTCB EXAM PRACTICE QUESTIONS

1. Which is the middle layer of the skin?
   a. subcutaneous
   b. epidermis
   c. dermis
   d. adipose

2. What is an acute, deep infection of the skin and connective tissue accompanied by inflammation?
   a. basal cell carcinoma
   b. eczema
   c. psoriasis
   d. cellulitis

3. What disease is caused by bacteria and an overproduction of sebum?
   a. eczema
   b. acne
   c. psoriasis
   d. cellulitis

4. What kind of skin infection is described as a mycosis?
   a. fungal
   b. bacterial
   c. viral
   d. parasitic

CHAPTER 25
Eyes and Ears

After completing Chapter 25 from the textbook, you should be able to:	Related Activity in the Workbook/Lab Manual
1. List, identify, and diagram the basic anatomical structure and parts of the eye and ear.	Review Questions, PTCB Exam Practice Questions
2. Describe the function or physiology of the ears and eyes.	Review Questions, PTCB Exam Practice Questions
3. List and define common diseases affecting the eyes and ears.	Review Questions, PTCB Exam Practice Questions

INTRODUCTION

Seeing and hearing are two of our basic senses. Although both the eyes and the ears are susceptible to a variety of disorders, these maladies can normally be prevented, controlled, or reversed with treatment, except in rare cases. A wide variety of treatment modalities is available to treat eye disorders. However, it is important that ophthalmic products be used safely and properly, because they are sterile. One of your most important responsibilities as a pharmacy technician is to thoroughly understand the basics of safe using of ophthalmic remedies. As a pharmacy technician, it is important for you to understand the basic anatomy and physiology of the eyes and ears and the conditions that affect them so that you have greater insight into how the drugs used to treat these conditions work.

REVIEW QUESTIONS

Match the following.

1. _____ humor
2. _____ asymptomatic
3. _____ blepharitis
4. _____ hordeolum
5. _____ cataract
6. _____ cycloplegic
7. _____ conjunctivitis
8. _____ tinnitus
9. _____ glaucoma
10. __a__ photoreceptors
11. __o__ iridotomy
12. _____ retinopathy
13. _____ mucopurulent
14. _____ otitis media
15. _____ mydriatic
16. _____ ophthalmic
17. _____ eustachian tube

a. rods and cones
b. a group of eye diseases characterized by an increase in intra-ocular pressure
c. a noninflammatory disease in which the retina of the eye is damaged
d. pertaining to the eye
e. causing relaxation and paralysis of the intraocular muscles
f. containing or composed of mucus or pus
g. acute or chronic inflammation of the eye conjunctiva
h. showing no evidence of disease or abnormal condition
i. causing dilation of the pupil of the eye
j. an ocular opacity or obscurity in the lens of the eye
k. a body fluid
l. inflammation of the eyelid margins accompanied by redness
m. infection and inflammation of the middle ear
n. ringing or buzzing in the ear that is not caused by an external source; may be caused by infection or a reaction to a drug.
o. an incision made in the iris of the eye to enlarge the pupil
p. an infection of one (or more) of the sebaceous glands of the eye
q. connects the middle ear with the nasopharynx of the throat

Choose the best answer.

18. The _____ is often referred to as the "film" of the camera.
    a. pupil
    b. cornea
    c. iris
    d. retina

19. The visual pathway for electrical impulses to the brain is the:
    a. cornea.
    b. sclera.
    c. iris.
    d. optic nerve.

20. The likely culprit of a stye is:
    a. *Staphylococcus aureus.*
    b. *Lactobacillus Casei.*
    c. *Streptococcus meningitis.*
    d. *Staphylococcus epidermis.*

PHARMACY CALCULATION PROBLEMS

1. A 5 mL bottle of olopatadine, 0.1%, is dispensed for allergic conjunctivitis. If the patient uses 1 gtt ou q8h, how many days will the bottle last?

2. How many milligrams of pilocarpine are in a 10 mL bottle of pilocarpine 6% ophthalmic gel?

3. Azithromycin 100 mg/5 mL suspension is prescribed for a child's inner-ear infection. If the patient is to receive 100 mg on day 1 and 50 mg on days 2–5, how many milliliters will the patient need for the entire course?

4. If cephalexin 250 mg is prescribed to a child one capsule qid for seven days, what is the total strength for the course of therapy that the child will receive? How many capsules will be dispensed?

5. Conversion: 1 pt. = _____ mL

PTCB EXAM PRACTICE QUESTIONS

1. What disease of the eye is characterized by increased intraocular pressure?
   a. conjunctivitis
   b. cataract
   c. glaucoma
   d. macular degeneration

2. What is a condition of the eye in which the lens becomes opaque and interferes with clear vision?
   a. conjunctivitis
   b. cataract
   c. glaucoma
   d. macular degeneration

3. Which common infection of the eye is most commonly referred to as "pinkeye?"
   a. conjunctivitis
   b. cataract
   c. glaucoma
   d. macular degeneration

4. A patient may experience ototoxicity if he or she is prescribed:
   a. amoxicillin.
   b. hydrochlorothiazide.
   c. gentamicin.
   d. celecoxib.

CHAPTER 26
The Gastrointestinal System

After completing Chapter 26 from the textbook, you should be able to:	Related Activity in the Workbook/Lab Manual
1. Identify the basic anatomical and structural parts of the digestive system.	Review Questions, PTCB Exam Practice Questions
2. Describe the physiology of the digestive system.	Review Questions, PTCB Exam Practice Questions
3. List and define common diseases affecting the gastrointestinal system and understand the causes, symptoms, and pharmaceutical treatments associated with each disease.	Review Questions, PTCB Exam Practice Questions, Lab 26-1, Lab 26-2

INTRODUCTION

The gastrointestinal system manages digestion in the body. Food is broken down, absorbed, or chemically modified into substances that are required by the cells to survive and function properly. Waste products that the body cannot use are eliminated. The gastrointestinal system extends from the mouth to the anus. Its six main parts are the mouth, esophagus, pharynx, stomach, and small and large intestines. Various supportive structures, accessory glands, and accessory organs also help to make up the complete digestive system. The main purpose of the digestive system is to fuel the body by taking in and metabolizing nutrients.

An estimated 70 million Americans suffer from one or more digestive disorders; this accounts for 13% of all hospitalizations. As a pharmacy technician, you should be aware of the most common digestive disorders that require pharmacological treatment, including conditions treated with OTC drugs.

REVIEW QUESTIONS

Match the following.

1. _____ chyme
2. _____ mastication
3. _____ protease
4. _____ lipid
5. _____ monosaccharide
6. _____ μg
7. _____ pepsinogen

a. fat
b. microgram
c. enzyme that begins protein breakdown
d. simplest form of carbohydrate
e. chewing
f. precursor to pepsin
g. liquid that food turns into before entering the small intestines

Choose the best answer.

8. Which of the following refers to LDL?
   a. bad cholesterol
   b. low-density lipoprotein
   c. a and b
   d. good cholesterol

9. Kilocalories (kcal) refers to:
   a. bad calories.
   b. food energy.
   c. good calories.
   d. a 1,000-calorie meal.

10. Good cholesterol is referred to as:
    a. high-density lipoprotein.
    b. DRI.
    c. HDL.
    d. a and c.

11. DRI stands for:
    a. dietary restriction information.
    b. diet reference index.
    c. dietary reference intakes.
    d. dietary recommendation index.

Fill in the blanks.

12. An added nutrient for enrichment is known as _____.

13. The liver produces _____, which is stored in the gallbladder.

14. As chyme enters the duodenum, it must be neutralized by bicarbonate; otherwise, a _____ ulcer will result.

15. _____ are nutrients needed by the body in larger quantities.

16. The only vitamin the body produces itself is vitamin _____.

Match the following.

17. _____ cecum
18. _____ tongue
19. _____ pharynx
20. _____ ileum

a. an accessory organ
b. a part of the small intestine
c. a part of the large intestine
d. part of main digestive system

True or False?

21. GERD occurs because the lower esophageal sphincter relaxes when it should contract.

    T   F

22. Ginger root is an herb that is known to combat nausea and vomiting.

    T   F

23. NSAIDs block the effect of the enzyme cyclooxygenase.

    T   F

24. Carbohydrates are bad for our health.

    T   F

PHARMACY CALCULATION PROBLEMS

1. You need to dispense omeprazole for a pediatric patient. The patient weighs 55 lbs. and the recommended dosage is 20 mg/kg. The dosing for this medication in the pediatric population is 20 mg if the patient is over 20 kg. Is this dosage safe for the patient to take?

2. Sucralfate comes in a concentration of 1 g/10 mL. If a patient is receiving 10 mL qid, how many milligrams of sucralfate is the patient receiving daily?

3. A 65-year-old woman weighing 156 lbs. is to receive a midazolam IVP dosed at 0.02 mg/kg prior to her colonoscopy. If midazolam contains 1 mg/mL, how many milliliters will the patient receive?

4. A standard pantoprazole drip at a hospital pharmacy contains 80 mg in 250 mL of 0.9% sodium chloride. If the patient is to receive 8 mg/hr, how many milliliters will be infused over each hour?

5. Conversion: 2.5 lb. = _____oz.

LAB 26-1: Treating GERD

Objective:

To understand the differences and protocols of various treatment options associated with gastrointestinal reflux disorder.

Pre-Lab Information:

• Review Chapter 26 in the textbook.

Explanation:

This exercise will help you to understand the protocol of therapies and treatment options that are most commonly prescribed for GERD.

Activity:

Using the WebMD website (http://www.webmd.com/ahrq/gerd-acid-reflux-treatments#top), please answer the following questions.

1. What is the very first type of treatment that a patient can invest in to quickly relieve the symptoms of GERD? Does this treatment require a prescription?

   _____

   _____

   _____

   _____

   _____

   _____

2. If the first line or type of treatment is not successful for a patient with relieving his or her GERD, what is the second type of treatment option that he or she can invest in to relieve the symptoms of GERD? Does this treatment option require a prescription?

   _____

   _____

   _____

   _____

3. If the second line or type of treatment is not successful for a patient with relieving his or her GERD, what is the third treatment option that he or she can invest in to relieve the symptoms of GERD? Does this treatment option require a prescription?

   _____

   _____

   _____

   _____

4. After these three prescribed and unprescribed treatment options have been proven to be ineffective for a patient, what is the final treatment option for a patient to consider in order to successfully alleviate his or her symptoms of GERD?

_____

_____

_____

_____

LAB 26-2: Treating Diarrhea

Objective:

To understand the role that probiotics have as a treatment option for diarrhea.

Pre-Lab Information:

• Review Chapter 26 in the textbook.

Explanation:

This exercise will help you to understand how probiotics can effectively treat diarrhea when the condition is brought on by the contributing use of an antibiotic.

Activity:

Using the following website: (http://www.onhealth.com/probiotics/article.htm#probiotics), please answer the following questions.

1. What are probiotics?

   _____
   _____
   _____
   _____

2. Please list the different types of probiotics.

   _____
   _____
   _____
   _____

3. Please list the different health benefits of probiotics.

   _____
   _____
   _____
   _____

4. Why do you think probiotics would be a good treatment option while a patient is taking antibiotics?

   _____
   _____
   _____
   _____

CHAPTER 27
The Musculoskeletal System

After completing Chapter 27 from the textbook, you should be able to:	Related Activity in the Workbook/Lab Manual
1. List, identify, and diagram the basic anatomical structure and parts of the muscles and bones.	Review Questions, PTCB Exam Practice Questions
2. Describe the functions of the muscles and bones and their physiology.	Review Questions, PTCB Exam Practice Questions
3. List and define common diseases affecting the muscles and bones.	Review Questions, PTCB Exam Practice Questions, Lab 27-1, Lab 27-2

INTRODUCTION

The musculoskeletal system, which consists of bones and skeletal muscles, provides the body with both form and movement. Its four main functions are to provide a framework or shape for the body, protect the internal organs, allow body movement, and provide storage for essential minerals. The musculoskeletal system is affected by numerous disorders, some of which cause only discomfort and pain, and some of which cause complete disability. Osteoporosis, the most prevalent bone disorder in the United States, affects approximately 20 million Americans and is a major cause of bone fractures. Osteoarthritis, a progressive disease of the joints, affects up to 40 million Americans.

A wide range of pharmaceuticals is used for the treatment of diseases of the musculoskeletal system, although many provide only symptomatic relief. However, as a result of intensive research, new products aimed at the prevention or retardation of disease, particularly osteoporosis and osteoarthritis, may provide hope for the millions of Americans afflicted with these debilitating diseases. As a pharmacy technician, you should be aware of the most common musculoskeletal disorders that require pharmacological treatment, including conditions treated with OTC drugs.

REVIEW QUESTIONS

Match the following.

1. _____ bones
2. _____ marrow
3. _____ cartilage
4. _____ hematopoiesis
5. _____ joints
6. _____ ligaments
7. _____ muscle
8. _g_ myocyte
9. _d_ sarcomere
10. _____ synovial fluid
11. _____ tendons

a. soft tissues that line every joint and give shape to the ears and nose

b. the location or position where bones are connected to each other

c. specialized tissue that contracts when stimulated

d. one of the segments into which a fibril of striated muscle is divided

e. strong fibrous bands of connective tissue that hold bones together

f. specialized form of dense connective tissue consisting of calcified intercellular substance that provides the shape and support for the body

g. a muscle cell

h. cords of connective tissue that attach muscle to bone

i. spongy type of tissue found inside most bones

j. liquid that fills the space between the cartilage of each bone; provides smooth movement by lubricating the cartilage

k. formation and development of blood cells

Choose the best answer.

12. Smooth muscles comprise or line all of the following *except*:
    a. stomach.
    b. lungs.
    c. neck.
    d. intestines.

13. An example of a bisphosphonate is:
    a. alendronate.
    b. celecoxib.
    c. calcitonin.
    d. tiludronate.

Match the following.

14. _____ osteoporosis
15. _____ bursitis
16. _____ myalgia
17. _____ anemia
18. _____ leukemia
19. _____ osteoarthritis
20. _____ rheumatoid arthritis
21. _____ gout
22. _____ osteomyelitis
23. _____ Paget's disease

a. a progressive form of arthritis that has devastating effects on the joints, body organs, and general health

b. when one or more white blood cells experience DNA loss or damage

c. bone brittleness due to lack of calcium

d. a progressive disease characterized by the breakdown of joint cartilage

e. changes the normal process of bone growth: Bone breaks down more quickly and then grows back softer than normal bone

f. failure of bone marrow to produce the components of the red blood cell

g. is an inflammation of the bursae, which are the small, fluid-filled pouches between bones and ligaments, or between bones and muscles, that serve as cushions

h. caused by an excess or overproduction of uric acid or by the inability of the kidneys to adequately excrete uric acid from the body

i. muscle pain

j. bacterial infection inside the bone that destroys bone tissue

PHARMACY CALCULATION PROBLEMS

Calculate the following.

1. If an employee gets paid $100/day and has to miss an average of 12 work days each year because of fibromyalgia, how much income is the employee losing each year due to illness?

2. Calculate the monthly medical (traditional and nontraditional) expenses for this fibromyalgia patient:

   medical insurance—$150/month

   medications—$89

   chiropractic and acupuncture—$119

   massage therapy—$45

   physician co-payments—$15

3. If an insurance company pays 60% of the retail price for medications, how much is the customer's co-pay if the total retail price is $223?

4. A patient comes in with a prescription for 30 leflunomide 20 mg tablets with the directions stated as 1 tab po qd. While checking the lab to see if this drug is in your inventory, you realize that you only have the 10 mg strength in stock. The pharmacist calls the physician to change the order and the physician is in compliance with changing the strength. What will the new directions be, and how many tablets will be dispensed to the patient?

5. 6 g of active ingredient is in 120 g of a compounded ointment. What is the concentration (w/w)?

PTCB EXAM PRACTICE QUESTIONS

1. An example of an NSAID is:
   a. carisoprodol.
   b. piroxicam.
   c. baclofen.
   d. aspirin.

2. Gout is a disorder involving the deposit of which of the following compounds in the joints and soft tissues, resulting in significant pain?
   a. potassium chloride
   b. hydrochloric acid
   c. uric acid
   d. calcium chloride

3. NSAIDs are a class of drugs used to treat:
   a. infection.
   b. inflammation.
   c. muscle weakness.
   d. bone loss.

4. A combination of salicylate and an antibiotic used to treat RA is:
   a. penicillamine.
   b. SMZ/TMP.
   c. sulfasalazine.
   d. hydroxychloroquine sulfate.

LAB 27-1: Treating Arthritis

Objective:

Familiarize yourself with the medications commonly prescribed and recommended for arthritis.

Pre-Lab Information:

• Review Chapter 27 in the textbook.

Explanation:

In our current market, there are many commonly prescribed medications that are used to effectively treat arthritis.

Activity:

Visit www.arthritis.org to locate the various treatment options that a patient may consider for his or her arthritis. Please answer all of the questions below and be sure to view the lists of drugs from each chart.

1. What are the nine classes of medications currently listed in the Drug Lookup section that are used to treat arthritis?

   • _____
   • _____
   • _____
   • _____
   • _____
   • _____
   • _____
   • _____
   • _____

2. Which class of medications has listed controlled substances that are used to treat arthritis?

   _____
   _____
   _____

3. What does the acronym DMARDs mean, and how are these medications effective in arthritis treatment?

   _____
   _____
   _____
   _____
   _____

4. Please provide the brand and generic names of the biologic response modifiers that are effective for arthritis.

Brand   Generic

_____   _____

_____   _____

_____   _____

_____   _____

_____   _____

5. Please provide the brand and/or generic manes of the corticosteroids that are effective for arthritis.

Brand   Generic

_____   _____

_____   _____

_____   _____

_____   _____

_____   _____

_____   _____

_____   _____

LAB 27-2: Treating Inflammation

Objective:

Familiarize yourself with the medications commonly prescribed and recommended for acute and chronic inflammation.

Pre-Lab Information:

• Review Chapter 27 in the textbook.

Explanation:

In our current market, there are many commonly prescribed medications that are used to effectively treat inflammation of the musculoskeletal system.

Activity:

Using the lists below, please match up the brand and generic names as well as the classes of the commonly prescribed and recommended medications that are used to effectively treat inflammation of the musculo-skeletal system.

Brand	Generic	Class
_____	_____	_____
_____	_____	_____
_____	_____	_____
_____	_____	_____
_____	_____	_____
_____	_____	_____
_____	_____	_____
_____	_____	_____
_____	_____	_____
_____	_____	_____

Celebrex	meloxicam	COX-II Inhibitor
Cortef	tramadol	NSAID
Medrol	prednisolone	Corticosteroid
Motrin	hydrocodone/IBU	
Ultram	ibuprofen	
Tylenol	celecoxib	
Mobic	methylprednisolone	
Feldene	hydrocortisone	
Vicoprofen	piroxicam	
Prednisone	acetaminophen	

CHAPTER 28
The Respiratory System

After completing Chapter 28 from the textbook, you should be able to:	Related Activity in the Workbook/Lab Manual
1. Identify and list the basic anatomical and structural parts of the respiratory tract.	Review Questions, PTCB Exam Practice Questions
2. Describe the function or physiology of the individual parts of the respiratory system and the external exchange of oxygen and waste.	Review Questions, PTCB Exam Practice Questions
3. List and define common diseases affecting the respiratory tract.	Review Questions, PTCB Exam Practice Questions, Lab 28-1, Lab 28-2

INTRODUCTION

The respiratory system is responsible for providing all cells of the body with the oxygen necessary to perform their specific functions. It is the system involved in the intake of oxygen through inhalation and the excretion of carbon dioxide through exhalation. The respiratory system is divided into two parts, the upper and lower respiratory tracts. The upper respiratory tract includes the nasal cavity, paranasal sinuses, pharynx, and larynx. The lower respiratory tract includes the trachea, two lungs, two main bronchi, secondary and tertiary bronchi, bronchioles, alveolar ducts, and alveoli.

The most common disease of the respiratory system is the common cold. Uncomplicated common colds are generally treated with over-the-counter (OTC) medications, including antihistamines, decongestants, cough suppressants, analgesics, antipyretics, and anti-inflammatories. The aim in treatment is to provide relief of symptoms. Naturally, the respiratory system is also prone to more serious diseases and conditions, such as asthma, which affect more than 15 million people and are responsible for as many as 1.5 million emergency room visits and 500,000 hospitalizations every year. If left uncontrolled, asthma can cause a long-term decline in lung function. Because many respiratory diseases are treated with some form of inhalation therapy, it is important for you, as a pharmacy technician, to be able to assist the pharmacist in educating clients as to the proper, safe use of inhalation products. You should also be aware of the most common respiratory disorders that require pharmacological treatment, including conditions treated with OTC drugs.

REVIEW QUESTIONS

Match the following.

1. _____ allergen
2. _____ allergy
3. _____ cilia
4. _____ COPD
5. _____ epiglottis
6. _____ larynx
7. _____ pharynx
8. _____ rhinitis
9. _____ trachea

a. the result of the immune system's reaction to a foreign substance

b. inflammation of the nasal passages

c. tiny hair-like organelles in the nose and bronchial passageways

d. the windpipe

e. a substance capable of causing a hypersensitivity reaction

f. a condition resulting from continual blockage of oxygen external exchange in the lungs

g. the voice box

h. small, leaf-shaped cartilage attached to the tongue that prevents substances other than air from entering the trachea

i. part of the throat from the back of the nasal cavity to the larynx

Choose the best answer.

10. The primary function of the respiratory system is to:
    a. transport air to and from the lungs.
    b. supply oxygen to the blood.
    c. exchange oxygen for carbon dioxide.
    d. keep the brain alive.

11. The two purposes of the respiratory system are:
    a. to prevent allergens coming into the airways and filter out contaminants.
    b. transport of air (gases) to and from the lungs and exchange of oxygen for carbon dioxide.
    c. exhaling and inhaling.
    d. maintaining an adequate supply of oxygen to the brain and exhaling carbon dioxide.

12. The exchange of gases between blood and cells is called:
    a. pulmonary ventilation.
    b. internal respiration.
    c. external respiration.
    d. cellular respiration.

13. Which does not belong to the conducting portion of the respiratory system?
    a. alveoli
    b. bronchioles
    c. nose
    d. pharynx

14. A common lay term for the larynx is:
    a. Bob's apple.
    b. Adam's apple.
    c. Adam's orange.
    d. Eve's apple.

15. The exchange of gases occurs in the:
    a. trachea.
    b. bronchioles.
    c. alveoli.
    d. bronchus.

PHARMACY CALCULATION PROBLEMS

Calculate the following.

1. If an inhaler contains 120 metered doses, how many days will the inhaler last if the patient is using 2 puffs qid prn?

2. A patient is using one levalbuterol 0.63 mg nebule in her home nebulizer tid. If levalbuterol comes in a box of 24 nebules, how many boxes will she need for a 24-day supply?

3. A patient is using an albuterol-ipratropium inhaler. The patient is using 2 puffs qid and prn, max 12 puffs/day. The inhaler contains 200 metered doses, calculate the day supply for this patient.

4. How many theophylline 200 mg tablets will be needed for a 30-day supply if the patient takes 1 po tid?

5. A five-year old female patient is prescribed albuterol syrup 0.2 mg/kg tid. The patient weighs 35 lbs. and the dosage is not to exceed 12 mg/day. Is the dose prescribed safe for this patient to take?

PTCB EXAM PRACTICE QUESTIONS

1. During respiration, the body inhales _____ and exhales _____.
   a. nitrogen, carbon dioxide
   b. oxygen, nitrogen
   c. oxygen, carbon dioxide
   d. carbon dioxide, oxygen

2. The common cold should *not* be treated with which medication?
   a. an analgesic
   b. an antibiotic
   c. a mucolytic
   d. a decongestant

3. Which of the following is *not* a respiratory disease?
   a. asthma
   b. GERD
   c. COPD
   d. emphysema

4. The Combat Methamphetamine Epidemic Act of 2005 requires nonprescription products to be sold from behind the pharmacy counter if they contain any of the following ingredients *except*:
   a. dextromethorphan.
   b. ephedrine.
   c. pseudoephedrine.
   d. phenylpropanolamine.

LAB 28-1: Treating Allergies

Objective:

To understand the different treatment options that allergic reaction and/or allergic condition from seasonal or yearly allergies are treated both pre and post reaction or condition.

Pre-Lab Information:

• Review Chapter 28 in the textbook.

Explanation:

Many consumers and patients, during the course of their lives, may experience the unfortunate effects and symptoms of an allergic reaction and/or allergic condition from seasonal or yearly allergies. There are many treatment options for these consumers and patients to consider and also to take precautions with so that their allergic reaction and/or allergic condition may not be bothersome and/or potentially fatal for them.

Activity:

Match the following allergic reaction and/or allergic condition to the class and medications from the following lists.

> **Hint:** Different OTC medications might be used by a consumer for an allergic condition or reaction.

Allergic Condition/Allergic Reaction

Poison Ivy _____

Allergic rhinitis _____

Sneezing _____

Foods _____

Runny nose _____

Antibiotics _____

Bee sting _____

Urticaria _____

Seasonal allergies _____

Poison oak _____

Watery eyes _____

Class/Medication

a) Nasal corticosteroids/beclomethasone, flunisolide, fluticasone, triamcinolone

b) H-1 antagonist/cetirizine, diphenhydramine, fexofenadine, hydroxyzine, loratadine

c) Topical antihistamine/diphenhydramine, fexofenadine

d) Topical corticosteroid/hydrocortisone

e) Vasopressor/sympathomimetic/epinephrine

f) Oral decongestant/phenylephrine

LAB 28-2: Treating Asthma

Objective:

To understand asthma and the different treatment options for patients who are diagnosed with asthma.

Pre-Lab Information:

- Review Chapter 28 in the textbook.
- Visit the website www.asthma.com

Explanation:

To date, there are more than 15 million individuals who have been diagnosed with asthma. There are many different classes of medications and medications within those classes that are prescribed for patients who are affected by this disease.

Activity:

While visiting the website www.asthma.com, take a few minutes to visit the toolbox and take the "DO I HAVE ASTHMA?" questionnaire, as well as take the "TEST YOUR ASTHMA CONTROL" "FOR ADULTS" questionnaire. Even if you do not have asthma, answering these questions may assist you with enhancing your customer service skills while working with the patients you know have asthma.

Next explore the MANAGE tab at the website. Please answer the following questions below.

1. What is a peak flow meter?

   _____

   _____

   _____

2. Peak flow readings can help a health care provider to determine:

   - _____

   - _____

   - _____

3. What is spirometry test? Is this test a common or uncommon test to diagnose asthma?

   _____

   _____

   _____

4. What is the class of medication within the "QUICK-RELIEF" tab?

   _____

5. What are the classes of medications within the "LONG-TERM" tab?

   _____

   _____

   _____

   _____

6. What is the class of medication within the "COMBINATION" tab?

_____

7. What are the classes of medications within the "OTHER" tab?

_____

_____

8. What are the four types of "DELIVERY DEVICES" that a patient might use to effectively treat his or her asthma?

_____

_____

_____

9. What are the "OTHER THERAPIES" that patients might consider to manage their asthma?

_____

_____

_____

_____

10. While visiting the "ASTHMA BASICS FOR PARENTS," what is the 2010 statistic of people with asthma who are children? _____

11. What should a parent do to help their child manage his or her asthma?

_____

_____

_____

_____

12. If a child is old enough to participate with managing his or her asthma, what should the parent do to help the child understand?

_____

_____

_____

_____

The Cardiovascular, Circulatory, and Lymph Systems

After completing Chapter 29 from the textbook, you should be able to:	Related Activity in the Workbook/Lab Manual
1. List, identify, and diagram the basic anatomical structure and parts of the heart.	Review Questions, PTCB Exam Practice Questions
2. Explain the function of the heart and the circulation of the blood within the body.	Review Questions, PTCB Exam Practice Questions
3. List and define common diseases affecting the heart, including the causes, symptoms, and pharmaceutical treatment associated with each disease.	Review Questions, PTCB Exam Practice Questions, Lab 29-1, Lab 29-2
4. List the total cholesterol, LDL, HDL, and triglyceride ranges for an average adult, and describe the differences between HDL, LDL, and triglycerides.	Review Questions, Lab 29-1, Lab 29-2
5. Describe the structure and main functions of the lymphatic system, and explain its relationship to the cardiovascular system.	Review Questions, PTCB Exam Practice Questions

INTRODUCTION

The cardiovascular system, or circulatory system, is responsible for transporting blood to all parts of the body. It includes the heart, arteries, arterioles, veins, venules, and capillaries. The arteries are responsible for carrying oxygen-rich blood to the cells, while the veins carry the deoxygenated blood back to the heart and lungs. The lungs and respiratory system work in tandem with the cardiovascular system to sustain life. To accomplish its primary purpose as a pumping mechanism that circulates blood to all parts of the body, the heart relies on a conduction system comprised of nodes and nodal tissues that regulate the various aspects of the heartbeat. In addition, the nervous system plays a vital role in regulating heart rate. The lymphatic system and circulatory system also work closely together as blood and lymph fluid move through the same capillary system. Lymph fluid removes wastes and debris from the body and supports the immune system by filtering out pathogens and draining excess fluid from the body.

The two common diseases affecting the cardiovascular system are congestive heart failure (CHF) and coronary artery disease (CAD). CHF occurs when the heart pumps out less blood than it receives, resulting in a weakened and enlarged heart, and in less blood being pumped to feed the other organs. CAD is a condition characterized by insufficient blood flow to the heart. Hypertension, or high blood pressure, and hyperlipidemia, or high blood cholesterol, are two additional conditions that affect the cardiovascular system. Often, both hypertension and hyperlipidemia go undetected, as these conditions do not cause substantial symptoms. As a pharmacy technician, you should also be aware of the most common cardiovascular disorders that require pharmacological treatment, including conditions treated with over-the-counter (OTC) drugs.

REVIEW QUESTIONS

Match the following.

1. _____ arterioles
2. _____ atrioventricular valves
3. _____ contractility
4. _____ DOC
5. _____ DVT
6. _____ dyscrasia
7. _____ hematuria
8. _____ hyperlipidemia
9. _____ leukocyte
10. _____ venules
11. _____ plaque
12. _____ pulmonary edema
13. _____ hematuria
14. _____ semilunar valves
15. _____ thrombophlebitis

a. the smallest veins
b. the smallest arteries
c. high concentrations of lipids in the blood
d. large quantities of protein in the urine
e. include the tricuspid and mitral valves of the heart
f. inflammation of a vein with a thrombus
g. the drug preferred for treatment of a particular condition or disease
h. the ability to contract; also, the degree of contraction
i. a blood clot in one of the veins of the legs or other deep veins
j. a white blood cell
k. abnormal condition of the body, especially a blood imbalance
l. include the aortic and pulmonary valves of the heart
m. blood in the urine
n. fluid collection in the pulmonary vessels or lungs
o. fatty deposits that are high in cholesterol

Choose the best answer.

16. The human body contains _____ of blood.
    a. 4,300 gallons
    b. 15.6 L
    c. 5.6 L
    d. none of the above

17. The heart muscle pumps _____ of blood daily.
    a. 4,300 gallons
    b. 16.6 L
    c. 5.6 L
    d. none of the above

18. The _____, a double layer of serous and fibrous tissue, is a fluid-filled sac that surrounds and protects the heart. It also permits free movement of the heart during contraction.
    a. endocardium
    b. myocardium
    c. septum
    d. pericardium

19. The two top chambers of the heart are called:
    a. ventricles.
    b. valves.
    c. atria.
    d. arteries.

20. The two bottom chambers of the heart are called:
    a. ventricles.
    b. valves.
    c. atria.
    d. arteries.

21. Which of the following is not a risk factor for high blood pressure?
    a. genetics
    b. stress
    c. race
    d. heart size

PHARMACY CALCULATION PROBLEMS

Calculate the following.

1. A patient is to receive lidocaine 2 g/250 mL IV that will run at 2 mg/min. What is the infusion rate in milliliters per hour?

2. If an amiodarone drip is to run at 33 mL/hr for six hours, how many milligrams of drug will be infused in that time if the bottle contains 500 mg/250 mL?

3. A patient weighing 240 lbs. is receiving dopamine 5 mcg/kg/min IV. The concentration of the dopamine bag is 400 mg/250 mL. What is the infusion rate in milliliters per hour?

4. An infant patient has been prescribed heparin 10 units q6–8h. On stock you have 100 units/mL. How many milliliters will you prepare to cover 24 hours?

5. What concentration (v/v) would be obtained when 20 mL of alcohol is combined with 60 mL of SWFI?

PTCB EXAM PRACTICE QUESTIONS

1. What is the American Heart Association's recommendation for healthy blood pressure levels?
   a. 80/120
   b. 140/90
   c. 120/80
   d. 90/140

2. Which of the following is used as the antidote for a heparin overdose?
   a. vitamin K
   b. protamine sulfate
   c. enoxaparin
   d. warfarin

3. In the cardiovascular system, _____ carries oxygenated blood to the cells and _____ carries deoxygenated blood back to the heart and lungs.
   a. arteries, veins
   b. veins, arteries
   c. arterioles, veins
   d. capillaries, veins

4. INR as it relates to blood coagulation stands for:
   a. independent normalized ratio.
   b. international nominal ratio.
   c. international normalized ratio.
   d. international normalized rations.

LAB 29-1: Treating High Blood Pressure

Objectives:

To understand the different treatment options for high blood pressure.

Pre-Lab Information:

• Review Chapter 29 in the textbook.

Explanation:

Many patients have been diagnosed with hypertension or high blood pressure. The American Heart Association has designated hypertension into the three categories of:

1.	Prehypertension	120–139	or	80–89
2.	High blood pressure (hypertension) Stage 1	140–159	or	90–99
3.	High blood pressure (hypertension) Stage 2	160 or higher	or	100 or higher

Whichever category their consistent blood pressure readings are, patients who require either lifestyle changes or prescribed regimens of medications to treat their hypertension can choose a course of action under the direction of a physician to produce a successful outcome.

Activity:

Using the website www.heart.org, please answer the following questions.

1. What are the eight ways that a person can control his or her blood pressure?

   • _____

   • _____

   • _____

   • _____

   • _____

   • _____

   • _____

   • _____

2. When a patient adopts a heart-healthy lifestyle, he or she can:

   • _____

   • _____

   • _____

   • _____

3. OTC decongestants that may raise a person's blood pressure are:

    - _____
    - _____
    - _____
    - _____
    - _____
    - _____
    - _____
    - _____
    - _____
    - _____

4. Is the sodium content in OTC medications important for patients with hypertension to consider? If so, why?

    _____

    _____

    _____

5. According to the American Heart Association, how many classes of blood pressure medications are there?

    _____

6. What is the generic suffix associated with the ACE inhibitor class?

    _____

7. What is the generic suffix most associated with the beta-blocker class?

    _____

8. What is the generic suffix associated with the alpha-blocker class?

    _____

9. The medication minoxidil is listed as a vasodilator. What is the another indication that minoxidil is approved for?

    _____

10. What are the cardiovascular risks associated with drinking alcohol?

    _____

LAB 29-2: Treating Cholesterol

Objectives:

To understand the different treatment options for cholesterol.

Pre-Lab Information:

• Review Chapter 29 in the textbook.

Explanation:

Many patients have been diagnosed with hyperlipidemia or high cholesterol. As the optimal range for most adults is 200 mg/dL or lower, the American Heart Association has suggestions to improve borderline and high cholesterol levels as well as the prevention of hyperlipidemia.

Activity:

Using the website www.heart.org, please answer the following questions.

1. What is the female sex hormone that contributes to raising HDL cholesterol?

    _____

2. What are the recommendations for a female with high LDL cholesterol?

    _____

3. What are the symptoms of high cholesterol?

    _____

4. How is cholesterol tested?

    _____

5. What three lifestyle changes can an individual make in order to affect his or her cholesterol levels?

    • _____

    • _____

    • _____

6. What are three cooking tips to help lower cholesterol suggested by the American Heart Association?

    • _____

    • _____

    • _____

7. What are the four classes of cholesterol medications currently available for patients with high cholesterol to consider?

    _____

8. What is the generic suffix most associated with HMG CoA reductase inhibitors?

_____

9. How often should cholesterol be checked?

_____

10. What situations might apply to an individual to where their cholesterol levels will have to be checked more often?

- _____
- _____
- _____
- _____

CHAPTER 30
The Immune System

After completing Chapter 30 from the textbook, you should be able to:	Related Activity in the Workbook/Lab Manual
1. Explain how the body's nonspecific and specific defense mechanisms work to keep the body safe from disease-causing microorganisms.	Review Questions
2. Understand the basic relationships between the immune system and the various body systems.	Review Questions, Lab 30-2
3. List and describe the different types of infectious organisms.	Review Questions, PTCB Exam Practice Questions, Lab 30-1
4. List the five stages of progression of HIV to AIDS.	Review Questions
5. Describe autoimmune disease and identify various types.	Review Questions, PTCB Exam Practice Questions
6. Understand how drug resistance develops and what steps can be taken to stop it.	Review Questions, Lab 30-1

INTRODUCTION

The immune system protects the body from foreign invaders that would otherwise destroy it, or parts of it, via infection or cancer. The immune system uses numerous kinds of responses to attacks from these foreign invaders and is amazingly effective most of the time. Its defensive barriers and mechanisms include nonspecific mechanisms such as the skin, mucus, and cilia in the linings of the respiratory and digestive passageways, and the blood clotting process. It also includes specific defense mechanisms such as the white blood cells, thymus gland, lymph nodes, antibodies, and lymphocytes (B-cells and T-cells).

Many different classes of medications affect the immune system. These include drugs for the treatment of HIV/AIDS, tuberculosis, and malaria, as well as for many other conditions and diseases of the immune system. Pharmacotherapeutic treatment of pathogens includes antibacterials, anti-infectives, and antifungals, to name a few. As a pharmacy technician, it is important for you to have a clear understanding of what these drugs are and how they work to protect the body.

In addition to fighting foreign invaders, sometimes the immune system is called upon to help defend against the autoimmune process in cases of autoimmune diseases, such as lupus erythematosus or rheumatoid arthritis, in which a person's immune system mistakenly attacks itself. The end result of this defense is often inflammation. These autoimmune diseases are treated both pharmacologically and nonpharmacologically. The pharmacotherapeutic goal of treatment is to reduce inflammation, or to stop or suppress the inflammatory process.

REVIEW QUESTIONS

Match the following.

1. _____ aerobic
2. _____ anaerobic
3. _____ antibodies
4. _____ antigens
5. _____ complement
6. _____ DNA
7. _____ epitopes
8. _____ cytoplasm
9. _____ hematopoietic
10. _____ genome
11. _____ lysis
12. _____ macrophage
13. _____ pathogen
14. _____ phagocytes
15. _____ RNA

a. a fluid where cell respiration takes place; usually contains RNA (a nucleic acid that enables protein synthesis)

b. the destruction of cells

c. specific molecules that trigger an immune response

d. blood-forming

e. a nucleic acid that carries genetic information and is capable of self-replication and synthesis of RNA

f. a nucleic acid needed for the metabolic processes of protein synthesis

g. a large group of proteins that is activated in sequence when cells are exposed to a foreign substance; activation eventually results in the death or destruction of the substance

h. white blood cell, found primarily in connective tissue and the bloodstream

i. region on the surface of an antibody that is capable of producing an immune response

j. specialized cells that engulf and ingest other cells

k. a disease-causing organism

l. requires oxygen for life

m. the complete hereditary material or code of an organism

n. does not require oxygen for life

o. proteins that specifically seek and bind to the surface of pathogens or antigens.

Choose the best answer.

16. Which of the following is not a defense against infection?
    a. mucus
    b. bone marrow
    c. vertebral column
    d. skin

17. Viruses are difficult to cure because:
    a. a capsid protects their DNA/RNA.
    b. they are resistant to antibiotics.
    c. they mutate constantly.
    d. a and c

18. What type of pathogen is TB?
    a. viral
    b. parasitic
    c. bacterial
    d. fungal

19. Which are protozoa that most often consume algae and bacteria?
    a. sporozoans
    b. zooflagellates
    c. ciliates
    d. amoeboids

20. Which have a specialized opening in the outer edge to capture their prey?
    a. sporozoans
    b. zooflagellates
    c. ciliates
    d. amoeboids

21. Which are parasites that live inside a host and often cause disease to the host by robbing the host of nutrients?
    a. sporozoans
    b. zooflagellates
    c. ciliates
    d. amoeboids

22. Which of the following is not a solution to resistance?
    a. Avoid using antibiotics unnecessarily.
    b. Complete each antibacterial regimen; do not have leftover pills.
    c. Use the widest spectrum antibiotic possible.
    d. Use the common antibiotics first.

True or False?

23. *Candida albicans* is also known as athlete's foot.
    T   F

24. Currently in the market, there are three generations of cephalosporin antibiotics that are available for use.
    T   F

25. About 20% of nosocomial bacterial infections (often acquired in hospitals) are resistant to at least one of the most commonly prescribed antibiotics.
    T   F

26. Some organisms are resistant to all FDA-approved antibiotics and can be treated only with experimental and potentially toxic drugs.
    T   F

Match the following.

27. _____ Stage 1
28. _____ hormonal treatment
29. _____ Stage 2
30. _____ chemotherapy
31. _____ Stage 3
32. _____ radiation
33. _____ Stage 4
34. _____ specific inhibitors
35. _____ Stage 5
36. _____ surgery

a. AIDS opportunistic infections begin; CD4 cell count or level at or below 200 per cubic millimeter of blood

b. usually the first line of treatment for solid tumors

c. final stage of wasting and infections; ends in death

d. may be used in conjunction with surgery and/or drug treatments

e. signs and symptoms of HIV begin to appear

f. uses cytotoxic agents—a wide array of drugs—to kill cancer cells

g. infection without presentation of signs or symptoms (may last 10 or more years)

h. prevent cancer cells from receiving the signals necessary for continued growth and division

i. initial transmission and infection with HIV

j. a relatively new class of drugs that works by targeting specific proteins and processes used by cancer cells

PHARMACY CALCULATION PROBLEMS

Calculate the following.

1. If cefuroxime 750 mg IV is administered to a patient tid × 3 days, how many grams will the patient receive over the entire course?

2. A patient has a prescription for acyclovir 200 mg capsules. If the script reads, "Take one capsule five times daily for 10 days," how many milligrams will the patient take during the entire course of treatment?

3. A patient who weighs 159 lbs. and is 5'8" is coming into the infusion center for his or her weekly dose of chemotherapy. What is the body surface area for this patient?

4. Your pharmacy marks up all herbal medication 40% above cost. If a bottle of Echinacea costs the pharmacy $3.25, what is the retail price?

5. Conversion: 180 lbs = _____ kg

PTCB EXAM PRACTICE QUESTIONS

1. All of the following are types of infectious organisms *except*:
   a. yeasts.
   b. bacteria.
   c. viruses.
   d. lipids.

2. How many different strains of HIV are in existence?
   a. one
   b. two
   c. three
   d. four

3. All of the following are considered to be autoimmune diseases *except*:
   a. cystic fibrosis.
   b. Crohn's disease.
   c. lupus.
   d. multiple sclerosis.

4. Which of the following antibiotics is a macrolide?
   a. amoxicillin
   b. tetracycline
   c. azithromycin
   d. clindamycin

LAB 30-1: Treating an Infection

Objectives:

To understand the different treatment options for methicillin-resistant staphylococcus aureus (MRSA).

Pre-Lab Information:

• Review Chapter 30 in the textbook.

Explanation:

The bacterial strain of MRSA has become very prevalent in our current fight toward combating dangerous microorganisms. As the arsenal of existing antibiotics has been proven to be ineffective against *Staphylococcus aureus*, which because of their overuse have assisted with evolving staphylococcus aureus into MRSA, new therapeutic approaches have been fostered and old ones have been modified to help slow down this microorganism's dangerous and sometimes fatal effects.

Activity:

Using the websites http://www.webmd.com/skin-problems-and-treatments/understanding-mrsa-methicillin-resistant-staphylococcus-aureus and http://www.webmd.com/skin-problems-and-treatments/understanding-mrsa-detection-treatment, please answer the following questions.

1. What areas or parts of the body system can MRSA infect?

   _____

   _____

   _____

   _____

2. What is MRSA sometimes called?

   _____

3. What four antibiotics are MRSA resistant to?

   • _____

   • _____

   • _____

   • _____

4. What is the term for MRSA that is showing up in healthy people who have not been hospitalized?

   _____

5. How is MRSA diagnosed?

   _____

   _____

   _____

6. What are the first two antibiotics used for an MRSA infection?

_____

_____

7. What are the other six antibiotics that are used optionally for an MRSA infection?

_____

_____

_____

8. Are antibiotics always necessary for an MRSA infection of the skin? If not, what other option might a physician choose for a skin boil?

_____

_____

_____

9. Why is it important for a patient to finish all of an antibiotic for an MRSA infection?

_____

_____

Research:

Use the Internet to find out more about the global problem of drug resistance. Visit the World Health Organization (WHO) website (http://www.who.int) to find out more on this topic. What options for action does the WHO propose? What can you, as a pharmacy professional, do to in relation to this global problem?

LAB 30-2: Treating Human Immunodeficiency Virus (HIV)

Objective:

To understand the different treatment options for the human immunodeficiency virus (HIV).

Pre-Lab Information:

• Review Chapter 30 in the textbook.

Explanation:

Ever since its modern-day discovery in the early 1980s, HIV has been on the forefront of the minds of our own government, the Centers for Disease Control, and the WHO. Ever since the first medication was approved for HIV/AIDS in 1990, the medication known as Retrovir or AZT, the discovery of the pipeline of medications used to treat HIV/AIDS has been of great importance during the last 30 years. These medications enable HIV positive patients to live a successful quality of life. Individuals, who are living with HIV and on the combination therapy regimen known as highly active antiretroviral therapy (HAART), will most likely to live their full life expectancy age.

Activity:

Using the website www.thebody.com, please answer the following questions below.

1. As of this writing, what are the names of the five current classifications of HIV medications?

    • _____

    • _____

    • _____

    • _____

    • _____

2. What is the goal of the design for the five classifications of HIV medications?

    _____

    _____

3. As there are many different HIV medications within each classification, currently there are eight medications that contain more than one medication in a single tablet. Please list those eight medications below.

    Brand Name   Generic Name(s)

    _____   _____

    _____   _____

    _____   _____

    _____   _____

    _____   _____

    _____   _____

    _____   _____

4. Why are the above-listed eight combination medications that are used to treat HIV developed this way?

_____

5. What are some of the side effects of the medication Sustiva? What schedule I substance might a patient test positive for while taking Sustiva?

_____

_____

_____

_____

6. Why is the adult single dose of the medication Viramune one 200 mg tablet (once a day) for 14 days rather than one 200 mg tablet (twice a day)?

_____

_____

7. What is the overall goal of HAART?

_____

_____

_____

8. Is an HIV positive individual more likely or less likely to pass on his or her HIV if he or she is taking HAART? Why?

_____

_____

_____

9. A new controversial therapy has been discovered for the treatment of leukemia, please discuss and notate this controversial therapy below.

_____

_____

10. What are some treatment options for individuals to consider for both pre and post exposure to HIV?

_____

_____

_____

CHAPTER 31
The Renal System

After completing Chapter 31 from the textbook, you should be able to:	Related Activity in the Workbook/Lab Manual
1. List, identify, and diagram the basic parts of the renal system.	Review Questions, PTCB Exam Practice Questions
2. Explain the functions of the nephron, kidney, and bladder.	Review Questions, PTCB Exam Practice Questions
3. List and define common diseases.	Review Questions, PTCB Exam Practice Questions
4. Explain how homeostasis of fluid and electrolytes affects the body.	Review Questions, PTCB Exam Practice Questions

INTRODUCTION

The renal system, or urinary system, is a fairly simple system with few components; however, its condition has a grave impact on many parts of the body. Genitourinary tract infections, poor kidney filtration, and water imbalance can indicate or cause diabetes, high blood pressure, or dehydration. The proper functioning of the kidneys is essential to maintain life. The drugs most commonly used to treat diseases of the renal system are anti-infectives and diuretics. The use of strong diuretics that help to remove excess water may also cause a loss of potassium, which may lead to muscle and heart problems. A delicate balance of electrolytes, kidney function, filtration, and waste removal must be maintained at all times during illnesses and while taking medications that affect or treat the urinary tract. As a pharmacy technician, you should be aware of the most common urinary system disorders that require pharmacological treatment, including conditions treated with OTC drugs.

REVIEW QUESTIONS

Match the following.

1. _____ acidosis
2. _____ bilirubin
3. _____ dialysis
4. _____ Kegel exercises
5. _____ ketone
6. _____ palliative
7. _____ pH
8. _____ specific gravity
9. _____ urobilinogen
10. _____ void

a. pelvic muscle training and toning exercises

b. empty the bladder

c. a by-product of fat metabolism

d. a measure of the density of a substance as compared to water

e. medical procedure that removes waste from the blood of patients with renal failure

f. substance produced by the breakdown of bilirubin

g. substance produced by the breakdown of hemoglobin

h. excessive acid in the body fluids

i. the measure of acidity or alkalinity of a solution

j. reducing the severity of symptoms

Choose the best answer.

11. The specific gravity of water is:
    a. 1.
    b. 2.
    c. 3.
    d. 4.

12. Microscopic kidney cells are known as:
    a. michrons.
    b. nephrons.
    c. nephews.
    d. microns.

13. What is the filter station of the kidney called?
    a. loop of Henle
    b. glomerulus
    c. distal convoluted tubule
    d. none of these

14. Phenazopyridine may cause the urine to be colored:
    a. red.
    b. orange.
    c. green/blue-green.
    d. brown/black.

15. Approximately how much urine collects in the bladder prior to signals being sent to the brain for voidance?
    a. 100–200 mL
    b. 300–400 mL
    c. 50–100 mL
    d. 200–300 mL

PHARMACY CALCULATION PROBLEMS

Calculate the following.

1. If a patient needs phenazopyridine 200 mg 1 po tid prn × 4 days, how many tablets should you dispense?

2. A new prescription has been dropped off for oxybutynin po, 10 mg bid. If the pharmacy carries only 5 mg tablets, how many tablets will be needed for a 30-day supply?

3. A woman is to receive a trimethoprim/sulfamethoxazole IV for a complicated UTI. Her dose is 200 mg based on the trimethoprim content. Trimethoprim (TMP)/sulfamethoxazole (SMZ) IV comes as TMP 80 mg/SMZ 400 mg per 5 mL vial. How many milliliters should be drawn up for the IV?

4. A patient took one hydrocodone/APAP tablet po qid × 5 days for pain from kidney stones. How many grams of hydrocodone would the patient be consuming for the full course of therapy, if each tablet contained 5 mg of hydrocodone and 500 mg of acetaminophen?

5. What is the day supply if the directions for a prescription for ciprofloxacin 500 mg are 2 tabs po STAT?

PTCB EXAM PRACTICE QUESTIONS

1. If the renal system does not maintain water and electrolyte balance then the body will not be in:
   a. stasis.
   b. homeostasis.
   c. homeopathic.
   d. homo sapiens.

2. What is the medical term for difficult or painful urination?
   a. dysuria
   b. hematuria
   c. pyuria
   d. anuria

3. The renal system is responsible for all of the following functions *except*:
   a. filtration of waste from the blood.
   b. maintenance of electrolyte balance.
   c. oxygen transport.
   d. maintenance of acid–base balance.

4. Diabetic kidney disease is also known as:
   a. diabetic nephropathy.
   b. diabetic ketoacidosis.
   c. peripheral neuropathy.
   d. end-stage renal disease.

LAB 31-1: Treating Prostatitis

Objective:

To understand about the pathology and treatment options for prostatitis.

Pre-Lab Information:

• Review Chapter 31 in the textbook.

Explanation:

Prostatitis can affect every male at a specific point in his lifetime. The condition may be either acute or chronic. The treatment options for a male to consider with his individual case may vary depending on the cause and severity of the inflammation of the prostate.

Activity:

Using the website (http://www.mayoclinic.com/health/prostatitis/DS00341), please answer the following questions.

1. Besides a bacterial infection, what are the three other causes of prostatitis?

    _____

    _____

    _____

2. What are the 10 risk factors for prostatitis?

    _____

    _____

    _____

    _____

    _____

3. What are the four complications of prostatitis?

    _____

    _____

    _____

    _____

4. What four preparations should a patient take prior to his appointment?

    _____

    _____

    _____

    _____

5. What six tests might lead to a diagnosis of prostatitis?

_____

_____

_____

6. What are the five treatment options for prostatitis?

_____

_____

_____

7. What are the home remedies and lifestyle changes that a male with prostatitis can do to lessen some of his prostatitis symptoms?

_____

_____

_____

_____

8. What are alternative therapies that the patient may choose to reduce his symptoms of prostatitis?

_____

_____

LAB 31-2: Treating Urinary Tract Infections (UTI)

Objective:
To understand the different treatment options for a UTI.

Pre-Lab Information:

• Review Chapter 31 in the textbook.

Explanation:
As of this writing, there are currently 20 different antibiotics and other medications that are approved and indicated for the treatment of a UTI.

Activity:
Match up the 20 antibiotics and other medications according to brand name, the generic counterpart, and the classification that the antibiotic or medication belongs to.

Generic	Brand	Classification
amoxicillin		
amoxicillin/clavulanate		
cefaclor		
cefadroxil		
cefpodoxime		
ceftriaxone		
cefuroxime		
cephalexin		
demeclocycline		
doxycycline		
flavoxate		
fosfomycin		
methenamine		
minocycline		
nitrofurantoin		
norfloxacin		
ofloxacin		
phenazopyridine		
sulfamethoxazole/ trimethoprim		
tetracycline		

Brand Names:

Vibramycin	Ceclor	Noroxin	Rocephin	Duricef
Bactrim, Bactrim DS	Sumycin	Urispas	Pyridium	Ceftin
Declomycin	Keflex	Augmentin	Macrobid, Macrodantin	Vantin
Urised, Urex	Floxin	Minocin	Amoxil, Trimox	Monurol

Classifications:

Cephalosporin (1st, 2nd, or 3rd generation)	Penicillin	Tetracycline
Urinary anti-infective	Analgesic	Sulfonamide
Nitrofuran antimicrobial agent	Broad-spectrum antibiotic	

CHAPTER 32
The Endocrine System

After completing Chapter 32 from the textbook, you should be able to:	Related Activity in the Workbook/Lab Manual
1. Identify and describe the glands of the endocrine system.	Review Questions, PTCB Exam Practice Questions
2. Describe male and female hormones.	Review Questions, PTCB Exam Practice Questions
3. Identify and describe the major diseases and conditions that affect the endocrine system.	Review Questions, PTCB Exam Practice Questions, Lab 32-1, Lab 32-2
4. Compare and contrast diabetes mellitus and diabetes insipidus.	Review Questions
5. Understand the effects of anabolic steroid use.	Review Questions

INTRODUCTION

The endocrine system is a collection of glands that produce hormones, substances that help regulate the body's growth, metabolism, and sexual development and function. The hormones, which are released into the bloodstream and transported to tissues and organs throughout the body, influence every cell in some way. The glands of the endocrine system are ductless. The hormones secreted from the endocrine glands are thus released directly into the bloodstream and travel in the body to specific target organs where they exert their effect.

The driving forces of the endocrine system are the hypothalamus, located in the brainstem, and the pituitary gland, which is attached to the base of the hypothalamus. The hypothalamus directs the pituitary gland, which, in turn, controls the thyroid, parathyroid, pancreas, adrenal glands, and the gonads. A complete review of these glands, their secretions, and their effects on body systems illustrates how important the endocrine system is to the proper functioning of the body. For example, every cell in the body depends on thyroid hormones for regulating metabolism.

Some diseases of the endocrine system, such as diabetes, are very familiar to most people; others, such as Graves' disease or Cushing's syndrome, are less common. As a pharmacy technician, you should be aware of the most common endocrine system disorders that require pharmacological treatment, including conditions treated with OTC drugs.

REVIEW QUESTIONS

Match the following.

1. _____ corticosteroid
2. _____ gonads
3. _____ homeostasis
4. _____ hormone
5. _____ isotonic
6. _____ negative feedback
7. _____ polydipsia
8. _____ polyphagia
9. _____ polyuria
10. _____ priapism

a. a chemical substance, produced by an organ or gland, that travels through the bloodstream to regulate certain bodily functions and/or the activity of other organs or glands

b. the process by which the body returns to homeostasis

c. painful, extended-duration erection

d. excessive hunger or eating

e. excessive urination

f. a stable and constant environment

g. steroidal hormones produced in the adrenal cortex

h. testes and ovaries

i. having the same salt concentration as that of blood

j. ingestion of abnormally large amounts of fluid

Fill in the blanks.

11. _____ is the study of the chemical communication system that provides the means to control a large number of physiologic processes.

12. The _____ is often referred to as the "master gland," because it controls many of the other _____.

13. Thyroid cells combine iodine and the _____ to make T3 and T4.

14. The _____ _____ are located on the upper part of each kidney.

15. The adrenal cortex secretes two types of corticosteroids or hormones: _____ and _____.

PHARMACY CALCULATION PROBLEMS

Calculate the following.

1. If the directions for conjugated estrogen cream read, "Apply 0.5 g PV qd," how long will a 60 g tube last?

2. A diabetic patient gives himself 20 units of insulin tid with meals. How many vials will the patient need for a 30-day supply? The vial contains 10 mL and has a concentration of 100 units/mL.

3. A patient requires a tapering prescription for methylprednisolone 4 mg tablets for a severe allergic reaction. It normally is stocked in a convenience pack, but that form is currently back-ordered. The patient agreed that he or she could take the tablets in a bottle as long as all the directions are included. The directions read:

Day 1: Take six tablets (at once or in divided doses)

Day 2: Take five tablets (at once or in divided doses)

Day 3: Take four tablets (at once or in divided doses)

Day 4: Take three tablets (at once or in divided doses)

Day 5: Take two tablets (at once or in divided doses)

Day 6: Take one tablet

How many tablets will you dispense?

4. A patient brings in a prescription for 0.75 mg of levothyroxine. How many micrograms would the patient take for a 30-day supply if the directions are 1 tab qd?

5. You just received a prescription for desiccated thyroid 180 mg tablets. The computer system only lists the product in grains. How many grains are in one tablet?

PTCB EXAM PRACTICE QUESTIONS

1. Which disease is characterized by the body's failure to produce insulin?
   a. type 1 diabetes
   b. type 2 diabetes
   c. gestational diabetes
   d. pre-diabetes

2. Insulin delivery technology has developed the following innovations *except* for:
   a. pens.
   b. oral tablets.
   c. external pumps.
   d. oral spray.

3. Glucotrol is to glipizide as Glucophage is to:
   a. acarbose.
   b. metformin.
   c. glyburide.
   d. glimepiride.

4. Male sex hormones are also referred to as:
   a. estrogens.
   b. progestins.
   c. insulins.
   d. androgens.

LAB 32-1: Treating Diabetes

Objective:
To become familiar with the management of diabetes.

Pre-Lab Information:

- Visit the website http://www.diabetes.org/

Explanation:
Depending on his or her type of diabetes that a patient is managing, many diabetics are prescribed a therapy regimen that will help control their glucose levels.

Activity:
Using the website www.diabetes.org, please answer the following questions.

1. When monitoring blood glucose levels, what is vital for a patient to do so that a provider can help the patient with a good care plan?

   _____

2. If a patient has type-2 diabetes, what therapy option is prescribed to him or her to manage his or her diabetes?

   _____

3. What are the six oral therapy classifications of diabetes medications currently available?

   _____

   _____

   _____

4. How many types of insulin are sold in the United States?

   _____

5. What are the four types of insulin?

   _____

   _____

   _____

   _____

6. If there are 100 units of insulin per 1 mL, how many milliliters are in 50 units of insulin?

   _____

7. According to "Site Rotation 101," what is the preferred infusion site for proper insulin delivery? What are the other alternate sites that a patient may consider?

   _____

   _____

   _____

   _____

LAB 32-2: Treating Menopause

Objective:

To become familiar with the management of menopause.

Pre-Lab Information:

• Review Chapter 32 in your textbook to learn more about menopause.

Explanation:

Estrogen replacement therapy is the primary resource for females who are experiencing menopause. The decline in a female's estrogen levels during this time in their lives presents both challenges and rewards with the proper use of hormone replacement therapy.

Activity:

Using your textbook as a resource, match up the following hormone replacement therapy medications with their brand name counterpart. Also notate the method of the delivery systems/dosage forms for each of the medications.

Generic	Brand Name(s)	Delivery System/ Dosage Form(s)
conjugated animal estrogen	_____	_____
estradiol	_____	_____
progesterone	_____	_____
conjugated plant estrogens	_____	_____
estrone estropipate	_____	_____
esterified estrogens	_____	_____
norethindrone acetate	_____	_____
medroxyprogesterone acetate	_____	_____
synthetic progesterone and animal estrogens	_____	_____
estradiol/norethindrone acetate	_____	_____

CHAPTER 33
The Reproductive System

After completing Chapter 33 from the textbook, you should be able to:	Related Activity in the Workbook/Lab Manual
1. List, identify, and diagram the basic anatomical structures and parts of the male and female reproductive systems.	Review Questions
2. Describe the functions and physiology of the male and female reproductive systems and the hormones that govern them.	Review Questions
3. List and define common diseases affecting the male and female reproductive systems.	Review Questions, Lab 33-1, Lab 33-2, Lab 33-3

INTRODUCTION

The reproductive system is made up of internal reproductive organs, associated ducts, and external genitalia. Its primary function is the reproductive process. Sex hormones are produced in the gonads: in males, in the testes; and in females, in the ovaries.

Although many diseases can affect the reproductive system, a pharmacy technician will most frequently encounter conditions involving contraception, infertility, sexually transmitted diseases (STDs), and benign prostatic hyperplasia (BPH). As a pharmacy technician, it is important for you to be well informed regarding the different types of contraceptives, as well as their side effects and contraindications, and to be familiar with common conditions and disorders of the reproductive system.

REVIEW QUESTIONS

Match the following. Some answers may be used more than once.

1. _____ contraception
2. _____ endometrium
3. _____ hyperplasia
4. _____ oocyte
5. _____ ovaries
6. _____ ovulation
7. _____ ovum
8. _____ STD
9. _____ STI
10. _____ testes

a. the reproduction of cells within an organ at an increased rate

b. female reproductive organs that produce eggs

c. process in which the ovarian follicle ruptures and releases the egg

d. a sexually transmitted disease

e. the male reproductive organs that produce sperm

f. a disease caused by a pathogen (virus, bacterium, parasite, or fungus) that spreads from person to person through sexual contact

g. birth control

h. the lining of the uterus

i. a mature egg

j. an immature egg

Choose the best answer.

11. The most abundant and active of the estrogens is:
    a. estrace.
    b. estropipate.
    c. estrodil.
    d. estradiol.

12. Federal law requires that all drugs containing estrogen:
    a. be dispensed with a patient package insert.
    b. also contain progesterone.
    c. be clearly labeled "do not take if pregnant."
    d. be redispensed for 28 days only.

13. Which of the following will not interact with oral contraception?
    a. antibiotics
    b. antipyretics
    c. antifungals
    d. antiepileptics

PHARMACY CALCULATION PROBLEMS

Calculate the following.

1. A female patient is prescribed Depo-Provera 150 mg IM for three months. What is the total day supply until this prescription can be refilled again?

2. A prescription for clomiphene 50 mg tablets is being processed for a quantity of 30 tablets. The insurance company will only adjudicate a five-day supply for every 30 days. How many refills will you have to add to the prescription?

3. A man has brought in a prescription for prazosin 5 mg capsules. The prescription indicates that he is to take 10 mg bid. How many capsules would you need to dispense for a 90-day supply?

4. For latent syphilis, the recommended treatment is penicillin g benzathine (long-acting), 7.2 million units, divided into three weekly intramuscular injections. How many milligrams will the patient receive per dose?

5. A man is receiving 50 mg of testosterone cypionate IM every two weeks for hormone replacement therapy. If the clinic pharmacy stocks testosterone cypionate 100 mg/mL, how many milliliters of drug will the patient receive over the course of eight weeks?

LAB 33-1: Treating Infertility

Objective:

To become familiar with the infertility treatment options for parents who are unable to conceive an infant naturally.

Pre-Lab Information:

- Visit the website http://www.webmd.com/infertility-and-reproduction/guide /infertility-reproduction-treatment-care.
- Review Chapter 33 in your textbook about infertility.

Explanation:

Many individuals who are unable to conceive an infant, for one reason or another, can now choose from various treatment options to help assist in the process of conception.

Activity:

Using the website (http://www.webmd.com/infertility-and-reproduction/guide/infertility-reproduction-treatment-care), please answer the questions below.

1. What are the eight assisted reproduction options that partners may choose from?

   _____

   _____

   _____

   _____

2. What is tubal ligation more commonly referred to as? What is a tubal ligation reversal?

   _____

   _____

   _____

3. How many medications are currently available for infertility treatment?

   _____

4. What are the six injectable medication names (brand and generic) for infertility treatment?

   _____

   _____

   _____

   _____

   _____

5. What is artificial insemination?

   _____

   _____

6. What is in vitro fertilization?

_____

_____

7. What is a surrogate? What two kinds of surrogate mothers are there?

_____   _____

_____

_____

LAB 33-2: Treating Erectile Dysfunction

Objective:

To become familiar with treatment options for male patients who have been diagnosed with ED.

Pre-Lab Information:

• Review Chapter 33 in your textbook about ED.

Explanation:

Many male patients who are unable to achieve an erection due to either inorganic or organic conditions can now choose from various treatment options to help assist them in the process of achieving a prolonged and successful erection.

Activity:

Match up the following generic medications to their brand-name counterparts.

Generic	Brand
yohimbine	_____
sildenafil	_____
alprostadil	_____
tadalafil	_____
vardenafil	_____

Brand Names:

Viagra	Muse	Aphrodyne	Levitra
Caverject	Cialis		

LAB 33-3: Understanding Pregnancy Categories

Objective:

To understand the importance of caution when pregnant women use prescription drugs.

Pre-Lab Information:

- Review Chapter 33 in your textbook.
- Visit the following U.S. Department of Health and Human Services website: http://www.womenshealth
  .gov/publications/our-publications/fact-sheet/pregnancy-medicines.pdf

Explanation:

Pregnancy categories are determined on the basis of the potential harm a drug may cause to the fetus. The five pregnancy categories are A, B, C, D, and X, with A being the lowest risk and X being the highest. As a pharmacy technician, it is important for you to understand the concept of risk versus benefit—especially as it applies to drugs taken during pregnancy.

Activity:

Visit the following U.S. Department of Health and Human Services website and use the information there to answer the questions related to drugs used in pregnancy: http://www.womenshealth.gov/publications /our-publications/fact-sheet/pregnancy-medicines.pdf

1. Write the definition of Pregnancy Category A as it applies to human studies only.

   _____
   _____
   _____

2. Write the definition of Pregnancy Category B as it applies to *human studies* only.

   _____
   _____
   _____

3. Write the definition of Pregnancy Category C as it applies to *human studies* only.

   _____
   _____
   _____

4. Write the definition of Pregnancy Category D as it applies to *human studies* only.

   _____
   _____
   _____

5. Write the definition of Pregnancy Category X as it applies to *human studies* only.

   _____
   _____
   _____

6. To which pregnancy category does the drug phenytoin (Dilantin) belong?

7. To which pregnancy category does the drug isotretinoin (Accutane) belong?

8. To which pregnancy category does the drug fluconazole (Diflucan) belong?

9. To which pregnancy category does the drug levothyroxine (Synthroid) belong?

10. To which pregnancy category does the drug ondansetron (Zofran) belong?

CHAPTER 34
The Nervous System

After completing Chapter 34 from the textbook, you should be able to:	Related Activity in the Workbook/Lab Manual
1. Explain the functions of the nervous system and its division into the central and peripheral nervous systems.	Review Questions
2. Compare and contrast the sympathetic and parasympathetic nervous systems.	Review Questions
3. Describe the function or physiology of neurons and nerve transmission and the various neurotransmitters.	Review Questions
4. Explain the relationship of the nervous system to the other body systems.	Review Questions, Lab 34-1
5. Explain the functions of the blood–brain barrier and describe what types of substances will and will not cross it.	Review Questions
6. List and define common diseases affecting the nervous system.	Review Questions, Lab 34-1, Lab 34-2

INTRODUCTION

The nervous system is a very complex system that interacts with every other system in the body to ensure homeostasis and regulate the body's responses to internal and external stimuli. The nervous system communicates with all cells in the body through nerve impulses that are conducted from one part of the body to another via the transmission of chemicals called *neurotransmitters*.

The nervous system is divided into two parts, the central nervous system (CNS) and the peripheral nervous system (PNS). The CNS includes the brain, the spinal column, and their nerves. The PNS is also divided into two parts: the somatic nervous system, which controls voluntary movement of the body through muscles; and the autonomic nervous system, which controls involuntary motor functions and affects such things as heart rate and digestion.

Diseases and conditions affecting the nervous system include anxiety, depression, bipolar disorder, Parkinson's disease, alcohol addiction, and seizures. Pain due to injury or cancer also affects the nervous system. *Neuropharmacology*, or pharmacology related to the nervous system, is one of the most diverse and complicated areas of pharmacology. As a pharmacy technician, you must have a solid understanding of the common diseases affecting the nervous system and the pharmaceutical treatments associated with these diseases.

REVIEW QUESTIONS

Match the following.

1. __e__ adjuvant
2. _____ afferent
3. _____ anxiety
4. _____ anxiolytic
5. _____ CNS
6. _____ cerebrospinal fluid
7. _____ EEG
8. _____ efferent
9. _____ gray matter
10. _____ hypotension
11. _____ PNS
12. _____ narcolepsy
13. _____ white matter

a. condition characterized by frequent and uncontrolled periods of deep sleep

b. all parts of the nervous system excluding the brain and spinal cord

c. component of myelinated nerve tissue in the CNS

d. low blood pressure

e. helping or assisting

f. a drug used in the treatment of anxiety

g. the part of the nervous system made up of the brain and spinal cord

h. an uncomfortable emotional state of apprehension, worry, and fearfulness

i. sending impulses away from the CNS

j. the fluid surrounding brain and spinal cord

k. a major component of the nervous system, composed of nonmyelinated nerve tissue with a gray-brown color

l. sending an impulse toward the CNS

m. a graphic record of the electrical activity of the brain

PHARMACY CALCULATION PROBLEMS

Calculate the following.

1. If chlorpromazine 25 mg/100 mL IV is to run over 30 minutes, what is the infusion rate in milliliters per hour?

2. A patient is to receive 37.5 mg of risperidone long-acting injection. The pharmacy only has 50 mg/2 mL in stock. How many milliliters are needed for the dose?

3. You need to fill a prescription for duloxetine 30 mg. The directions read "3 caps po qd." The patient only wants a 14-day supply. How many capsules will you need to fill the prescription?

4. If a patient is receiving 1 mg of alprazolam bid for 15 days, how many milligrams is the patient receiving each day? How much will the patient receive for the course of therapy?

5. If a patient weighs 132 lbs., what is his or her weight in kilograms?

LAB 34-1: Treating Attention Deficit Hyperactivity Disorder (ADHD)

Objective:

To understand about the different treatment options for attention deficit hyperactivity disorder (ADHD).

Pre-Lab Information:

Review Chapter 34 in your textbook to learn more about ADHD.

Explanation:

ADHD is prevalent in the preadolescent to adolescent age ranges as well as in some adults. There are a few treatment options for parents and adults to consider; after proper assessment, observation can be made for a diagnosis of ADHD.

Activity:

Using your textbook as a resource, match up the following medications that are commonly used as a treatment option for ADHD. Please match the generic medications with their brand-name counterpart. Also notate if the medication is a controlled substance and what schedule it belongs to.

Generic	Brand Name(s)	Controlled Substance Schedule
atomoxetine	_____	_____
dextroamphetamine dextroamphetamine sulfate, dextroamphetamine saccharate, amphetamine aspartate,	_____	_____
amphetamine sulphate	_____	_____
methylphenidate	_____	_____
methylphenidate (once daily)	_____	_____

LAB 34-2: Treating Migraines

Objective:

To understand about the different treatment options for migraines.

Pre-Lab Information:

Review Chapter 34 in your textbook to learn more about migraines.

Explanation:

Migraines can be both debilitating and bring about many uncomfortable symptoms for the migraine sufferer. Currently, there are 11 different kinds of medications to help patients either abort a migraine after its sudden onset or there is a prophylactic treatment option to prevent a migraine.

Activity:

Using your textbook as a resource, match up the following migraine therapy medications with their brand-name counterpart. Also notate the method of the delivery systems/dosage forms for each of the medications.

Generic	Brand Name(s)	Delivery System/ Dosage Form(s)
almotriptan	_____	_____
amitriptyline	_____	_____
naratriptan	_____	_____
ergotamine + caffeine	_____	_____
frovatriptan	_____	_____
sumatriptan	_____	_____
propranolol	_____	_____
rizatriptan	_____	_____
eletriptan	_____	_____
methysergide	_____	_____
zolmitriptan	_____	_____

Brand Name:

Amerge	Elavil	Sansert	Frova
Axert	Maxalt	Relpax	Inderal LA
Imitrex	Zomig		

CHAPTER 35
Medication Errors

After completing Chapter 35 from the textbook, you should be able to:	Related Activity in the Workbook/Lab Manual
1. List and describe the five rights of medication administration.	Review Questions, PTCB Exam Practice Questions, Activity 35-1, Activity 35-2, Activity 35-3, Lab 35-1, Lab 35-2
2. Outline and define the various categories of medication errors.	Review Questions, PTCB Exam Practice Questions, Activity 35-1, Activity 35-2, Activity 35-3, Lab 35-1, Lab 35-2
3. Discuss key statistics related to medication errors and pharmacy practice.	Review Questions, PTCB Exam Practice Questions, Activity 35-1, Activity 35-2, Activity 35-3, Lab 35-1, Lab 35-2
4. Identify look-alike, sound-alike drugs and tall man lettering.	Review Questions, PTCB Exam Practice Questions, Activity 35-1, Activity 35-2, Activity 35-3, Lab 35-1, Lab 35-2
5. Review specific case studies of medication errors, and discuss the causes, outcomes, and recommended preventable solutions.	Review Questions, PTCB Exam Practice Questions, Activity 35-1, Activity 35-2, Activity 35-3, Lab 35-1, Lab 35-2
6. Outline and describe best practices for preventing medication errors.	Review Questions, PTCB Exam Practice Questions, Activity 35-1, Activity 35-2, Activity 35-3, Lab 35-1, Lab 35-2
7. List various agencies involved in the monitoring and reporting of medication errors and describe their role(s).	Review Questions, PTCB Exam Practice Questions, Activity 35-1, Activity 35-2, Activity 35-3, Lab 35-1, Lab 35-2

REVIEW QUESTIONS

Match the following.

1. _____ medication error
2. _____ right patient
3. _____ right drug
4. _____ right route
5. _____ right dose
6. _____ right time
7. _____ right technique
8. _____ right documentation

a. the patient must receive the right dose. A dose that is too high or too low is considered a medication error

b. correct documentation must be completed

c. the patient must receive the medication within the prescribed time frame

d. the drug must be given via the correct route of administration. If the correct drug and dose are given, but via the wrong route, a medication error has occurred

e. the right drug must always be chosen

f. correct technique must be used when preparing the drug

g. the drug must always go to the correct patient

h. any preventable event that may cause or lead to inappropriate medication use or patient harm while the medication is in the control of the health care professional, patient, or consumer

Fill in the blanks.

9. An _____ or _____ is defined as administration of a dose of medication that was never ordered for that patient.

10. An _____ is counted if a dose is given in excess of the total number of times ordered by the physician, such as a dose given on the basis of an expired order, after a drug has been discontinued, or after a drug has been put on hold.

11. If a patient fails to receive a dose of medication that was ordered, an _____ _____ is noted if no attempt was made to administer the dose.

12. A _____ occurs when any dose is given that contains the wrong number of preformed dosage units (such as tablets) or was, in the judgment of the observer, more than 17% greater or less than the correct dosage.

13. _____ are typically defined as those situations where a medication is administered to the patient using a different route than was ordered.

14. _____ are typically defined as the administration of a dose more than 30 minutes (or 60 minutes depending on the site) before or after the scheduled administration time, unless there is an acceptable reason for this time difference.

15. A _____ involves the administration of a dose form different from that ordered by the physician, provided the physician specified or implied a particular form.

Choose the best answer.

16. The recommended dosage of digoxin for a child who is 5–10 years is:
    a. 10–15 mcg.
    b. 35–60 mcg/kg.
    c. 20–35 mcg.
    d. 35–60 mcg/kg.

17. More people die each year from:
    a. AIDS.
    b. motor vehicle accidents.
    c. breast cancer.
    d. medical errors.

18. Which medication is associated with medication errors?
    a. propofol
    b. heparin
    c. levothyroxine
    d. magnesium sulfate

19. The ultimate tool in preventing medication errors will always be:
    a. education.
    b. training sessions.
    c. becoming nationally certified.
    d. all of the above.

20. What piece of technology is most likely to reduce medication errors?
    a. personal electronic devices
    b. e-prescribing
    c. automated dispensing units
    d. none of the above

PHARMACY CALCULATION PROBLEMS

Calculate the following

1. How many milligrams are in 0.75 mcg if the direction for the patient is 1 tab po bid?

2. The order for cefazolin is 1 g/500 mL IV q12h for two days. The pharmacy has just run out of the 500 mL bags but there are 500 mg/250 mL bags currently in stock. The flow rate for the infusion of the 500 mL bag was for 60 minutes. How many bags will the patient now receive for the duration of the therapy, and what will the infusion rate in mL/hr be for each 250 mL bag?

3. The oncologist has prescribed gemcitabine 1,000 mg/mL over 30 minutes once weekly for up to seven weeks followed by one week of rest for a patient with pancreatic cancer. The patient's current height and weight are 79.5 kg and 5'10", respectively. The direction for reconstitution is to add 25 mL of 0.9% Sodium chloride to make a solution 38 mg/mL. Shake to dissolve. How many milliliters will you prepare for this patient?

4. You have a stock vial of sodium bicarbonate 0.5 mEq/mL. How many milliliters are needed to provide 60 mEq?

5. You have a stock vial of potassium chloride 2 mEq/mL. How many milliliters are needed to provide 35 mEq?

PTCB EXAM PRACTICE QUESTIONS

1. An environmental factor that can deter or distract health care professionals from their tasks is:
   a. heat.
   b. screaming babies.
   c. pollution.
   d. dust.

2. An example of a cardiovascular medication is:
   a. HCTZ.
   b. GABA.
   c. AZT.
   d. ASA.

3. A prescription for an antibiotic eardrop is prescribed to a patient who has otitis media. The direction is 1gtt bid × 7 days. How should the directions be translated for the patient?
   a. Instill one drop into the left eye twice a day for seven days
   b. Instill one drop into the right eye twice a day for seven days
   c. Instill one drop into the left ear twice a day for seven days
   d. Instill one drop into both ears twice a day for seven days

4. The correct way to type or write out 500 mg after converting it to a grams weight is:
   a. .5 g.
   b. 5 g.
   c. 0.05 g.
   d. 0.5 g.

5. Coumadin is to warfarin as Xanax is to:
   a. lorazepam.
   b. temazepam.
   c. alprazolam.
   d. diazepam.

ACTIVITY 35-1: Case Study—Recognizing Dangerous Abbreviations

Please match up the following dangerous abbreviations with their intended meanings and the common errors from the lists below.

Abbreviation	Intended Meaning	Common Errors
U	_____	_____
		_____
μg	_____	_____
		_____
Q.D.	_____	_____
		_____
Q.O.D.	_____	_____
		_____
SC or SQ	_____	_____
TIW	_____	_____
D/C	_____	_____
		_____
		_____
HS	_____	_____
Cc	_____	_____
AU, AS, AD	_____	_____
		_____
		_____
IU	_____	_____
MS, MSO$_4$, MgSO$_4$	_____	_____

Units	International Unit	Half strength	Confused for one another
Three times a week	Every other day	Cubic centimeters	Subcutaneous
Discharge; also discontinue	Both ears; left ear; right ear	Every day	Micrograms

Mistaken for "mg" (milligrams), resulting in an overdose.

Misinterpreted as "QD" (daily) or "QID" (four times daily). If the "O" is poorly written, it looks like a period or "I."

Misinterpreted as "three times a day" or "twice a week."

Mistaken as "SL" (sublingual) when poorly written.

The period after the "Q" has sometimes been mistaken for an "I," and the drug has been given "QID" (four times daily) rather than daily.

Mistaken as "U" (units) when poorly written.

Mistaken as IV (intravenous) or 10 (ten).

Patient's medications have been prematurely discontinued when D/C (intended to mean "discharge") was misinterpreted as "discontinue," because it was followed by a list of drugs.

Misinterpreted as the Latin abbreviation "HS" (hour of sleep).

Misinterpreted as the Latin abbreviations "OU" (both eyes), "OS" (left eye), and "OD" (right eye).

Mistaken as IV (intravenous) or 10 (ten).

Can mean morphine sulfate or magnesium sulfate.

Mistaken as a zero or a four (4), resulting in an overdose. Also mistaken for "cc" (cubic centimeters) when poorly written.

ACTIVITY 35-2: Case Study—Wrong Drug, Wrong Patient

Instructions: Read the following scenario and then answer the critical thinking questions.

Mr. Price is a consistent patient at the retail pharmacy to where you are the lead technician. You have had a positive and strong rapport with Mr. Price, and you are also very familiar with his patient profile. His list of medications comprises of atorvastatin, timolol, and esomeprazole 20 mg. He has just phoned in his refill requests for the three medications to you, and he will pick them up later on in this afternoon.

Another consistent patient at your pharmacy, Ms. Prince, has been taking the medication omeprazole 20 mg for the past four months for GERD. She has also phoned in her refill request and will also be picking up her prescription this afternoon. A few minutes after you completed the call with Ms. Prince, four patients arrive at the drop-off counter with new orders for you and the pharmacy team to process. You successfully convey to the team that the expected wait time for each patient is now 15–30 minutes. To your knowledge, the four new orders as well as the refill requests have all been successfully processed.

Mr. Price comes into the pharmacy at 4:00 p.m., and Ms. Prince comes into the pharmacy a few minutes after Mr. Price does. Both Mr. Price and Ms. Prince pay for their prescriptions and thank you for your service. A half hour later, Ms. Prince calls the pharmacy and asks to speak with the pharmacist. Soon after that, Mr. Price calls also asking to speak with the pharmacist. After the pharmacist has completed the calls with both patients, he asks to speak with you and the two other technician colleagues.

He explains to you all that both Ms. Prince and Mr. Price took the wrong prescription home with them. He further explains to you all that the major indicator for the two of them that they received the wrong medication was that the colorings of the capsules were different than what they have been receiving with their prior refills. Both patients are immediately returning to the pharmacy to exchange their prescriptions per the pharmacist's instruction. Fortunately, neither patient has taken any of his or her medication that was incorrectly dispensed.

1. What two medications were incorrectly dispensed to Ms. Prince and Mr. Price?

    _____

    _____

2. What type of medication error has occurred in this case?

_____

_____

3. What should have been done to prevent this medication error from happening?

_____

_____

4. What were the two factors that contributed to this medication error?

_____

_____

5. Is this type of medication error reportable by law? Why or why not?

_____

_____

6. Which team member is to blame for this error?

_____

_____

ACTIVITY 35-3: Case Study—Dispensing an Antibiotic Suspension

Instructions: Read the following scenario and then answer the critical thinking questions.

The morning at the retail pharmacy has been very busy. Along with five refill requests for five different patients, three new orders have been phoned in by physicians along with four new walk-in orders, one of those new walk-in orders has been brought in by Amy's grandmother. For the first time in her life, three-year-old Amy has been prescribed amoxicillin and clavulanate potassium suspension 125 mg/mL with the quantity as 100 mL after reconstitution.

One of the pharmacy clerks has called in sick for the day; therefore, you have been delegated to run the front counter and register as well as process all new walked-in prescription orders at the drop-off counter.

Amy's order is ready and her grandmother is eager to get home so that Amy can take the medication and feel better. You hurriedly ring the grandmother up while at the same time noticing that something feels different about the weight of the bag. The other prescriptions for the patients who have been waiting are also ready for pick-up as Amy's grandmother denies a consultation from the pharmacist. She figures that she can just read the directions on the label.

An hour goes by and Amy's grandmother calls the pharmacy in a panicked mode. She asks to speak with the pharmacist and tells the pharmacist that Amy has been crying loudly for the past 25 minutes since she gave her a teaspoonful of the powder. The pharmacist instructs Amy's grandmother to immediately call poison control and that the poison control team may tell Amy's grandmother to take Amy to the emergency room.

1. What type of medication error has occurred in this case?

_____

_____

2. What harm may come to Amy after she has been given 5 mL of the powder?

_____

_____

3. What should have been done to prevent this medication error from happening?

_____

_____

4. Is this type of medication error reportable by law? Why or why not?

_____

_____

5. Which team member is to blame for this error?

_____

_____

LAB 35-1: Preventing Errors

Objective:
To understand as a technician, how to prevent errors from happening inside and outside of the pharmacy.

Pre-Lab Information:
Review Chapter 35 in your textbook to learn more about preventing errors.

Explanation:
From the time a physician prescribes a medication to a patient until the time the patient starts and ends his or her medication therapy, there are 12 types of medication errors that could occur. The pharmacy technician is strongly relied upon to assist the health care team and the patient with preventing errors.

Activity:
Match up the following cases to strategies in order to be aware of and also to prevent errors.

Case	Strategy
1. AD, AS, AU, OD, OS, OU _____	**A.** Look for duplicate therapies and interactions
2. Celexa/Celebrex _____	**B.** Do not take shortcuts around technology safeguards
3. Patient is taking Alka-Seltzer PM and loratadine for a cold. She takes the Alka-Seltzer PM for her heartburn and the loratadine so that she does not fall asleep at work. _____	**C.** Recognize prescription look-alike/ sound-alike medications
4. Ketamine, propofol _____	**D.** Report errors to improve process
5. A geriatric patient has arthritis and is medication risking compliance. _____	**E.** Avoid abbreviations and nomenclature
6. Patient is taking two different brand-name drugs with the same generic ingredient. _____	**F.** Increase awareness of at-risk confusing her arthritis medication for the other populations
7. The patient talks with the pharmacist about the "5 Rights" for medication safety. _____	**G.** Control the environment
8. Pharmacist gives the technician initials to override alerts. _____	**H.** Educate the patient
9. The technician witnesses the pharmacist throwing away all evidence of an error. _____	**I.** Focus on high-alert medications
10. Lighting, shift changes, workload increases. _____	**J.** Beware of OTC family extensions and standardized labeling

LAB 35-2: Reporting an Error

Objective:

To understand how to report an error once it occurs.

Pre-Lab Information:

Review Chapter 35 in your textbook to learn more about reporting errors.

Explanation:

As the safety of a patient is imperative for pharmacy professionals to protect, the responsibility of a pharmacy technician to report any error, which may compromise the safety of the patient, is just as imperative.

Activity:

Using the website www.nccmerp.org, please follow the procedures and answer the following questions.

1. Click onto "Report a Medication Error."
2. Click "Go" for the ISMP Medication Errors Reporting Program (MERP).
3. What are the seven examples of medication and vaccine errors?

   _____
   _____
   _____
   _____
   _____
   _____
   _____
   _____

4. Which kind or types of submissions are reporters encouraged to provide to ISMP?

   _____
   _____
   _____

5. Click on the "Healthcare Practitioners" tab.
6. Click on the "Report Medication Errors (ISMP MERP)" tab.

7. What content is needed to report a medication error? What other information is necessary to provide?

_____

_____

_____

_____

_____

_____

_____

_____

_____

8. Is the information reported kept confidential? Why or why not?

_____

_____

CHAPTER 36
Workplace Safety and Infection Control

After completing Chapter 36 from the textbook, you should be able to:	Related Activity in the Workbook/Lab Manual
1. Define and describe the importance of workplace safety.	Review Questions, PTCB Exam Practice Questions
2. Explain the difference between an accident and an incident.	Review Questions, PTCB Exam Practice Questions
3. Outline the four key elements of workplace safety.	Review Questions, PTCB Exam Practice Questions
4. Identify specific workplace safety concerns related to pharmacy practice.	Review Questions, PTCB Exam Practice Questions
5. Outline the key requirements as prescribed by OSHA, state regulations, and institutional policies.	Review Questions, PTCB Exam Practice Questions
6. Define and describe infection control.	Review Questions, PTCB Exam Practice Questions

INTRODUCTION

The concerns of workplace safety and infection control are of great importance for pharmacy technicians. It is critical to understand that workplace safety is a must whether the technician is working in an institutional or community-based pharmacy practice setting. There are a variety of rules and best practices regarding workplace safety and infection control, for pharmacy professionals, based on the specific state, practice setting, and institution, in addition to federal regulations. In this chapter, we will review the major provisions of workplace safety and infection-control measures.

REVIEW QUESTIONS

Match the following.

1. _____ workplace safety
2. _____ infection control
3. _____ PPE
4. _____ HEP B, HIV
5. _____ TCJ
6. _____ OSHA

a. proper hand hygiene

b. blood-borne pathogens

c. the organization that provides protocols for the safe removal of different hazards and substances, chemicals, needles, body fluids, blood, fire safety and control, and emergency plans in case of a fire

d. formed to assist health care organizations and health care programs in improving quality health care standards, accreditation, and certification for better, safe, and effective workplaces for health care workers and patients

e. gloves, gowns, hair covers, and masks

f. prevention of injury and illness of employees, and volunteers, in the workplace

Fill in the blanks.

7. An _____ refers to a specific event that results in unintended harm or damage, whereas an _____ is an event that has the potential to result in unintended harm or damage.

8. An _____ of all workplace conditions should be performed on a regular and timely basis to identify or eliminate existing and potential hazards.

9. Workplace training sessions must be available to _____ in the pharmacy.

10. A _____ area for preparing dangerous chemicals and drugs, such as _____, should be designated along with safety posters and signs restricting access to only qualified personnel.

PHARMACY CALCULATION PROBLEMS

Calculate the following

1. The patient has been ordered clindamycin 450 mg IM STAT in both gluteal areas of the body while in the emergency room. Then upon the patient's admission to the hospital, the order will be 450 mg IV q8h for 48 hours. The patient will be discharged with an order to take clindamycin 150 mg po tid for 10 days. How much clindamycin has this patient been prescribed for the entire course of therapy?

2. A physician orders for a patient requiring anticoagulation therapy: 2 mg of warfarin for days Monday, Wednesday, Friday, and Sunday and 5 mg of warfarin for days Tuesday, Thursday, and Saturday for a 30-day supply. How many tablets of each strength will be dispensed?

3. A patient has been ordered prochlorperazine 25 mg suppositories for 10 days. The directions are 1 supp PR bid prn N/V. You currently have in stock prochlorperazine 25 mg suppositories that come in quantities of 12 per box. How many suppositories will you dispense to the patient?

4. 6 oz. = _____ mL

5. 1 oz. = _____ tsp.

PTCB EXAM PRACTICE QUESTIONS

1. Material Safety Data Sheets contain all of the following information except:
   a. trade name.
   b. date of manufacturing.
   c. synonyms for the chemical.
   d. manufacturers name.

2. OPIM stands for:
   a. other prevalent infectious materials.
   b. obvious prevalent infectious materials.
   c. other potentially infectious materials.
   d. obvious potentially infectious materials.

3. The CDC has stated that proper hand hygiene techniques include:
   a. decontaminating hands with an alcohol-based hand rub.
   b. washing the hands for at least 15 seconds.
   c. using disposable towels to thoroughly dry hand rub the hands.
   d. all of the above.

4. Chemotherapy medications/hazardous agents must be compounded in what type of airflow hood?
   a. horizontal laminar airflow hood
   b. compounding aseptic isolator
   c. vertical laminar airflow hood
   d. both b and c

5. An example of an OPIM is:
   a. vaginal secretions.
   b. plasma.
   c. sweat.
   d. athlete's foot.

CHAPTER 37
Special Considerations for Pediatric and Geriatric Patients

After completing Chapter 37 from the textbook, you should be able to:	Related Activity in the Workbook/Lab Manual
1. Discuss the physiological changes that occur in pediatric and geriatric patients.	Review Questions, PTCB Exam Practice Questions
2. Explain how the processes of pharmacokinetics in pediatric patients affect drug dosing.	Review Questions, PTCB Exam Practice Questions
3. Discuss pediatric drug administration and dosage adjustment considerations.	Review Questions, PTCB Exam Practice Questions
4. List two common childhood illnesses or diseases in pediatric patients.	Review Questions, PTCB Exam Practice Questions
5. Discuss the physiological changes that occur in geriatric patients.	Review Questions, PTCB Exam Practice Questions
6. List several factors that affect pharmacokinetic processes in geriatric patients.	Review Questions, PTCB Exam Practice Questions
7. Discuss polypharmacy and noncompliance in pediatric and geriatric medication therapy.	Review Questions, PTCB Exam Practice Questions
8. Discuss Medicare Part D and its effects on medication dispensing to the geriatric population.	Review Questions
9. Explain ways in which geriatric medication dispensing will change in the future, and how extended life expectancy will change pharmacy practice.	Review Questions

INTRODUCTION

Providing medical and pharmaceutical care for pediatric and older patients is a bit more challenging than caring for adults who need medications. Drug dosing is different for children than adults and carries the same responsibility for accuracy and attention to detail when filling prescriptions for this age group. For older adult patients, there is often more concern about side effects and how well the drug is tolerated by them. These two age groups need extra care and consideration when it comes to pharmaceutical services and care. As a pharmacy technician, you need to understand the unique factors involved in caring for pediatric and geriatric patients.

REVIEW QUESTIONS

Match the following.

1. _____ absorption
2. _____ adverse effects
3. _____ bioavailability
4. _____ distribution
5. _____ excretion
6. _____ geriatric
7. _____ half-life
8. _____ metabolism
9. _____ noncompliance
10. _____ OTC drugs
11. _____ polypharmacy
12. _____ side effects
13. _____ toxicity

a. drug poisoning; can be life-threatening or extremely harmful

b. chemical change of drugs or foreign compounds in and by the body

c. when a patient does not follow a prescribed drug regimen

d. amount of a drug that is available for absorption

e. amount of time it takes the body to break down and excrete one-half of a drug dosage

f. refers to persons over the age of 65

g. elimination of a drug from the body; usually occurs through urine, feces, or the respiratory system

h. undesirable and potentially harmful drug effects

i. the process by which a drug enters the bloodstream

j. drug effects other than the intended one; usually undesirable but not harmful

k. administration of more medications than clinically indicated

l. drugs that can be purchased without a prescription

m. the process by which a drug reaches the various organs and tissues of the body

Choose the best answer.

14. _____ are newborn babies from birth to one month of age; _____ are between the ages of one month and two years.
    a. neonates/toddlers
    b. infants/neonates
    c. infants/toddlers
    d. neonates/infants

15. Because the kidneys, liver, and brain are the organs that require the most blood flow to function properly, the _____ and _____ processes slow as people age.
    a. metabolism, excretion
    b. metabolism, absorption
    c. excretion, absorption
    d. kidneys, liver

16. Which of the following is a common reason for noncompliance by the elderly?
    a. dosing schedule is confusing
    b. difficulty understanding or remembering what the drug is
    c. inability to afford the drug
    d. all of the above
    e. none of the above

True or False?

17. Organ size generally increases in the elderly, as do blood flow and cardiac output.

    T   F

18. Significant cognitive impairment in the geriatric population includes loss of eyesight and loss of hearing.

    T   F

19. By the year 2050, the elderly population will increase to approximately 72 million.

    T   F

20. Common childhood conditions include infections of the skin.

    T   F

PHARMACY CALCULATION PROBLEMS

Calculate the following.

1. A normal adult requires 0.1 mcg/kg/min of remifentanil for continuous IV infusion. However, in geriatric patients, the dosage should be reduced by half. How many micrograms will a 192 lb. geriatric patient receive over 10 minutes?

2. A pediatric patient is receiving an antibiotic for an impetigo infection. The pediatrician has prescribed cephalexin 25 mg/kg q8h. The patient weighs 85 lbs. How much will the patient receive per dose?

3. Zaleplon 10 mg is usually given qhs. If a geriatric patient is prescribed half of this dose, how many milligrams will the patient receive over a 14-day period?

4. A pediatric patient has been prescribed a medication at 2 mg/kg q12h. The patient weighs 70.4 lbs. How much will the patient receive per day?

5. A geriatric patient is ordered DuoNeb (ipratropium bromide 0.5 mg/albuterol sulfate 3.0 mg) nebulizer treatments q4h. How many milligrams of albuterol sulfate is the patient receiving per day?

PTCB EXAM PRACTICE QUESTIONS

1. Adults experience a decrease in many physiological functions between the ages of:
   a. 18 and 30 years.
   b. 20 and 40 years.
   c. 30 and 50 years.
   d. 50 and 70 years.

2. Syrup of ipecac is used for:
   a. gastric lavage.
   b. whole bowel evacuation.
   c. gastric decontamination.
   d. vomiting.

3. Which of the following drugs can cause elderly patients to become dizzy, unsteady on their feet, and possibly fall if the dosage is not adjusted appropriately?
   a. benzodiazepines
   b. diuretics
   c. acetaminophen
   d. ibuprofen

4. Treatment for pediatric patients with asthma often includes a combination of:
   a. anti-inflammatory agents and bronchodilators.
   b. inhalers and syrups.
   c. bronchodilators and corticosteroids.
   d. anti-inflammatory agents and corticosteroids.

5. To help solve the problem of polypharmacy and avoid complications and adverse drug interactions, pharmacists and pharmacy technicians must record *every* medication their patients are taking and keep a current patient profile by the:
   a. "white bag method."
   b. "brown bag lunch method."
   c. "bag lunch method."
   d. "brown bag method."

LAB 37-1: Pediatric Dosing

Objective:

To understand the relationship between Clark's Rule and Young's Rule to accurately calculate the dose for a cough/cold medication for a pediatric patient.

Pre-Lab Information:

• Review Chapter 37 in your textbook.

Explanation:

Pediatric dosing of cough and cold medications has to be calculated with the importance of accuracy being at the forefront of the allied health professional's mindset. The two common methods used for calculating pediatric dosing of cough and cold medications are Clark's Rule and Young's Rule.

Activity:

Please refer to Chapter 37 in your textbook to use Clark's Rule and Young's Rule for the following problems.

Clark's Rule

1. A child who weighs 95 lbs. is prescribed prednisolone syrup. The normal adult dosage is 10 mg. What is the appropriate dose for this child?

2. A child who is weighing 75 lbs. is prescribed pseudoephedrine syrup as a decongestant. The normal adult dosage is 45 mg. What is the appropriate dose for this child?

Young's Rule

1. A child who is nine years old is prescribed dextromethorphan polistirex for a cough. The normal adult dose is 60 mg. What is the appropriate dose for this child?

2. A child who is six years old is prescribed acetaminophen for a fever. The normal adult dose is 500 mg. What is the appropriate dose for this child?

LAB 37-2: Geriatric Dosing

Objective:

To understand how a geriatric patient may not be noncompliant with his or her multiple drug regimens.

Pre-Lab Information:

• Review Chapter 37 in your textbook.

Explanation:

With 55% to 59% of the geriatric population are on more than one class of medications for various disease states and conditions, the pharmacy technician is often relied upon to assist this population with their polypharmacy needs.

Activity:

Select a team of three, which will include a "pharmacist," a "technician," and a "patient." Decide upon which team member will take on each of the roles in this activity/scenario.

Scenario:

An older adult patient comes into the pharmacy with three new prescriptions. Two of those prescriptions are for hypertension and another one is for high cholesterol. The three medications are very close in size and shape as the patient has both vision and hearing conditions as well as arthritis.

1. What steps can you take to ensure that the patient will not make his or her own medication errors and be in full compliance with his or her medications?

   _____
   _____
   _____
   _____

2. The patient tells you that his or her grandchildren come to visit him. Should this patient have safety caps for his or her vials of medications? Why or why not?

   _____
   _____
   _____

3. Does this patient take any over-the-counter medications? If so, what other assistance should you offer to the patient for better compliance?

   _____
   _____
   _____
   _____

CHAPTER 38
Biopharmaceuticals

After completing Chapter 38 from the textbook, you should be able to:	Related Activity in the Workbook/Lab Manual
1. Name at least two drugs developed by using recombinant DNA technology, and outline their uses.	Review Questions
2. Discuss the four steps in the genetic engineering process.	Review Questions
3. Explain briefly how a company gets approval for a biopharmaceutical drug from the FDA.	Review Questions
4. Discuss why biopharmaceuticals, genetic engineering, and stem cell research are important in the future of pharmacy and the practice of medicine.	Review Questions

INTRODUCTION

Biopharmacology is the branch of pharmacology that studies the use of biologically engineered drugs. Biopharmaceuticals are substances created using biotechnology. They can be proteins like antibodies, and even consist of DNA and RNA. Research is being conducted to find new therapeutic medications, or biopharmaceuticals, to treat such life-threatening diseases as AIDS, various cancers, and Parkinson's disease.

Large majorities of biopharmaceuticals are derived from existing life forms, such as plants and animals, although they are produced by means other than direct extraction from a biological source. Genetic engineering is another way to create new drugs; stem cell research also offers opportunities to discover new therapeutic treatments and is making significant strides in the development of new medications used today. As a pharmacy technician, you should be familiar with some of the concepts of biopharmacology, their impact on the pharmaceutical industry, and their role in the future of pharmacology.

REVIEW QUESTIONS

Match the following.

1. _____ allergenic
2. _____ biologics
3. _____ biopharmaceuticals
4. _____ biopharmacology
5. _____ biotechnology
6. _____ Gaucher's disease
7. _____ GMO
8. _____ Stem cells
9. _____ neutropenia
10. _____ rheumatoid arthritis
11. _____ transform
12. _____ vector

a. autoimmune disease that causes chronic inflammation of the joints

b. organism that does not itself cause disease, but spreads disease by distributing pathogens from one host to another

c. alteration of an organism itself or the cell in the genetic engineering process

d. disease in which there are an abnormal number of the white blood cells that are responsible for fighting infections

e. substances created using biotechnology

f. a substance that can cause an allergic reaction

g. use of biological substances or microorganisms to perform specific functions, such as the production of drugs, hormones, or food products

h. branch of pharmacology that studies the use of biologically engineered drugs

i. organism whose genetic material has been altered using the genetic engineering techniques known as recombinant DNA technology

j. disease in which fatty materials collect in the liver, spleen, kidneys, lungs, and brain and cause the person to be susceptible to infections

k. have a special ability to renew themselves many times through cell division, in a process called proliferation

l. a group of varied medicinal products, such as vaccines, blood products, allergenics, and proteins

True or False?

13. Genetic manufacturing is another way to create new drugs.

    T   F

14. After the successful completion of all three IND phases, the company can then file a NDA with the FDA.

    T   F

15. Erythropoietin is used for anemia for cancer therapy.

    T   F

PHARMACY CALCULATION PROBLEMS

Calculate the following.

1. A female patient who has rheumatoid arthritis has been prescribed infliximab 2.5 mg/kg for her first dose. What is the strength of her therapy if she weighs 145 lb.? On stock, you carry the medication in a vial where the concentration is 100 mg/20 mL. How much of the infliximab will you prepare for this patient?

2. Etanercept is usually dosed at 50 mg SC twice a week for three months for severe plaque psoriasis. How many grams will a patient with psoriasis receive for a three-month regimen?

3. A patient who is prescribed abatacept weighs 195 lb. According to the manufacturer's recommendation, a patient weighing less than 60 kg should receive a 500 mg dose. If a patient weighs between 60 and 100 kg, the patient should receive a 750 mg dose. If the patient weighs more than 100 kg, the patient should receive a 1,000 mg dose. What is the correct dose for this patient?

4. A patient is to receive rituximab 700 mg IV in 250 mL 0.9% sodium chloride. If the IV is to be infused at 100 mg/hr, how long will it take for the IV to be completely infused?

5. 10 mL = _____ minims.